Building the Russian State

The John M. Olin Critical Issues Series

Published in cooperation with
The Harvard University Davis Center for Russian Studies

BOOKS IN THIS SERIES

Building the Russian State, edited by Valerie Sperling

The Rule of Law and Economic Reform in Russia,
edited by Jeffrey D. Sachs and Katharina Pistor

The Sources of Russian Foreign Policy After the Cold War,
edited by Celeste A. Wallander

Central Asia in Historical Perspective, edited by Beatrice F. Manz

FORTHCOMING

Business and the State in Contemporary Russia, Peter Rutland

The Collapse of the Soviet Union, Mark Kramer

Building the Russian State

Institutional Crisis and the Quest for Democratic Governance

EDITED BY
Valerie Sperling

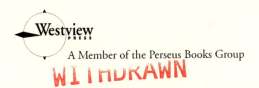

Westview
PRESS

A Member of the Perseus Books Group

The John M. Olin Critical Issues Series

Published in 2000 in the United States of America by Westview Press, 5500 Central Avenue, Boulder, Colorado 80301-2877, and in the United Kingdom by Westview Press, 12 Hid's Copse Road, Cumnor Hill, Oxford OX2 9JJ

Find us on the World Wide Web at www.westviewpress.com

Library of Congress Cataloging-in-Publication Data
Building the Russian state : institutional crisis and the quest for democratic governance/
    edited by Valerie Sperling.
        p.   cm. — (The John M. Olin critical issues series)
    Includes bibliographical references and index.
    ISBN 0-8133-3742-9 (hc)—ISBN 0-8133-3805-0 (pb)
    1. Russia (Federation)—Politics and government—1991—Congresses.   2. Elite (Social sciences)—Russia (Federation).   I. Sperling, Valerie.   II. Series.

JN6695 .B85   2000
947.086—dc21

00-022087

The paper used in this publication meets the requirements of the American National Standard for Permanence of Paper for Printed Library Materials Z39.48-1984.

PERSEUS
POD
ON DEMAND   10   9   8   7   6   5   4   3   2

Contents

Tables and Figures

Preface

The chapters in this volume began as papers for the 1998–1999 John M. Olin Critical Issues Series, "Building the Russian State: Institutions and Capacity," held at Harvard University's Davis Center for Russian Studies. The yearly series, as well as the publication of the volume arising from it, are supported by generous funding from the John M. Olin Foundation. As the chairperson of this year's series, I am grateful to all the speakers who contributed their knowledge and expertise, and also to those who attended the seminars and helped the authors of the chapters in this volume shape and refine their arguments.

I would particularly like to thank Tim Colton, director of the Davis Center, and Lis Tarlow, associate director, for asking me to serve as chair, and for their support of my goals for this year's series. Linda Kitch provided efficient administrative assistance, enabling the series to run smoothly. Rob Williams at Westview Press was instrumental in endorsing the concept for this volume and working to ensure its timely publication. Joyce Wilson, the copyeditor, brought the chapters into line with Westview's specifications in a speedy and good-humored fashion.

As editor, I have tried to hold the chapters in this volume to a difficult standard: one of scholarship that is specialized without being esoteric; accessible to undergraduates, yet also of interest to experts on Russia. If I have succeeded in this venture, it is only because I had the support of friends, family, my steady sweetheart, and those mentioned above, especially the series authors, who met and exceeded my rigorous standards.

Valerie Sperling

List of Contributors

Eva Busza is an Assistant Professor specializing in Comparative Politics in the Department of Government at the College of William and Mary. She is currently on research leave completing a book comparing the development of civil-military relations in postcommunist states. She has been a research fellow at the Kennan Institute (Woodrow Wilson Center), Columbia University's Harriman Institute, Ohio State University's Mershon Center, the Brookings Institution, and Stanford University's Center for International Security and Arms Control. She is the author of a number of articles on the military in Russia, Poland, Hungary, and the Czech Republic. Her research interests include civil-military relations, postcommunist security and political affairs, globalization, and cyberspace terrorism.

Virginie Coulloudon is director of the research project on "Elite and Patronage in Russia," based at the Davis Center for Russian Studies, Harvard University. She received her Ph.D. in History from the Ecole des Hautes Etudes en Sciences Sociales, Paris. Prior to this, she wrote three monographs published in French. The first focuses on the younger generation under *perestroika* (*Génération Gorbatchev*, foreword by Michel Heller, Paris, 1988). The second book (*La Mafia en Union Soviétique*, Paris, 1990) is one of the first nonfiction books in the West on Soviet organized crime and patronage. The third book (*Le Russisme*, Paris, 1992) is a political analysis of the new Russian elite after the collapse of the Soviet Union. She has also published several articles on the Russian elite and patronage, mainly in the French review *Politique Internationale*, and also in *The East-European Constitutional Review*, *The Fletcher Forum*, and *Demokratizatsiya*. Working for the Media and Opinion Research Department of Radio Liberty for six years (1987–1993), she directed a dozen qualitative surveys (in-depth interviews and focus group discussions) in Moscow, the Russian provinces, Belarus, and Uzbekistan.

Stephen Crowley, an Assistant Professor of Politics at Oberlin College, is the author of *Hot Coal, Cold Steel: Russian and Ukrainian Workers from the End of the Soviet Union to the Postcommunist Transformations* (University of

Michigan Press, 1997), in addition to a number of articles on labor in Russia and other postcommunist countries.

M. Steven Fish is Associate Professor of Political Science at the University of California, Berkeley. He has also taught at the University of Pennsylvania. He is the author of *Democracy from Scratch: Opposition and Regime in the New Russian Revolution* (Princeton University Press, 1995). His interests include comparative politics, political parties and organizations, social movements, regime change, constitutionalism, leadership, and political economy.

Pamela Jordan is a specialist in comparative politics and Russian studies. She received her Ph.D. in political science from the University of Toronto in 1997. She has taught as an Adjunct Professor of Political Science at the University of Vermont and Norwich University and is currently an independent scholar living in the New York City area. Her research focuses on legal politics in post-Soviet Russia.

Pauline Jones Luong is an Assistant Professor in the Department of Political Science at Yale University. She received her Ph.D. from Harvard University in 1997 and held a postdoctoral fellowship at the Harvard Academy for International and Area Studies from 1997 to 1998. She has published several articles on political and economic development in Central Asia and Russia in *International Negotiation, Journal of International Affairs, Central Asian Monitor, Europe-Asia Studies,* and *Comparative Political Studies.* Her current research focuses on the short- and long-term impact of natural resource endowments on state formation in developing countries, focusing on the energy-rich former Soviet republics.

Corbin Lyday is a Senior Policy Analyst in the Bureau for Europe and New Independent States at the U.S. Agency for International Development. His dissertation, "From Coup to Constitution: Dilemmas of Nation-Building in Russia's 'First Republic,'" was completed at the University of California at Berkeley in December 1994.

Louise Shelley is a Professor in the Department of Justice, Law, and Society and the School of International Service at American University and founder and Director of the Center for Transnational Crime and Corruption (TraCCC). She is a leading United States expert on crime, law, and law enforcement in the former Soviet Union, as well as an expert on transnational organized crime and corruption. She studied at the Law Faculty of Moscow State University on IREX and Fulbright Fellowships and holds a Ph.D. in sociology from the University of Pennsylvania. She is the recipient of Guggenheim, NEH, Kennan Institute, and Fulbright fellowships, and received a MacArthur Grant to establish the Russian Organized Crime Study Centers. Dr. Shelley is the author of *Policing Soviet Society* (Routledge, 1997), as well as numerous articles and book chapters. Professor Shelley is presently coeditor of *Demokratizatsiya*, the journal of post-Soviet democratization, and *Trends in Organized Crime*.

Steven Solnick is Associate Professor of Political Science at Columbia University and Program Coordinator for Russian Studies at Columbia's Harriman Institute. He is the author of *Stealing the State: Control and Collapse in Soviet Institutions* (Harvard University Press, 1998) as well as numerous articles on Soviet and post-Soviet politics. He is currently completing a book on territorial politics, federal institutions, and state-building in Russia and other large states.

Valerie Sperling is an Assistant Professor in the Department of Government and International Relations at Clark University, in Worcester, Massachusetts. She received her Ph.D. from the University of California, Berkeley, in 1997, and held a postdoctoral fellowship at the Davis Center for Russian Studies, Harvard University, in 1997–1998. In 1998–1999, she chaired the Olin Critical Issues Series at the Davis Center. She has published several articles on gender politics in Russia, as well as a book, *Organizing Women in Contemporary Russia: Engendering Transition* (Cambridge University Press, 1999). Her current research interests include the domestic and international influences on social movements, and the intersection between globalization and state-building.

Mark Clarence Walker is an Assistant Professor of Comparative and Regional Studies in the School of International Service at American University in Washington, D.C. He received his Ph.D. from the University of California at Berkeley in 1999 and his B.S. from MIT in 1991. His teaching and research focus upon electoral politics, new democratic institutions, leadership, and the methodology of political science.

Introduction:
The Domestic and International
Obstacles to State-Building in Russia*

VALERIE SPERLING

Speaking to the Eighth Congress of Soviets on December 23, 1920, in the afterglow of his party's assumption of power in Russia, Vladimir Ilyich Lenin, leader of the Bolsheviks, expressed his enthusiastic vision of the future in terms of an equation: "Communism is Soviet power plus the electrification of the whole country."[1] Although Soviet power was imposed relatively quickly, and electricity followed in due course, the equation proved false, and communism was never reached. Similarly, after the conclusion of the Cold War, scholars and politicians alike were eager to derive an equally simple formula for creating democracy on the ruins of Soviet autocracy. Although it was never expressed as pithily as Lenin's, the equation might look like this: "Liberal democracy is the end of Soviet power plus capitalism."[2] But, a decade later, the political mathematicians had to return to the drawing board. Although Soviet power had collapsed by the close of 1991, the Soviet Union having joined the tsarist empire on the ashheap of history, and although a hybrid capitalism in Russia had spread nearly as far as electrification, the result of the proposed equation proved elusive. Despite its leaders' declared intentions, the Russian state did not transform itself into a liberal democracy, and quickly developed a reputation for being able to guarantee neither the public welfare and safety of its citizens, nor the rule of law on which liberal democracy is founded.

The chapters in this volume explore the reasons behind the Russian state's failure thus far to develop into a liberal democracy, looking specifically at the interactions between Russia's elites and Russia's state institu-

---

*I am grateful to Sam Diener and Pauline Jones Luong for their comments on an earlier draft of this chapter.

tions, including the military, the police, economic institutions, political institutions, and the legal system. The three chapters in Part I of the volume focus on Russia's elites, their values, and their economic and political behavior, while the remaining chapters, in Part II, critically assess the varied condition of Russia's political, economic, legal, and military institutions, and analyze Russia's capacity for long-term stability and democratic governance. Below, in this introductory chapter, I provide various definitions of the state and its purposes, and identify the challenges that Russia and other states face that can prevent them from effectively performing their tasks and achieving their goals. In so doing, I explore a series of obstacles that deter the Russian state specifically from strengthening state institutions and from fulfilling the promise of building a liberal democracy.[3]

Defining the State

At the center of analyses of Russia's changing political and economic systems lies the state and the policies that it promotes. It seems obvious that the new Russian state would have to play a key role in the major restructuring effort occurring in the wake of the collapse of the Soviet Union and its single-party polity and centrally planned economic system. But when we speak of the state, what do we mean? What is the state and how does it function?

Theorists have defined the state in a variety of ways, although most agree that the state is essentially an organization, institution, or set of institutions that governs a polity.[4] The work of German sociologist Max Weber has been influential in discussions of the nature of the state. In his famous essay, "Politics as a Vocation," Weber defined the state as "a human community that (successfully) claims the *monopoly of the legitimate use of physical force* within a given territory."[5] Following Weber, John Hoffman defined the state as "an institution claiming to exercise a monopoly of legitimate force within a particular territory."[6] From this perspective, states are *institutions*, composed of bureaucracies or other kinds of organizations, combining four interrelated elements: monopoly, territory, legitimacy, and force.[7]

Numerous theorists further tend to regard the state as the source of law—the rules that govern life within its territory.[8] However, the state is not alone in the polity. Political scientist Joel Migdal pointed out that the "state" is only one of the many organizations that comprise "society," along with families, factories, interest groups, and so forth. Yet, what sets the state apart from these other entities is the fact that the officials running the state "seek predominance over those myriad other organizations." Migdal continues:

That is, they aim for the state to make the binding rules guiding people's behavior or, at the very least, to authorize particular other organizations to make those rules in certain realms. By "rules" I mean the laws, regulations, decrees, and the like, which state officials indicate they are willing to enforce through the coercive means at their disposal.[9]

Just as states are said to have authority in the rule-making realm, states are also considered to be "sovereign," that is to say, as having "supreme authority" within their territory, and being recognized abroad as such.[10] For example, the United Nations (UN) recognizes (or assumes) that the Russian state is the only legitimate ruling authority on Russia's territory. However, in the global age of the late twentieth century, there is some discussion as to whether states are truly sovereign, or whether global associations (such as the UN), transnational corporations (such as Nike), or global civic organizations (such as Greenpeace) are in fact eroding states' "supreme authority" by compelling states to act in particular ways, whether it be lowering tariffs or disposing of nuclear waste more safely. Similarly, social movements at home may also constrain states' behavior (witness the effects of popular protest in the United States compelling southern states to recognize African Americans' voting rights in the 1960s).

In essence, then, the "state" is the set of institutions that "makes the rules" in a given territory. Whether it is a strong or weak state is determined by how successfully it succeeds in getting the people on its territory to follow those rules, whatever they may be, and however just or unjust they are. Moreover, as noted, the state may be held back in this regard by both domestic and international circumstances, a point to which we will return more extensively below.

Theorists also view states as having varying levels of "autonomy," by which is meant "insulation from the pressures of societal groups or powerful individuals." In other words, for theorists who believe that the state enjoys a high level of autonomy, state institutions and those who staff them can derive their own goals and set policies intended to implement those goals, "independently from societal interests."[11] In contrast to this view of states, however, Marxist political theorists generally see state autonomy as being rather limited.[12] In *The Communist Manifesto*, Marx and Engels dismissed the capitalist state as the mere handmaiden of the ruling class, an organization that could not be labeled an autonomous set of institutions: "The executive of the modern state is but a committee for managing the common affairs of the whole bourgeoisie."[13] In other words, for Marx and Engels, in a bourgeois capitalist society, the state serves as an instrument of domination over the lower, laboring classes, and will continue to exist, serving that function, only as long as capitalism and its unjust and unequal distribution of wealth persist. With a victorious working class revolution over the bourgeoisie, followed by the worldwide establishment of proletarian rule, the state, Marx believed, would wither away, having lost its function in a world now run by the international proletariat, who would have no further need for borders. For Marx, the state was "captured"—it was a mere reflection of the interests of whatever socioeconomic class held power at the time.

These various definitions raise fundamental questions about the state and its purpose. Does the state reflect the interests of all organized societal groups, as a pluralist model of the state might suggest? Or does the state merely meet the needs of elites, of the narrow stratum of wealthy people in a given society, as Marx and Engels argued? What is the purpose of the state? And what sort of state exists in contemporary Russia?

The Purposes of the State

Having sketched out various theoretical conceptions of what the state *is*, we may now move on to determine what it is that the state *does*. According to Adam Smith, author of *The Wealth of Nations*, states have three specific functions:

> First, the duty of protecting the society from the violence and invasion of other independent societies; secondly, the duty of protecting, as far as possible, every member of the society from the injustice or oppression of every other member of it, or the duty of establishing an exact administration of justice; and, thirdly, the duty of erecting and maintaining certain public works and certain public institutions which it can never be for the interest of any individual, or small number of individuals, to erect and maintain, because the profit could never repay the expense to any individual or small number of individuals, though it may frequently do much more than repay it to a great society.[14]

In short, then, Smith's view holds that the three duties of a state are (1) defending the country from external attack, (2) protecting individual citizens under a rule of law, applied equally to all, and (3) providing for what we might label the "public good."

Smith's description of the state's purpose is only one perspective, however. Scholars and philosophers debate at length how extensive the state's role should be, and of what that role should consist. According to political scientist Michael Desch, states vary in "scope," among other things. Scope signifies the range of duties assigned to the state, which can be maximal or minimal. The minimal scope reflects only three state functions: providing "internal order, external defense, and basic public infrastructure." Maximal scope would add other functions, "such as adjudication, redistribution, and extensive infrastructural development."[15] Thus, an extensive public healthcare system, welfare, state-provided unemployment benefits, and other policies that "redistribute" wealth could fall within the functions of a maximal state.[16]

At a minimum, then, "The one duty of the state, that all citizens, except the philosophical anarchists, admit, is the obligation to safeguard the commonwealth by repelling invasion and keeping the domestic peace." It is for this reason that states almost always maintain armed forces: police (to maintain order on the local level) and militaries (to defend the state's territory from outside enemies).[17] Thus, the monopoly on the legitimate use of force that Weber indicated is, in this view, ostensibly used to serve the purpose of maintaining domestic order and defense against external powers.[18]

To this minimum of "maintaining order," others add the function of preserving or fostering the public or common good, although the content of that good is disputed across and within political systems.[19] The public good may include, for instance, the state's responsibility for maintaining the institutional and other infrastructures necessary for a functioning capitalist economy.[20] The market is not an invisible hand after all, and without state regulation and enforcement of property rights, contracts, and so forth, a capitalist economy will not operate smoothly. In order to perform these functions (ranging from supporting a market economy to providing for internal and external defense), the state requires resources, achieved sometimes through conquest or, more typically, through taxation.

Whether state leaders operate with an eye toward furthering the public good will in large part determine whether or not a given state's institutions can achieve legitimacy. Thus, the three chapters in Part I of this volume address the Russian elite's understanding of the public or common good.

In **Chapter 1**, Pauline Jones Luong, analyzing the implications of Russia's energy resource development policies, finds that a self-interested set of Russian political and economic elites privatized the energy resource sector in a way that benefited themselves, and largely excluded the rest of the public from the profits, thereby appearing to value pursuit of private goods (or profits) over the public good and general welfare. Mark Walker, in **Chapter 2**, draws similar conclusions about the Russian elite's tendency to be guided by the primacy of their own power, rather than ruling in the interest of the public good. Investigating the use of political referenda in Russia, Walker finds that Russia's leaders used referenda as a tool with which to perpetuate their own power, rather than as a means of gauging public sentiment. And, in **Chapter 3**, Virginie Coulloudon's exploration of Russia's elite circles suggests that the elite is in fact divided between those profiting from state backing and those whose political and economic fortunes have been made more independently. She finds, however, that the latter elite group remains amorphous and is inherently no more democratically inclined than the former.

In addition to fostering an economic and political climate that benefits more than a narrow spectrum of elites, the enforcement of existing laws is another crucial aspect of maintaining the public good. When law enforcement or contract enforcement is left in private hands, rule of law will not be applied consistently, and laws will not achieve legitimacy.[21] Thus, many scholars view the state as a guarantor of individuals' rights and the rule of law. Indeed, some theorists argue that rule of law is the "central attribute of the modern impersonal state."[22]

The extent of Russia's success in establishing the rule of law is widely debated. In **Chapter 9**, Pamela Jordan expresses a limited optimism regarding the rule of law in Russia. Her analysis of the Russian courts suggests progress toward a more decentralized legal system, where jury trials have been established in some areas (guided by Western assistance), and civil rights are more adequately guaranteed than they were under the Soviet system. Yet the legal system is still plagued with problems, including a lack of state funding. This drives some local courts to seek financial support from private businesses and local political executives, with the obvious potential for biased outcomes.

Finally, perhaps the highest purpose of the liberal state is to control itself, to renounce absolutism, and be responsive to the populace. Franklin Giddings, extolling what he labels the "responsible" state, writes, "And the state, the mightiest creation of the human mind, is also the noblest expression of human purpose. Were it, however, absolute, it would defeat all purpose. Finite and relative it is, of necessity. To fulfill its destiny it must hold itself responsible."[23] That most states are excluded from this "responsible state" definition goes without saying. Where Russia lies will be considered below.

States' goals and purposes vary, in the view of theorists of the state and of state officials and politicians across the world. The extent to which a state fulfills its purposes or lives up to them may be a means by which we can judge the *strength* or *weakness* of that state, its capacity to rule effectively.

State Strength and State Weakness

Political scientist Joel Migdal defines a "strong" state as one that has "high capabilities" to achieve its goals, including "the capacities to penetrate society, regulate social relationships, extract resources, and appropriate or use resources in determined ways."[24] Others define state capacity as "the ability of the state to govern effectively," that is, not on the basis of strength or coercion alone, but relying also or mostly on legitimacy.[25] State capacity is also a measure of how strong the state is in comparison to other forces, both in domestic society and globally. Assessing state capacity and state strength is thus quite challenging.

Moreover, state strength is sometimes understood as signifying strong, repressive states that abuse their power, using bureaucratic and military institutions to repress the population and destroy political enemies or threats (real or imagined). But state strength carries a second meaning, namely that a strong state is one capable of enforcing the population's civil and other rights. This is state strength in the liberal sense—meaning a strong liberal democratic state that protects individual rights, including public services, capitalistic property rights, an honest court system to protect the rule of law and apply it, and an honest bureaucracy to implement regulations.[26] Mere military or police strength may indicate that a state has to rely on the use or threat of force in order to be effective, rather than on strong institutions that the majority of the population supports and views as legitimate. Thus, the distinction between strong states that are repressive dictatorships and strong democratically oriented states deserves emphasis.

Obstacles to the Formation of a Strong State in Russia

The Russian state's problems are manifold, ranging from a failure to collect taxes, implement laws and decrees, fight crime, prevent the fire sale of natural resources, forestall the concentration and massive flight of capital, and reverse the collapse of the social welfare system. Poverty has reached alarming levels: During the first half of 1999, official government statistics in Russia showed that 35 percent of the population was living below the poverty line, earning less than 36 dollars per month.[27] Russia's state weakness is further manifested in widespread corruption, the total cost of which has been estimated at $15 billion per year; even foreign aid has fallen prey to embezzlement.[28]

In trying to explain the persistence of these destructive phenomena, scholars have suggested that "the fundamental problem in Russia's transition is the existence of an enfeebled and profoundly dysfunctional state,"[29] one whose capacity is challenged in many ways. The remainder of this chapter lays out a set of seven obstacles to Russia's achievement of a high level of state capacity: the presence of "strongmen" challenging central authority; the underdevelopment of civil society; widespread reliance on personalism; failure to build institutions; corruption; a lack of clarity about the citizenship boundaries of the Russian state; and Russia's location in

the global political and economic system. Together these illustrate a daunt-
ing set of domestic and international obstacles to the achievement of high
state capacity and the formation of a strong liberal state in Russia.

States Versus "Strongmen"

One technique in a state's arsenal for achieving its aims is to mobilize the
population in support of those goals, whether that means encouraging
popular education in order to provide increasing numbers of state administrators, building a larger and more effective army, or getting the population to pay more of the state's burden through taxes.[30] Such mobilization
can be achieved in different ways, but at a minimum, it involves explaining the goals to the population, and involving the population in state activities, through state agencies or political parties. A state that lacks these
institutional links to the population will have trouble enlisting popular
support, but such structures are difficult to build.[31] Migdal has identified
this as a problem for states in the Third World, but it is not dissimilar to the
problem that postcommunist elites have in Russia today. Deprived of the
Soviet Communist Party, whose tentacles reached into every corner of the
population's life and simultaneously prevented the formation of independent civic groups, Russia's political elites today are left with few available
channels through which to inform and elicit the support of the population.

Although building strong state agencies would seem an appropriate
way to reach the population, in his studies of Third World states, Migdal
was struck by the peculiar behavior of state leaders, many of whom
"have persistently and consciously undermined their own state agencies—the very tools by which they could increase their capabilities and
effect their policy agendas."[32] Migdal explained this phenomenon in part
as a result of *societal structure*, specifically, by the presence of "strongmen"—regional or local leaders or classes who resist the state's policies,
and to whom segments of the population are loyal and/or upon whom
they are dependent.[33]

When such strongmen are present, building state institutions becomes a
risky business. In weak states, central state leaders hesitate to create strong
institutions, because they then run the risk of those very institutions being
"captured" by rival leaders and used to undermine their power (this is
particularly problematic in the case of building a strong army, for example).[34] Migdal terms central state leaders' attempts to undermine strongmen and rivals as "the politics of survival," the result of which is to
weaken central state agencies overall. These methods include several common to today's Russian political scene, such as shuffling appointees
among various state agencies (to prevent any of them from building a patronage network), appointing top officials who have strong personal ties

to the state leadership (personalism), and building shadow institutions or multiple institutions that serve the same purpose (such as paramilitary-internal security forces, in addition to the existing police force and army).[35]

A state's tendency toward minimalist goals may also be explained by this politics of survival. When leaders choose to prioritize their own short-term power over the long-term goal of building support among the population, the goal of public welfare can fall by the wayside. Political scientist William Reno, discussing weak states in Africa, argues that rulers will use state resources to "provide for essential allies, whereas large numbers of state officials—such as teachers [and] health care workers . . . —who consume state resources" but do little to strengthen a ruler or regime against rivals, are dropped.[36] Thus, shrinking state responsibilities for public welfare can be explained in the context of leaders conserving their resources in an attempt to undermine their rivals. This too has been observed in Russia, where teachers, health care workers, and other laborers whose salaries are paid out of the state budget have seen their wages withheld and delayed for months at a time.

When state capacity is eroded in this way, state autonomy may be endangered. In countries with regional "strongmen," state autonomy may be compromised when these domestic societal actors are able to exert influence over the state's policy choices, manipulating the leadership into handing out state resources in exchange for the strongmen's temporary support. The Russian state's failure to institutionalize or regularize economic arrangements like taxation and market competition closely echoes Migdal's argument. Namely, Russia confronts the problem of "strongmen"—although these are both regional officials (who make demands on the state for exemptions and tax breaks for their regions, and thus retain the favor of local populations, as Steven Solnick discusses in **Chapter 6**) as well as the leaders of certain businesses and industries (particularly the oil and gas industries, as described by Pauline Jones Luong in **Chapter 1**), who extracted favors from Yeltsin's government.

In essence, then, as Migdal argued, the central state's ability to build institutions will be inversely proportional to the strength of such "strongmen" in society. As long as they are present it will be hard for a central state to "apply a single set of rules" (or "rule of law") throughout the society, and "to build channels for widespread, sustained political support."[37] Thus far, the new Russia has shared this challenge with the states Migdal studied in the developing world.

Underdevelopment of Civil Society

One way in which Russia may be distinguished from the Third World states that Migdal analyzed is the long institutional legacy of monopolistic rule by the Soviet Communist Party, and the attendant weakness of Russian civil society.[38] While Migdal found the presence of "strongmen" to be the main obstacle to central state capacity, in Russia this problem is exacerbated by the history of Communist Party domination, which weakened the potential for social movement and interest group development that could serve as a counterweight to Russia's regional and economic strongmen. This is often referred to as Russia's lack of "civil society."

It appears that a relationship like that which exists in Russia, between a weak central state and a weak civil society, is a reciprocal one. There is little reason for social movements and interest groups to exert the energy needed to mobilize in order to shape state policies, if those policies are unlikely to be carried out in any case.[39] Stephen Crowley, in **Chapter 7** of this volume, uses the absence of a vibrant labor movement to illustrate this point, arguing that the Russian state has increasingly absented itself from responsibility to the working class, and has been unable or unwilling to enforce laws that would protect workers from wage arrears and other violations. From the state's point of view, this has been a somewhat successful strategy, in that workers, on the whole, do not seem to be directing mass social protest against the state. The virtual absence of well-organized, mass-based constituencies that could demand accountability from their state leaders in the executive branch and legislature is thus a key "missing link" in attempts to create liberal democracy in Russia.

The organization of Russia's political system, with a powerful presidency and a relatively weak parliament, further reinforces both the state's ineffectiveness and the weakness of societal organizations, as M. Steven Fish argues in **Chapter 8**. Indeed, Russia's "superpresidential" system erodes rather than increases the state's capacity for good government, and exacerbates the trend toward an illegitimate and personalistic politics.

Personalism in Russian Politics

Personalism denotes "loyalty to persons rather than to impersonal ideologies, institutions, or rules."[40] This loyalty can have diverse bases, from personal affection for a leader to patronage benefits that leaders give to clients in exchange for political support. Typically, personalism is counterpoised to institutionalization[41] as a means for organizing a state, a political party, or a religious movement, for example; it tends to discourage organization-building and focus instead on a particular leader who provides benefits to supporters.[42]

Russia has a long history of conflating the state with its ruler. According to historian Richard Pipes, "Until the middle of the seventeenth century, Russians had no notion of either 'state' or 'society'. The 'state', in so far as they thought of it at all, meant to them the sovereign, the 'gosudar' or dominus, that is, his [sic] person, his private staff and his patri-mony."[43] Indeed, in tsarist Russia, as in other European states, all state property was associated with that of the king or queen; public and private ownership were thus indistinguishable from each other.[44]

This conflation of economics and politics continues apace in contemporary Russia, where political office is sought after, in large part, as a source of nonsalaried revenue.[45] Sociologist Max Weber might have labeled Russia a regime reliant on "traditional" authority, where the leadership is supported by a "staff" of officials whose services are reimbursed in kind, through patrimony and personal favors from the ruler, rather than by receiving a fixed salary.[46] By contrast, in what Weber described as a rational-legal (or impersonal) system of authority, state bureaucrats—the "staff"—must be "completely separated from ownership of the means of production or administration."[47] In other words, state officials' jobs should bring them no monetary advantage aside from their salaries. This is precisely what is absent from the current Russian system. In the words of one Russia observer, "Almost every Russian official has both an impersonal bureaucratic role and a personal profit-making role; almost every Russian official serves and profits from two masters."[48]

Because of this overlap between the spheres of public service and private economic gain, some scholars see present-day Russia as having reverted to a Weberian "traditional" or "clientelistic" form of government, where, "in exchange for support or the carrying out of a service, the state turns over to an official a resource to be exploited." The Yeltsin government's "loans-for-shares" policy in 1995, for example, effectively granted control over Russia's most valuable state resources to a small number of bankers (now often referred to as "oligarchs"), in return for support in the 1996 presidential campaign, and can be viewed in this light.[49] Among those who financed Yeltsin's campaign, two received government positions afterwards, from which they were able to push against the establishment of a state-regulated, competitive market economy (which would have worked to their detriment).[50] Under such conditions, the state can hardly be said to be autonomous, or insulated from societal pressure groups—one of the characteristics of a strong and effective state.[51]

In other words, state capacity-building may have failed to occur in Russia because "sharp elite conflict and weak links between state and society dramatically reduced the incentives of incumbents to devote the political capital and resources necessary to build state capacity and counter efforts by the winners of initial reforms to block their continuation."[52] Driven by the desire to remain in office, Russia's new political elites chose to use the state resources at their disposal as a means of proffering incentives and favors to potential supporters and powerful allies. Simultaneously, Yeltsin and his team allowed less "useful" segments of the population to fall into poverty, as money that could have been used for social programs was diverted. This route was chosen in part, as Migdal might point out, because Russian civil society is weakly institutionalized and lacks powerful and organized interest groups that could mobilize support for political programs.

Many of the authors in this volume note personalism as a detrimental aspect of Russia's present political and economic course, from the privatization of state property into the hands of a small and well-connected elite (Pauline Jones Luong, **Chapter 1**), to Yeltsin's strategy of promoting only his own supporters within the military (Eva Busza, **Chapter 5**), and the ongoing tendency for the police and court systems to be vulnerable to criminal control and bribery (Pamela Jordan, **Chapter 9**). Ultimately, however, the most damaging result of such pervasive personalism is that it is self-perpetuating. The few people who end up with a stake in the existing system will not be driven to support institution-building or law-building, but rather will support the personal ties and legal loopholes from which they profit. The majority of the population, meanwhile, is left out of the picture. As Stephen Holmes put it, "Russia seems to be a broken-hourglass society in which the privileged do not exploit or oppress or even govern but simply ignore the majority."[53] Only time will tell whether this situation is sustainable.

Failure to Create Strong State Institutions

Russia's state-institutional weakness is perhaps most evident in the economic sphere. In seeking to explain Russia's persistent economic crisis, numerous scholars have reached the conclusion that Russia's economic problems are traceable to a long-standing neglect of institutional development. Building a successful market economy in Russia, according to one such observer, would require an "institutional framework that would protect property rights, allow for the transfer of such rights to foreigners, enforce contracts, ensure the rights of stockholders, and so forth."[54] Institutions are also needed to prevent monopoly and to regulate competition. Instead, after the collapse of the Soviet Union, Russia's political leaders failed to institutionalize a new political and economic system, and allowed the transition from a centralized state-run economy to a criminalized market economy to take place without building in a strong place for state regulation.[55]

Russia's state institutions responsible for taxation provide a striking illustration of incapacity. According to recent reports by Russia's Federal

Tax Police, as little as one percent of Russia's population pays their taxes in full.[56] Among businesses, tax collection also runs low; in 1996, half of Russia's businesses were paying taxes "only sporadically," and one-third were paying none at all.[57] Tax evasion is exacerbated by intentional personal grants of tax freedom by the state to major companies, such as Gazprom. Part of the reason for the state's failure in the realm of taxes is that the very complexity of the tax system discourages compliance, with "over 1,200 contradictory presidential decrees, government orders, and ministerial instructions" confusing the picture.[58] The low salaries of tax police (who can be bribed) and the danger of running afoul of one's intended targets (murders and assaults on tax police are not uncommon) also reduce state capacity in this area.[59]

State institutional weakness in providing the infrastructure to support a market economy (including sufficient police protection of businesses, clear property rights, a court system able to execute its decisions, and so on) has led to the privatization of state functions, particularly in the sphere of enforcement. The growing diffusion of the use of violence by organized criminal groups may be viewed as a means of enforcing the rules of Russia's new market economy. As a result, the state's monopoly on the legitimate use of force is disintegrating rapidly, as entrepreneurs have come to view the use of private security (including both legal and criminal protection organizations) as a legitimate aspect of business dealings.[60]

The purpose of enhancing Russia's state institutions, such that they could more effectively regulate economic interaction and resource collection, is not to achieve a strong state that then abuses its power, as did the Soviet regime and other dictatorships. Rather, the goal is to achieve an accountable set of state institutions that follow transparent and established rules: "People must be able to trust that when the state uses its power, it is for the benefit of society as a whole, not for those with connections, or even the government itself."[61]

Corruption Within State Institutions

Perhaps the most direct drain on state capacity in Russia is corruption. Corruption includes the misappropriation of funding, diversion of resources, evasion of taxes, bribery, and so forth. The privatization of state economic assets in Russia took place in a highly corrupt environment, such that resources which could have been available to the state for general welfare purposes were instead rerouted to a small circle of elites. This misuse of state resources has drastically reduced the funds available to the state for social programs, debt repayment, and infrastructural investment.

Russia's failing economy has even affected resources earmarked for the military. As described by Eva Busza in **Chapter 5**, low salaries, delayed wages, and lack of food and supplies have led to moonlighting by Russian soldiers, who now work as security guards or even form private security services to defend businesses. It is not difficult to imagine entire military units soon seeking out ways to raise funds on their own. Indeed, Busza's analysis of the Russian military reveals a civilian leadership increasingly unable to control soldier behavior (including selling weapons to potentially hostile forces). The state monopoly over the legitimate use of physical force that Weber offered as a defining condition of a state can be achieved only if there is state control over the military, a condition that is on the verge of being dangerously undermined in the new Russia.

Widespread state corruption and a lack of funding for the military also combine to produce a disturbing outcome for public safety. Specifically, the state's monopoly over its weapons stocks is eroding rapidly, as improperly guarded police and military facilities become open to pilfering. The numbers of illegally owned firearms are increasing, and statistics suggest that one-third of these illegally owned weapons originated in Defense Ministry stockpiles.[62]

Finally, just as state leaders and business elites may be wary of strengthening Russia's economic regulatory institutions, they may also be reluctant to build up strong legal mechanisms against corruption, because these could be used against these selfsame politicians and "entrepreneurs," thereby undermining their political and economic positions. This and other aspects of corruption are treated extensively in **Chapter 4** of this volume. There, Louise Shelley presents a dramatic description of the Russian state's failure to cope with organized crime and corruption. In her view, rapid privatization in a highly corrupt environment recentralized economic control in the hands of a small stratum of elites, and possibly threatened the very survival of the Russian state.

Lack of Clarity About the Citizenship Boundaries of the Russian State

Ironically, another obstacle to achieving a high level of state capacity in Russia may be the institutionalization of ethnicity and regionalism, both strengthened over the seven decades of Soviet rule. The fact that the Soviet Union was composed of fifteen republics, each with a "titular" or main ethnicity, provided institutional backing for nationalism to develop once Gorbachev permitted it, although previous Soviet rulers had discouraged this strongly.[63] Within Russia, regional subdivisions similarly based on ethnicity now threaten to provide a parallel basis for Russia's disintegration as a nation-state.[64] Demands on the central government by some of these regions range from Chechnya's assertion of independence (followed by war with Russia in 1994 to 1996) to a recent declaration by the president of the largely Islamic south Russian republic of Ingushetia, establishing that male residents of the republic would henceforth be entitled to have up to four wives. In theory, this would require amending the Russian Family Code, which must be approved by the Russian legislature.[65] Meanwhile, Russia's central government in Moscow lacks regular institutions with which to adjudicate wide-ranging center-regional disputes. Steven Solnick, in **Chapter 6** of this volume, depicts the multiple demands on the center made by Russia's eighty-nine subregions, and argues that, increasingly unable to maintain its authority and leverage over Russia's many and diverse regions, Russia's decaying central government may be endangering the state itself.

Moreover, even ethnic Russians living in Russia lack a sense of unified nationhood, a common understanding of what it means to be "Russian," as opposed to "Soviet." This absence of a unified identity makes it difficult to consolidate Russia's central state. Russia and the other successor states to the USSR, according to Rogers Brubaker, are "incipient states . . . their sociological 'stateness' remains to be established. . . . They are states in the making."[66] Among the contested aspects of their statehood is that of citizenship and nationhood: The answer to the question "Who belongs?" remains unclear. Russia is a multiethnic country, containing dozens of non-Russian nationalities. Given this situation, some politicians are calling for an exclusive, nationalist type of citizenship, where Russia is "for Russians." Others favor a more inclusive, "civic" definition of citizenship, one not based on ethnicity. Citizenship in the Russian case is further complicated by the fact that 25 million Russians presently live outside of Russia in the other former Soviet successor states, such as the Baltics and Kazakhstan. Russia is, in this sense, what Brubaker calls a "national homeland" state and a "nationalizing" state simultaneously—one that serves as "home" to a diaspora and claims that diaspora as its own, and one that is trying to build a sense of "nationhood" around its main ethnic group, in this case, Russians, at the expense of citizens of non-Russian background.[67] Under these circumstances, defining the limits of Russia's territory and striving to find a set of common cultural symbols present another domestic challenge to Russian state capacity.

Russia's Disadvantaged Location in the Global Political and Economic System

With the advent of transnational social movements and global communication systems, scholars acknowledged that politics was no longer solely a "national" affair, but rather a transnational one. Nongovernmental organizations (NGOs) and social movements both domestic and transnational have, for example, pressured states to change their environmental policies and to stop human rights abuses. Politics and economics now take place across borders and are no longer confined by them.[68] In this global era, then, state sovereignty is less than complete. Numerous issues have become transborder issues that individual states do not (and cannot) have the administrative capacity to solve. These include refugee flows, and environmental pollution originating inside one state but affecting others.[69]

Yet states in this international system have varying *degrees* of state autonomy and capacity. Some boast state institutions with high capacity and rule of law; others, like Russia, lack institutions to protect property rights and regulate markets, and are riven by corruption. For such states, this increasingly global system is particularly problematic. Indeed, the international mobility of capital—a key aspect of the global economy—may even further undermine weak states' institutional capacity.[70]

In Russia's case, corruption, the weakness of the state, and the international mobility of capital combine to produce a vicious cycle of under-institutionalization and disinvestment. One might argue that Russia's current business elite will, sooner or later, seek a stable government and economic system at home, so that they can invest, repatriate their profits, and so forth, instead of moving their money into offshore accounts in territories managed by "strong" states, able to provide secure financial guarantees. Russia's "oligarchs" and gangsters alike seem singularly unlikely to make this transition, however. By comparison to their counterparts profiting off of drug money in Columbia and Mexico, who route the majority of their profits back to their home countries, Russians are distinctly "unpatriotic" in this regard.[71] Businesses and corporations in Russia prefer to put their proceeds from trade into foreign accounts, or real estate abroad.[72] Although the extent of this capital flight is distinctly difficult to capture accurately, according to Russian government estimates up to $350 billion worth of Russia's assets have already left the country.[73] Meanwhile, members of the new Russian elite vacation elaborately on the French Riviera and purchase multimillion-dollar beachfront villas.[74] Yet, investment in the Russian economy remains low: By 1997, "investment in key production sectors" had declined to a mere 17 percent of the 1990 level.[75] Altering this situation would necessitate providing Russia's miniature moneyed class with incentives to invest at home, which, in turn, would require a stronger institutionalization of property rights, among other things.

Given this state of affairs, who will convince Russia's leaders of the potential benefits of forming a competent state? Historically, propertied classes in Western Europe and elsewhere have recognized the value of having a strong state (to guarantee their property), and have demanded state protection, followed by demands for other liberal democratic ideals, such as state accountability to voters. But now, given the globalization of capital and financial flows, we may be seeing a globalization of state capacity itself. In other words, some countries that have already established stable and law-governed states will continue to have them, but the elites in other countries will have no reason to expend the effort to create such law-governed states and institutions, because they have discovered that they can profit by stripping resources from their own countries and safeguarding their money in markets attached to stable, law-governed states. In short, the globalization of the economy has changed the rules of the game. As sociologist Peter Evans put it, "As long as private economic actors were dependent on the political environment provided by a particular state, it made sense for them to identify with the political successes and aspirations of that state."[76] This is no longer true for economic elites living in a global economy. Pillaging one's own state (as Russia's elite has done) will not affect one's future, as long as international capital mobility remains in effect.

In this context, Evans argues that globalization has not in fact eroded the need for states, but rather that the contrary may be true.[77] Transnational corporations in the global economy prefer countries with "high" measures of state capacity (that is, with strong public institutions). In short, a high level of state capacity is necessary in order to attract global capital; corporations will show interest only in states that will "protect [transnational economic actors'] returns."[78] The global economic system rewards state administrative competence, whether it is based on repression or on legitimacy, and punishes "weaker" states that have less capacity to protect property, guarantee financial contracts in court, and so on. Thus, states that already have high capacity are at a tremendous advantage over those that lack it, as low-capacity states become entrenched at the bottom of the transnational heap.

A final way in which being part of the global political system may hinder Russian institutional development concerns the internationalization of the legal system. Pamela Jordan, in **Chapter 9**, explains that as of February 1998, the European Court of Human Rights began to hear Russian cases; within a few months, 800 complainants from Russia had already brought suits, thereby going over the heads of Russia's own domestic court system. Turning to international courts instead of domestic ones again suggests a reliance on a foreign government to solve individuals' problems. This represents another example of taking advantage of international state capacity (in this case, judicial institutions) instead of working toward domestic institution-building.[79]

What we are seeing here is how the globalization of civil society, justice systems, and the economy may affect state-building in weak states. Russia's status as a former superpower has spurred international financial aid, as well as assistance from abroad in fighting corruption and administering justice more effectively, particularly through U.S. government, European Community, and other programs, as described by Corbin Lyday in **Chapter 10**. However, the very weakness of Russia's civil society, legal system, state agencies, and economic regulation, vis-à-vis that available in various strong liberal states, may paradoxically be reducing Russia's impetus toward state institution-building. In short, in Russia's case, a combination of internal and external pressures may result in making a weak state even weaker.

Conclusion

> The true forms of government, therefore, are those in which the one, or the few, or the many, govern with a view to the common interest; but governments which rule with a view to the private interest, whether of the one, or of the few, or of the many, are perversions. (Aristotle, *Politics*, Book III, Chapter VII)[80]

Upon the official collapse of the Soviet Union at the close of 1991, the new Russian state inherited a set of institutions in varying states of decay and disarray. In his recent book, *Stealing the State*, political scientist Steven Solnick described the looting-from-within of state-Party institutions like the Communist Youth Organization (Komsomol), which peaked toward the end of the Gorbachev period. That period of accelerated decay now seems like only the beginning of state administrative weakness, or, viewed differently, as the survival strategy of state-Party officials. In other words, the state-institutional weakness observed in Russia at the close of the 1990s is no novelty. As Solnick argues, it had its roots in the Gorbachev era reforms, if not in the establishment of the Party-run, centrally planned economic system itself, and in the opportunism of the bureaucrats who staffed Soviet bureaucracies at all levels. Hastening the process was the decay of authority relations within these bureaucratic institutions under Gorbachev, when the hierarchies were effectively disabled. Gorbachev's reforms altered the incentive structure for bureaucrats, leading to rampant stealing of state assets and the eventual collapse of the state from within.[81] Thus, today's profit-seeking bureaucrats are taking advantage of state resources and assets as part of a long tradition of parasitism.[82]

The use of state assets for personal profit, particularly in the face of collapsing authority relations, is common to the Gorbachev and Yeltsin periods alike. However, while it may make more sense in the short term to take the money and run, in the long term, official encouragement of such behavior is a destructive strategy with potentially ruinous consequences. Indeed, the weakness and undermining of Russia's state institutions leaves the new Russia in an unfortunate position vis-à-vis the other industrialized states, nearly all of which enjoy solidly built state institutions capable of guaranteeing property rights, rule of law, and some degree of political and economic predictability.[83]

If Karl Marx were alive today, it is hard to say how he would interpret Russia's present status within his political-economic schema. Marx's dream, after all, was a communist world without borders, where the state, as such, would wither away. The rise of globalism is surely contributing to the erosion of state borders, as I have argued above, although not for the reasons Marx imagined. Moreover, Marx envisioned that the eventual withering away of the state would occur when the dictatorship of the proletariat gave way to a communist utopia, not to crony capitalism. Perhaps Marx would recognize in Russia precisely his own vision of the state under capitalism: the bourgeois class—albeit, a rather tiny one—ruling through the state, exclusively in their own interests.[84] In the latter case, according to Marx's understanding of history, eventually these conditions would give way to a revolution by the masses against the rich state-elites. For now, however, Russia's state leaders show little sign of trepidation, and Russia's population has eschewed large-scale protest. Whether the Russian state will ultimately wither away from within, grow more stable and effective, or be destroyed from below remains to be seen.

Notes

1. See "Communism and Electrification," in Robert C. Tucker, ed., *The Lenin Anthology* (New York, N.Y.: W.W. Norton and Co., 1975): 492–495.

2. This is not to suggest that all scholars and politicians in Russia and the West saw liberal democracy and capitalism as the best form of government and economic organization, despite the predominance of these ideologies at the close of the twentieth century. On the latter subject, see Francis Fukuyama, *The End of History and the Last Man* (New York, N.Y.: Free Press, 1992).

3. Russia meets the minimalist standards for a democratic political system, having undergone several rounds of multiparty parliamentary elections since December 1993. Russia may thus be labeled an "electoral democracy," if not a "liberal democracy." Indeed, competitive elections constitute an achievement in which some scholars find grounds for a limited optimism about Russia's eventual development toward a liberal democracy. See Michael McFaul, "Democracy Unfolds in Russia," *Current History* (October 1997): 319–325.

4. For an extensive discussion of the "state" as a concept, see John Hoffman, *Beyond the State: An Introductory Critique* (Cambridge, U.K.: Polity Press, 1995).

5. Max Weber, "Politics as a Vocation," in H.H. Gerth and C. Wright Mills, eds., *From Max Weber: Essays in Sociology* (New York, N.Y.: Oxford University Press, 1958): 78; emphasis in the original.

6. Hoffman, *Beyond the State*, 3. Joel Migdal also sees Weber's definition of the state as "institutional"—the state is an organization. See Joel Migdal, *Strong Societies and Weak States: State-Society Relations and State Capabilities in the Third World* (Princeton, N.J.: Princeton University Press, 1988): xiii, fn. 2.

7. Hoffman, *Beyond the State*, 35–37.

8. Andrew Vincent, *Theories of the State* (Oxford, U.K.: Basil Blackwell Ltd., 1987): 20.

9. Joel Migdal, "Strong States, Weak States: Power and Accommodation," in Myron Weiner and Samuel P. Huntington, eds., *Understanding Political Development* (Boston, Mass.: Little, Brown, and Co., 1987): 396–397.

10. Vincent, *Theories of the State*, 20. For extensive discussion of the conceptual importance of the state, see J.P. Nettl, "The State as a Conceptual Variable," *World Politics* 20 (1968): 559–592.

11. Steven Solnick, *Stealing the State: Control and Collapse in Soviet Institutions* (Cambridge, Mass.: Harvard University Press, 1998): 245.

12. There is more than one "Marxist" view of the state; here I refer to Marx's viewpoint as expressed in *The Communist Manifesto*.

13. "The Communist Manifesto," in David McLellan, ed., *Karl Marx: Selected Writings* (New York, N.Y.: Oxford University Press, 1977): 223.

14. Adam Smith, *The Wealth of Nations*, Vol. II, pp. 180–181, as quoted by Alfred Stepan, *The State and Society: Peru in Comparative Perspective* (Princeton, N.J.: Princeton University Press, 1998): 8–9.

15. Desch adds that states vary in "cohesion" as well, which measures the degree to which a state is "unified." Unified states find it easier to fulfill maximal goals. Michael Desch, "War and Strong States, Peace and Weak States?" *International Organization*, vol. 50, no. 2 (Spring 1996): 240–241.

16. The scope of totalitarian states like the Soviet Union is far greater than that encompassed by the "maximal" definition, including a state-run, centrally planned, command economy, and extensive state intrusion into everyday life.

17. Franklin H. Giddings, *The Responsible State* (Boston, Mass.: Houghton Mifflin Co., 1918): 81. For a discussion of contemporary anarchist perspectives, see Howard J. Ehrlich, ed., *Reinventing Anarchy, Again* (San Francisco, Calif.: AK Press, 1996).

18. Vincent, *Theories of the State*, 20.

19. For a more extensive discussion of the "common good," see Alexander Passerin D'Entreves, *The Notion of the State* (New York, N.Y.: Oxford University Press, 1967), chapter 8.

20. Alfred Stepan, *The State and Society: Peru in Comparative Perspective* (Princeton, N.J.: Princeton University Press, 1998): 9.

21. See Joseph Dresen, citing Stephen Holmes, "Can Foreign Aid Promote the Rule of Law?" a seminar at the Woodrow Wilson International Center for Scholars, Washington, D.C., April 15, 1999, posted by [ccsi@u.washington.edu] to the [neww-rights@neww.org] listserv.

22. Yossi Shain and Joan Linz, "Introduction," in Yossi Shain and Joan Linz, *Between States: Interim Governments and Democratic Transitions* (Cambridge, U.K.: Cambridge University Press, 1995): 10.

23. Franklin H. Giddings, *The Responsible State* (Boston, Mass.: Houghton Mifflin Co., 1918): 48.

24. Migdal, *Strong Societies and Weak States*, 4.

25. Cynthia Roberts and Thomas Sherlock, "Bringing the Russian State Back In: Explanations of the Derailed Transition to Market Democracy," *Comparative Politics* (July 1999): 480.

26. For an excellent discussion of the necessity of state strength for a liberal state, see Stephen Holmes, "What Russia Teaches Us Now: How Weak States Threaten Freedom," *The American Prospect* (July-August 1997): 30–39.

27. "Mental Illness, Poverty Increasing," *Radio Free Europe/Radio Liberty Newsline*, vol. 3, no. 149 (August 3, 1999).

28. Nigel Gould-Davies and Ngaire Woods, "Russia and the IMF," *International Affairs*, vol. 75, no. 1 (January 1999): 20.

29. Roberts and Sherlock, 478.

30. Migdal, *Strong Societies and Weak States*, 21–22.

31. Migdal, "Strong States, Weak States," 402.

32. Migdal, *Strong Societies and Weak States*, xv.

33. Migdal, *Strong Societies and Weak States*, 33.

34. William Reno, *Warlord Politics and African States* (Boulder, Colo.: Lynne Rienner, 1998): 19.

35. Migdal, "Strong States, Weak States," 406–415. Migdal also mentions "dirty tricks," such as applying death squads and assassination of one's political rivals, a tactic that was certainly used under Stalin, and has been used less in contemporary Russian politics, although there are many contract killings each year, whose victims include politicians, bankers and other businessmen, and crime figures.

36. Reno, 22.

37. Migdal, "Strong States, Weak States," 428.

38. For an overview of the constraints on creating a liberal democracy in Russia, see Michael McFaul, "The Perils of a Protracted Transition," *Journal of Democracy*, vol. 10, no. 2 (1999): 4–16.

39. For analysis of the varied opportunities and obstacles to social movement development in Russia, see Valerie Sperling, *Organizing Women in Contemporary Russia: Engendering Transition* (Cambridge, U.K.: Cambridge University Press, 1999).

40. Christopher K. Ansell and M. Steven Fish, "The Art of Being Indispensable; Noncharismatic Personalism in Contemporary Political Parties," *Comparative Political Studies*, vol. 32, no. 3 (May 1999): 286.

41. Institutionalization is "the process by which organizations and procedures acquire value and stability." In other words, a practice or an institution can become institutionalized once people become familiar with it, accept it, and expect it to continue to exist. See Samuel Huntington, *Political Order in Changing Societies* (New Haven, Conn.: Yale University Press, 1968): 12.

42. In a recent article, two political scientists have identified a type of political party based on a noncharismatic personalist leadership, which is not inherently

anti-institutional and which exhibits definite organization-building tendencies. See Christopher K. Ansell and M. Steven Fish, "The Art of Being Indispensable: Noncharismatic Personalism in Contemporary Political Parties," *Comparative Political Studies*, vol. 32, no. 3 (May 1999): 283–312.

43. Richard Pipes, *Russia Under the Old Regime*, 2nd edition (New York, N.Y.: Macmillan, 1992): 127.

44. Vincent, *Theories of the State*, 64.

45. Nor was this practice unknown under the Soviet regime.

46. Talcott Parsons, ed., *Max Weber: The Theory of Social and Economic Organization* (New York, N.Y.: Free Press, 1964): 345.

47. Parsons, ed., 331.

48. Charles Fairbanks, Jr., "The Feudalization of the State," *Journal of Democracy*, vol. 10, no. 2 (1999): 49.

49. Fairbanks, 48. The loans-for-shares deal was a phase of the privatization of state property in late 1995, in which, in a series of rigged auctions, the state received loans from certain banks, in exchange for shares of major state-owned companies, which then reverted to the banks when the state was unable to repay the loans.

50. Roberts and Sherlock, 487.

51. Roberts and Sherlock, 493.

52. Roberts and Sherlock, 478.

53. Holmes, "What Russia Teaches Us Now: How Weak States Threaten Freedom," 38.

54. James Millar, "Creating Perverse Incentives," *Journal of Democracy*, vol. 10, no. 2 (1999): 90.

55. Roberts and Sherlock, 478.

56. "Bulk of Russians Avoid Paying Taxes," *Radio Free Europe/Radio Liberty Newsline*, vol. 3, no. 138 (July 19, 1999).

57. Anotol Lieven, "Chechnya: Tombstone of Russian Power," (New Haven, Yale University Press, 1998): 170.

58. Roberts and Sherlock, 493.

59. Lieven, 170.

60. See Vadim Volkov, "Organized Violence, Market Building, and State Formation in Post-Communist Russia," unpublished paper, 1999; and Vadim Volkov, "Violent Entrepreneurship in Post-Communist Russia," *Europe-Asia Studies* 5 (June 1999).

61. See Dresen, citing Holmes.

62. "Unguarded Weapons Caches Leading to Scourge of Illegal Guns," *Radio Free Europe/Radio Liberty Newsline*, vol. 3, no. 121 (June 22, 1999).

63. On the institutionalization of multinationality, see Rogers Brubaker, *Nationalism Reframed* (Cambridge, U.K.: Cambridge University Press, 1996), chapter 2.

64. For analysis of the risks of Russia's disintegration, see Mikhail Alexseev, ed., *Center-Periphery Conflict in Post-Soviet Russia: A Federation Imperiled* (New York, N.Y.: St. Martin's Press, 1999).

65. "Ingush President Approves Polygamy," *Radio Free Europe/Radio Liberty Newsline*, vol. 3, no. 140 (July 21, 1999).

66. Brubaker, 43.

67. Brubaker, 112, fn. 112, and 83–84.

68. On the ways that the globalization of politics and economics affects the state, see Joseph A. Camilleri, Anthony P. Jarvis, and Albert J. Paolini, eds., *The State in Transition: Reimagining Political Space* (Boulder, Colo.: Lynne Rienner, 1995), especially Part I and Part III.

69. See Joseph A. Camilleri, "State, Civil Society, and Economy," in Camilleri, et al., 212.

70. International mobility of capital refers to the possibility for money to flow easily and quickly across borders, including into foreign bank accounts.

71. See Louise Shelley, "Following the Trail of Rubles," *The New York Times* (February 26, 1999).

72. Peter Rutland, "Russia's Unsteady Entry into the Global Economy," *Current History* (October 1996): 324.

73. Shelley, "Following the Trail of Rubles," *The New York Times* (February 26, 1999).

74. Marlise Simons, "New Russians Spread Money on Riviera, but Lack the Panache of the Czars," *The New York Times* (July 24, 1999): A5.

75. Roberts and Sherlock, 487.

76. Peter Evans, "The Eclipse of the State? Reflections on Stateness in an Era of Globalization," *World Politics* (October 1997): 66.

77. See Evans, 74–87.

78. Evans, 78.

79. Globalization has also enabled a shift toward the transnational provision of military protection. For example, William Reno argues that globalization allows the rulers of weak states in Africa to rely on external forces (such as South Africa's firm, "Executive Outcomes") for functions that are usually provided by states, such as armed security. Given the availability of such foreign support, rulers have even less reason to try to gain domestic support by appealing to the population with public goods, or to a rising middle class with rule of law. See Reno, 61–68.

80. Cited in Stepan, 31.

81. For this argument, see Steven Solnick, *Stealing the State: Control and Collapse in Soviet Institutions* (Cambridge, Mass.: Harvard University Press, 1998).

82. On corruption among state officials in the tsarist era, see Pipes, 282–286.

83. Although the industrial democracies are often described as "rule of law" states, the fact remains that these states operate within the bounds of racist, sexist, homophobic societies, with great class disparities, and do not truly provide equality under the law to all citizens.

84. I am grateful to Pauline Jones Luong for her description of the new Russia as Marx's ideal bourgeois-ruled state, in her lecture for the Olin Series, October 14, 1998, Harvard University, Cambridge, Mass.

PART I

The Elite:
Ruling in Whose Interests?

1

The "Use and Abuse" of Russia's Energy Resources: Implications for State-Society Relations[*]

PAULINE JONES LUONG

When Russia emerged as an independent state in 1991, its massive oil and gas reserves held both the promise of economic growth and the potential for building strong political links with society during the transition from Soviet rule.[1] The former could be achieved by using energy to revitalize key domestic industries while simultaneously generating revenue from energy exports abroad. The latter was attainable through investing a portion of these export-generated revenues in basic social services so as to cushion the impact of a short-term rise in unemployment and decline in living standards. Indeed, Russian policymakers seemed acutely aware that the energy sector was crucial to the economic and political success of the transition. One of President Boris Yeltsin's first official responses to the Soviet Union's disintegration in the fall of 1991 was to issue a number of decrees that effectively transferred the authority to control oil and gas exports from the collapsed Soviet state to the newly emergent Russian one.[2] As a result, Russia claimed ownership over 90 percent of the Soviet Union's energy reserves; that is, "one-seventh of the world's proven oil reserves (6.7 billion tons) outside the Middle East, [or] ... the same order of magnitude as the oil reserves of Mexico."[3] Yet, several years into the transition, the energy sector's great promise remained elusive. Long before the spread of the Asian financial crisis and the se-

*The author gratefully acknowledges the critical reading and/or valuable comments of Steve Hanson, Rory MacFarquar, Valerie Sperling, and Erika Weinthal. She takes full responsibility for the final product.

vere decline in world oil prices in mid-1998, Russia's leaders faced
mounting debts to unpaid workers, pensioners, and foreign lenders, and
an increasingly impoverished and disgruntled population.

This outcome is surprising considering not only the aforementioned
expectations for Russia at independence, but also the common experiences of other petroleum-rich states. Natural resource wealth is charac-
teristically found in tandem with nondemocratic political systems, which
are often described as *rentier states*. This is because the possession of substantial petroleum reserves engenders a reliance on oil and gas exports,
which, in turn, leads to state dependence on revenue derived from external sources, such as international trade, rather than from a productive
domestic sector, such as manufacturing and agriculture. The fact that the
state derives its income abroad allows its leaders wide discretion over the
allocation and distribution of resources. Society thus becomes increasingly dependent upon the state for its economic needs, while the state becomes increasingly independent from society for its survival—both economically and politically. In contrast, in nonrentier states, taxation serves
as a lever for society to exercise some political influence over state leaders and has historically served as a basis for demanding popular enfran-
chisement.[4]

The Russian Federation, however, is somewhat unique in that it has
not joined the ranks of the rentier states, but rather has witnessed the
emergence of what I call a "rentier oligarchy." Rentier states seek to exert
social and political control over their populations by creating and maintaining economic dependencies through their sole authority to allocate
and redistribute income obtained from natural resource exports abroad
(i.e., *rents*).[5] Thus, a strong link develops between state leaders and society based on direct economic subsidies to the latter in exchange for concentrated political power for the former. In Russia, however, there has
been little or no attempt to use oil and gas rents to either maintain or re-
formulate state-societal links. Instead, these rents have been captured by
a group of increasingly powerful self-interested elites who have "used"
and "abused" Russia's vast energy wealth to enrich themselves at the expense of society, and without regard for the broader social consequences.
This is the result, I argue, not solely of Russia's polices in the oil and gas
sector, but also of the social-historical context in which these policies
were made. These two factors combined both facilitated and reinforced
an extreme form of rent-seeking behavior among Russia's political and
economic elites, who unabashedly usurped the country's most valuable
natural resources for private gain. The widespread occurrence and increasing acceptance—or normalization—of this behavior has implications not only for the future of economic growth in Russia, but also for
the viability of the Russian state itself.

In this chapter, I highlight the role that the use and abuse of Russia's oil and gas reserves has played in the emergence of a rentier oligarchy, and its implications for the future of the Russian state. In order to do so, I first provide an overview of the social-historical context that enabled political and economic elites to successfully exploit Russia's primary source of revenue for their own ends. Second, I briefly describe the nature of the Russian government's policies toward the energy sector, which amounted to insider privatization of oil and gas production and continued state efforts to control their sale and distribution. I then turn to the specific and general effects that these policies have had on the entrenchment of rent-seeking behavior among elites and the erosion of links between the state and society. Finally, I conclude by exploring the implications of these effects for the future of democracy and the state in Russia.

Social-Historical Context

In order to understand the ability of elites to systematically use and abuse Russia's most valuable resources for their own ends, it is necessary to frame energy sector policies and their effects in a larger social-historical context—that of the Soviet legacy. Three aspects of this legacy are particularly important: first, the critical role that energy resources played in the Soviet economic and political system; second, and perhaps most important, the fact that Russia inherited the remnants of the Soviet state, which had already collapsed by 1991; and finally, the predominance of personalism over institutions for governing political behavior and distributing economic rewards.

The Soviet Union as a Quasi-Rentier *State*

A state must meet three conditions to earn the title of a rentier state: (1) its economy relies upon substantial income from abroad, or "external rent"; (2) few people are actually engaged in generating this rent; and (3) "the government is the principal recipient [and distributor] of the external rent in the economy."[6] The Soviet Union was like a classic rentier state in that it relied heavily on external rents to sustain its economy and to maintain social and political stability, yet departs from this classic model in that its ideology and economic system prevented it from utilizing these resources in an efficient manner. Thus, it is more appropriately classified as a *quasi-rentier* state.

If rents are substantial enough, "[they] can sustain the economy without a strong productive domestic sector," such as manufacturing or agriculture.[7] Under these circumstances, the state does not have to rely upon its population for generating income. Rather, it can utilize its privileged access to external rents to engender societal dependency. Since revenue is extracted from a third party outside the state, society has no economic and hence political leverage over the state. This situation is akin to the manner in which the Soviet economic and political system operated, particularly since the expansion of oil and gas production and the discovery of new reserves in the 1960s.[8] Under Brezhnev and Gorbachev, the Soviet Union increasingly exported its oil and gas in exchange for hard currency and consumer products to subsidize its dwindling productive sector and to maintain its bloated social welfare system. By the 1980s, it "generated approximately forty percent of its budget through collecting rents from oil and gas," which it used primarily to "indirect[ly] subsidiz[e] the domestic economy."[9] Thus, the Soviet Union can be characterized as a "rentier state" because it relied upon external rents to sustain its economy and placate its population.

Yet, the Soviet Union departed significantly from classic rentier states in its approach toward the utilization of its rents from oil and gas. In particular, what made the Soviet Union a quasi-rentier state was the preponderance of ideology and inefficiency in its economy. Marxist-Leninist ideology led the Soviet leadership to undervalue the country's natural resources, and thus the potential rents it could derive from them, as well as to utilize them inefficiently. Inefficiency was then compounded by the centrally planned economy, in which government ministries determined prices for goods internally rather than based on world market indicators. The Soviet Union could thus attribute whatever value it desired to its oil and gas reserves. Both for ideological reasons and in keeping with its centralized economic system, however, it actually chose to price them well below their full market value—both domestically and in its foreign trade arrangements with other socialist countries. Natural resources were viewed as a "free good," and hence, little or no cost was assigned to them as an input in the production of industrial or agricultural goods. At the same time, the allocation-based production system, in which resources were assigned to various sectors based on a central economic plan regardless of economic efficiency or profitability, meant continued reinvestment in the energy sector despite rising production costs. There was thus no accountability, either within the energy sector for costs of production, or on the part of enterprise directors and the general population for the efficient use of energy, all of whom came to expect low-cost energy from the state. The state, in turn, used its energy resources to placate the domestic population by charging next to nothing for domestic electricity and heat, and used the revenue derived from energy exports to subsidize social services and the import of consumer goods. Low fuel prices also enabled the Soviet regime to maintain control over its empire in Eastern Europe and to win political support in the developing world.

The newly independent Russian Federation inherited not only the Soviet Union's vast oil and gas reserves, but also the role and apparatus of the Soviet quasi-rentier state. In sum, this inheritance entailed (1) a heavy reliance upon the energy sector as a source of external rents and cheap fuel; (2) a costly system of cradle-to-grave social welfare and an inefficient industrial base that relied upon the distribution of these external rents and cheap fuel; and (3) a stable social and political situation contingent upon the continuation of huge state subsidies to the energy sector, industry, and society. To be sure, the nature of this "inheritance" sheds light on the difficulties involved in reforming Russia's energy sector. Yet, this alone does not explain why the government adopted certain policies—in particular, policies that amounted to a wholesale shift away from the traditional state role of using its vast energy wealth to maintain a bloated social welfare system. To understand this phenomenon, one must also understand what is perhaps the most crucial inheritance of the Russian Federation—a state in collapse. As will become clear below, the atmosphere of a collapsed state directly influenced elite attitudes and behavior such that they preferred to pursue short-term private interests rather than to adopt long-term goals involving the provision of public goods.

The Legacy of State Collapse

The fact that the Soviet Union was itself a collapsed state when the Russian Federation emerged as its chief successor is crucial to understanding the elite attitudes and behavior that both shaped and were shaped by Russia's approach toward its newly acquired energy sector. Like most states undergoing simultaneous political and economic transition, the Russian Federation began its passage from Soviet to independent rule with a great deal of uncertainty regarding both present circumstances and future outcomes. Thus, it is understandable that Russian elites would be focused on achieving their short-term goals. In fact, the transition produced a situation similar to the anarchical one described by Mancur Olson in which Russian elites acted like "roving bandits" without regard for the future and thus without interest in making long-term investments.[10]

Yet, the legacy of the collapsed Soviet state exacerbated the effects of uncertainty by sanctioning this behavior as "normal practice." As Steven Solnick's account of the Soviet Union's institutional demise makes clear, unbridled opportunism became the norm under Mikhail Gorbachev as a result of his attempts to reform and decentralize the Soviet system. In response to the breakdown of hierarchy around them, Soviet administrative elites took advantage of every opportunity to seize state assets and claim them as their own property.[11] Hence, the mentality and practice of "stealing the state" that Solnick describes were already well entrenched at the beginning of Russia's transition to independent statehood. This meant that, rather than building a new state, elites were continuing to actively dismantle the old one—piece by piece.[12] Considering their immense potential wealth and ready-made export market, it is not surprising that oil and gas reserves ranked highest among preferred state assets that these elites wanted to appropriate.

Moreover, the inheritance of a collapsed state apparatus meant that the Russian leadership lacked the necessary administrative capacity and collective will either to regulate the appropriation of state assets effectively or to put an end to this process. Viewed in this light, Yeltsin's failure to build (or rebuild) institutions after the collapse of the Soviet Union did not create the conditions under which short-term goals and self-interested behavior continued to be rational, but rather, perpetuated them. Michael McFaul's depiction of the privatization process in Russia is consistent with this claim, though he adopts the perspective that Russia inherited a very weak state rather than a wholly collapsed one. In short, he argues that the weakly institutionalized Russian state was incapable of redistributing property rights de jure once these had already been established de facto under the late Soviet regime. As a result, the official privatization program launched in October 1992 did not promote the Russian government's plan to transform the country's economic system, but rather, furthered enterprise directors' parochial interests to maintain their privileged position in the status quo.[13]

Yet, attitude and behavior alone are insufficient to account for the success of these elites at actually achieving their shortsighted goals. The missing link here comes from the Soviet system's promotion of personal ties over institutions as a mechanism for governing political behavior and distributing economic rewards. This legacy contributed directly to the Russian government's failure to lay the institutional foundations for a successful economic transition.

Personalism over Institutions

The significance of the Soviet system's predilection for personal ties over institutions is that it actually facilitated Russian elites' ability to succeed in realizing their own private interests. One of the primary tenets guiding Russian policymaking since the election of Boris Yeltsin to the presidency in 1991 is the sanctity of personalistic politics. As a result, the central government continued to rely upon personal ties and informal networks that developed under the Soviet system to formulate and implement policy, rather than investing in institution-building. Rather than institutionalizing the popular authority he had achieved in 1991 by constructing a new political party or holding new parliamentary elections, for example, Yeltsin chose to centralize the policymaking process among a few select individuals. These individuals were thus in a convenient position to utilize their political influence to further their own economic gain. In fact, those who were best situated to take advantage of Gorbachev's economic reform program (*perestroika*) in the mid-to-late 1980s (i.e., Communist Party officials and factory directors) actually acquired their *real* wealth under Yeltsin's government.

The privatization process once again serves to illustrate. Russia launched its official privatization program for large state enterprises in 1992 as the hallmark of its transition to a market economy. This program proceeded in two phases: (1) the transfer of state ownership to Russian citizens through issuing vouchers, which they could then use to acquire stock or re-sell to other Russian citizens; and (2) money privatization, whereby Russian citizens could purchase state enterprises directly.[14] Both phases of privatization occurred without either a regulatory regime or the necessary legal foundations in place, such as clearly defined property rights and an effective court system. The first phase (voucher privatization) enabled entrepreneurial Russians, who were already well entrenched in the expanding commercial and criminal structures, to accumulate the majority of vouchers from ill-informed citizens either by purchasing them for nominal fees or by guaranteeing high dividends that never materialized. Similarly, in the second phase (money privatization) Russian industry was sold at undervalued prices to favored insiders through the manipulation of documents and auctioning procedures at all levels of government.[15]

Russian Energy Sector Policies

The three aspects of the Soviet legacy described above—a quasi-rentier political and economic system, a collapsed state, and the predominance of personalism over institutions—provide the setting in which the Russian government developed and implemented its policies toward the energy sector. These legacies served to constrain policymakers' choices in the energy sector as well as their ability to implement these policies effectively. In sum, the Russian government's strategy for energy sector development consisted of privatizing the Soviet oil and gas industry, but without either completely divesting the state of ownership and control or allowing significant foreign involvement. While intended to maintain a strong state presence in the energy sector, this strategy instead enabled private actors to gain control over the energy sector and to deny the state its primary source of much-needed revenue.

Although they inherited the apparatus of the Soviet quasi-rentier state, Russian policymaking elites were not "locked in" to continuing past Soviet practices with regard to the energy sector. In fact, they could have pursued two very different paths that might have improved the Soviet Union's utilization of energy reserves as a source of state revenue (through increased taxation) and/or for redistribution to placate society. Namely, they could have (1) completely privatized the energy sector with full foreign participation so as to realize the true market value of its state oil and gas companies; or (2) increased exports abroad under the full control of the state—that is, turned the quasi-rentier state into a real one. Instead, they pursued a minimalist approach to reform, which amounted to neither fully devolving control over the production, sale, and distribution of oil and gas to private owners nor adopting full state ownership and control over these processes.[16]

The first stage of reforming the energy sector consisted of breaking up the Soviet oil monopoly through the restructuring and partial privatization of the oil industry. Initially, a large state holding company for oil—Rosneft—was set up in order to direct this process and then to temporarily manage the remaining state enterprises and shares.[17] Subsequently, the oil industry was reorganized into several smaller companies, including some private, vertically integrated companies (VICs) that "combine crude production, refining, and distribution and retailing in one integrated structure," companies based in Russia's resource-rich regions, and state-owned enterprises.[18] Privatization in the energy sector mirrored the Russian privatization process as a whole in that it proceeded without the necessary legal institutions in place. Thus, as was the case with large state enterprises in other economic sectors, it was based on personal ties rather than competitive bidding. The Siberian Oil Company (SIDANKO), for example, originated as a renamed production association from the Soviet period that "was . . . given by decree, in the absence of any competition, priority rights to exploitation of 20 fields" without taking into consideration the substantial capital investments that the government had already made in these fields.[19] The selling price was thus much lower than what the company might have been worth on the open market, or if it had taken prior investment into account.

At the same time, since energy sector privatization occurred later than in other sectors of the Russian economy, it was also affected by the nature and outcomes of these other "insider-style" privatizations. Those who had acquired the capital to establish commercial banks, for example, were well positioned to acquire ownership in Russian industries through a "loans for shares" agreement between the central government and several newly formed banks with close ties to the executive branch. Because of its efforts to meet pressure from international financial institutions to cut inflation and balance the budget, the Russian government was forced to borrow money from commercial banks to meet its obligations. Beginning in late-1994, they used shares in state-owned enterprises as collateral. When they failed to repay the loans, the ownership transferred directly to the banks. Banks acquired some of Russia's largest and most valuable enterprises in this manner. These included Russia's main producer of nickel, Norilsk Nickel, as well as three of Russia's most lucrative newly formed vertically integrated oil companies—Sidanko (Oneksimbank), YUKOS (Menatep Bank), and Sibneft (Boris Berezovsky's National Oil Company with the help of Menatep and Stolichnyi Bank).[20] As a result, "[t]he proceeds of the export industries [were] divided between the elites who [controlled] the extractive industries and those who [ran] the new commercial banks . . . 65 to 75 percent of [whom came] out of the ranks of the old [Soviet] nomenklatura."[21]

At the end of 1997, there were ten VICs (East Oil Company, Lukoil, ONAKO, Sibero-Uralskaya, Sibneft, SIDANKO, Slavneft, Surgutneftegas, Tyumen Oil Company, and YUKOS), four regional companies (Bashneft in Bashkortostan, Komitak in the Komi Republic, Tatneft in Tatarstan, and Yunko in Chechnya), and two state-owned enterprises (Rosneft and Transneft).[22] The state retained a number of shares in each private company, ranging from 17 percent (Lukoil) to 51 percent (Tyumen Oil Company), as well as a controlling interest in Rosneft, but, for the most part, has allowed them a considerable degree of autonomy in production and exploration.[23] These companies have also enjoyed a "special relationship with the state" through which they have secured continued access to inputs for production based on their privileged status rather than any economic criteria, such as "efficiency and profitability."[24] Regional governments also have benefited from this system, both through assuming outright ownership over oil enterprises and obtaining privileged access to revenue from oil production and export within the territory under their administration.[25]

The Russian government has been much less willing, however, to loosen its controls over the sale and distribution of oil. It continued to set prices for the sale of oil on the domestic market until the spring of 1995, when it allowed domestic oil prices to rise to three-quarters of the world market price.[26] More important, although the state officially discontinued the Soviet practice of exporting oil directly by 1995, it continued to exert formidable influence over the export process through limiting access to pipelines, issuing export licenses, and assigning export quotas.[27] In 1991, the government achieved this by "[appointing] . . . various Russian companies . . . as 'export coordinators' for each of the major oil export routes."[28] Similar to privatization, selection of these companies was based on their personal relations with government officials, rather than through competitive bidding. In response to continued pressure from the international community, Yeltsin officially abolished this system by decree in March 1995. Yet, provisions in this decree and one passed subsequently maintained state control over access to pipelines through Transneft.[29] Thus, by 1995, Russia had "shifted to a more decentralized licensing system based on export quotas" and moved closer toward the liberalization of oil exports.[30] Nonetheless, the state reserved the right to proceeds from a certain percentage of exports.[31] Until the end of 1997, oil producers were still required to sell a portion of their output to traders at low domestic-market prices rather than export directly. This oil was then sold at world market prices by oil companies designated "state-needs exporters" who "split the difference with the government."[32] Such a system enabled the state to control the flow of exports so that it could simultaneously ensure domestic deliveries to industry and households and earn some hard currency, while maintaining strong political links with the oil barons.

Reform of the gas sector has followed this same general pattern, although it has proceeded at a much slower pace. The Soviet gas monopoly, rather than being dismantled, was simply reconfigured into a holding company called Gazprom, which, like Rosneft, was set up "in order to manage state enterprises in the sector . . . [and to] carry out the necessary restructuring prior to privatization in the strict sense," in accordance with the 1992 Law on Privatization.[33] In this sense, "Gazprom . . . was privatized as well, but *in toto* as a single entity controlling the entire cycle of gas production, gas transportation, and processing."[34] This move was harshly criticized in the Russian media at the time as "'actually [securing] the firm's monopoly position in the Russian gas market.'"[35] The government's decision to "[allow] Gazprom to leave 38 percent of its [hard] currency abroad," and then to halt an investigation into the fate of its foreign bank accounts, also received harsh criticism.[36] In fact, many observers have attributed these policies to the position and superior lobbying techniques of then Prime Minister Viktor Chernomyrdin, who headed the Soviet oil and gas ministry under Gorbachev and Russia's fuel and energy ministry under Yeltsin, as well as the government's need to maintain long-term contracts that private companies would not honor.

Similar to the oil industry, Gazprom was allowed a substantial degree of autonomy in its operations, but was greatly constrained by government interference in the form of price controls and export quotas. For example, through a series of decrees approved in the first half of 1993 that raised the wholesale prices for gas, Gazprom was able to "[index] prices (except for gas sold to the population) to adjust for inflation . . . [such that] by June 1995, the average wholesale price was . . . an astonishing sixty percent of the border [i.e., world market] price."[37] Nonetheless, as of the end of 1995, "wholesale and retail prices for gas continue to be administered directly by the government."[38] In addition, "[t]he state . . . maintain[ed] a more direct interest in gas export revenues, with a proportionally larger volume of 'state exports'" and much higher export taxes.[39] This has changed somewhat over time in response to Gazprom's objections. For example, in 1994 the government set new quotas that reduced state exports to an even level with that of Gazprom's own exports, and exempted gas exports from taxation "if exported in payments against government loans or to pay for goods imported under government contracts, [including] natural gas exported as payment for transit to East European countries" in order to honor previous government contracts.[40]

Privatization in the energy sector shared not only a preference toward insiders but also an exclusion of foreign investors from this process. In fact, a strong bias remained among the Yeltsin government, parliamentary deputies, regional leaders, and the oil and gas industry as a whole *against* direct foreign investment in the oil and gas sector, particularly any form of ownership. Much of this stems from the notion that energy is a strategic sector and that Western owners would deliberately undermine Russia's competitiveness on the world market. Even as late as February 1998, when the Russian Duma finally realized some foreign investment in the energy sector was necessary, a prominent member of a reformist party cautioned his fellow deputies and countrymen to "choose foreign investors carefully."[41] Similarly, despite the recognized benefits of selling some of Gazprom's shares on the international market, foreign ownership of more than 9 percent of its shares was prohibited by law until November 1998, when Yeltsin issued a decree raising the limit to 14 percent.[42]

Contrary to the hopes and expectations of the international community, in the first few years of independence Russia failed to create an atmosphere conducive to attracting and maintaining foreign investment in the oil and gas sector. This included the slow pace with which both the Russian government and parliament drafted and adopted a law on oil and gas. When the law was finally adopted in July 1995, moreover, it still lacked adequate legal guarantees to attract foreign investment.[43] The Russian government and parliament also continued to oppose the expansion of production-sharing agreements (PSAs) through 1997 and into early 1998, despite the country's increasing financial difficulties.[44] This opposition comes from within the conservative State Duma as well as among regional governments, both of which apparently fear losing control and profits to foreign companies. The highly complex and arbitrary taxation system as well as the government monopoly over export routes have provided further disincentives for foreign companies to invest in Russia's oil and gas sector.[45] Thus, despite the initial eagerness of the international community to become active participants in Russia's oil sector following independence,

> very little investment has actually taken place. By the summer of 1995 no more than $1–2 billion of the $50–70 billion that the oil industry needed and the foreign companies were willing to invest had actually been committed. Oil output from joint ventures in 1995 accounted for less than six percent of the Russian total.[46]

Some form of foreign involvement might have broken the cycle of elite control over energy reserves as well as provided greater revenue to the Russian government in the form of royalties and bonuses. Instead, the exclusion of foreign investors from the privatization process served to reinforce the privileged position of insiders in securing ownership of the oil and gas industry. This exclusion also ensured that insiders would pay much less than the actual market value of these resources to acquire ownership. As a result, the state essentially forfeited a significant amount of revenue from the sale of its most valuable assets. Ironically, domestic-production-associations-turned-independent-oil-companies have benefited directly from accusations in the media and the Duma that foreigners would "cheat" society.[47] They could then do the "cheating" themselves.

Effects of Energy Sector Policies

The Russian government's policies toward the energy sector can be linked to both a set of specific consequences and a general outcome. First of all, the method of restructuring the oil and gas industry into holding companies has multiplied rather than replaced the functions of former ministries in terms of allocating resources and "sharing out investment."[48] Thus, this restructuring has neither streamlined production nor increased investment, as intended. Second, continued price controls meant that the central government extracted rents by exploiting the differential between world and domestic prices through the "state-needs exporters" system, yet, at the same time, forfeited potential income from oil and gas exports by indirectly subsidizing domestic energy use.[49] This situation has been compounded by the problem of nonpayments, since both private oil companies and Gazprom claim they are unable to meet their tax burden in large part because of their customers' unpaid debts. Third, the system of export controls created incentives for oil companies to enlist the support of organized crime to obtain licenses and to actively organize against any reforms to this system that would threaten their privileged position.[50] It also enabled designated oil companies to hide their export earnings from government tax inspectors in overseas bank accounts.[51]

Finally, and most importantly, the nature of the privatization process itself reinforced the atmosphere created by the inheritance of a collapsed state and the Soviet legacy of personalism over institutions. At the same time, it has undermined the practice of using rents primarily for societal redistribution (i.e., to finance healthcare, education, housing, and other state-sponsored social services). First and foremost, privatization has multiplied the number of actors involved in the collection and distribution of oil and gas rents, with whom the state must now compete. Second, in the absence of direct foreign investment, privatization greatly undervalued the worth of the state's most important resource, such that the *real* worth of the oil and gas industry was neither assessed nor possible to procure from capital-poor domestic "buyers."

In sum, the combination of a preference for insiders and the exclusion of foreign investors directly contributed to the rise of a "new" set of rent-seeking elites who actively compete with the state for the capture of oil and gas rents.[52] The most striking manifestation of this competition is the ongoing struggle between the VICs and the central government over taxes. On the one hand, the VICs have accused the central government of imposing such an unreasonable tax burden that they are unable to make even a small profit. On the other, the central government has complained that these companies fail to contribute their fair share to the state budget, and yet, it has been unable to manage either tax collection or its shrinking budget effectively. The collection and distribution of oil and gas rents, therefore, is determined by competition among these political and economic elites, after which there is very little left over for redistribution at the societal level. As a result, the Russian state has lost both the authority and the capacity to collect and allocate oil and gas rents at its sole discretion.

Together, these factors have resulted in the destruction of the Soviet quasi-rentier state and the rise of a "rentier oligarchy" in its place. In contrast to rentier states, the Russian government competes directly with industry for control over rents rather than conspiring with industry to capture and redistribute rents, and relatively little of the rent income it is able to secure is redistributed to the population as a form of political and social control. In contrast to both rentier states in general and the Soviet quasi-rentier state in particular, it has abandoned the practice of utilizing rents to provide public goods. Whereas the Soviet Union used its rents, however inefficiently, primarily to subsidize both its domestic industry and maintain social support among its population, the Russian elite abuses oil and gas rents for its own personal economic gain. In sum, Russia is not a rentier state, or even a quasi-rentier state, but rather, a country whose economic and political system is governed by a set of rent-seeking elites with little or no connection to society-at-large. It is more appropriate, therefore, to think about Russia as a "rentier oligarchy," or an administration that sustains itself through dependence upon substantial external rents in which the only real allocation and distribution of those rents takes place at the level of elites themselves.

Implications for Democracy and Russian Statehood

The failure of the Russian government to utilize its oil and gas rents in order to provide public goods has significant implications for Russia's future, both as a democracy and as a state. The erosion of links between state and society that has occurred as a result of this blatant violation of the Soviet "social contract" undermines the process of democratization that began in Russia in 1991.[53] It is widely recognized that democracy requires a certain form of state-society relations—direct and reciprocal—in order to function properly. In fact, the very purpose of democracy is to devise domestic institutions that effectively channel societal demands to the country's leadership.[54] One of the mechanisms that makes this possible is the collection and redistribution of taxes. In such a system, leaders are compelled to be responsive to societal demands for two reinforcing reasons: to win reelection and to generate revenue. The spheres of state and society in Russia, however, have become increasingly detached. Domestic institutions are essentially ineffective in both channeling societal demands to state leaders and facilitating state administrative capacity to penetrate society. A fully functioning party system, which closely links state and society in other democratic systems, for example, has not yet materialized. Nor has the state established a viable taxation system through which to sustain itself and provide basic social services. Rather, state elites rule by negotiating pacts with one another that have little to do with the society they are supposedly "governing," and societal forces are disengaged from virtually all state functions rather than either supporting or protesting elite behavior.[55]

The implications for the future of Russian statehood are even more striking. If indeed Russia is governed by an administration that exists for the sole purpose of extracting and enjoying oil and gas rents, the future of the Russian state may be tenuous at best. On the one hand, the type of "state" that appears to be emerging in Russia closely resembles the model of the "predatory state" found in either premodern Europe or modern-day Africa. On the other, the question arises as to whether Russia *really* constitutes a state at all.

Undoubtedly, the contemporary situation in Russia shares several similarities with the system of "predatory rule" described by Margaret Levi and the "predatory state" described by Peter Evans. The former refers to state leaders who are "rational" in that they "always try to set terms of trade that maximize their personal objectives, which require them to maximize state revenues."[56] The latter refers to a state that

> extract[s] at the expense of society, undercutting development even in the narrow sense of capital accumulation [and] lack[s] the ability to prevent individual incumbents from pursuing their own goals [because] personal ties are the only source of cohesion, and individual maximization takes precedence over pursuit of collective goals.[57]

Yet, the situation in contemporary Russia also has some crucial distinctions. First of all, both the behavior of Russian political elites and the outcome of their behavior depart from the expectations of these models. Unlike predatory rulers, the Russian government does not appear to concern itself with "maximiz[ing] state revenues" either in the short or long term. In contrast to the leaders of a predatory state, in which patronage coupled with some redistribution serves as the link between state and society, the Russian "state" does not attempt to penetrate society, but rather hovers over it in a detached fashion.[58] Second, it is not at all clear that the Russian "state" is the agent of political and economic policy in the same way that the "state" is in these models. The former requires a state with a great deal of administrative capacity, which the Russian government clearly lacks—in particular the ability to collect taxes. In contrast to the latter, it is not the Russian "state" that is being predatory, since that would require an identifiable set of actors within the governing apparatus; rather, it is a small number of autonomous individuals.

Thus, we might instead consider whether Russia really constitutes a state at all—predatory or otherwise. At a minimum, we would expect a state to have an interest in providing some public goods, such as social stability and economic growth. Yet, Russia's political and economic elites do not seem to have either an interest in providing public goods or a clear understanding of why they should. Doing so requires a long-term investment, which is counter to their short-term goals.

This leads us full circle to the social-historical context in which Russia emerged an as independent political unit. Particularly important here is the fact that Russia inherited, if not a fully collapsed state, then a greatly weakened one, particularly in terms of its ability to collect and distribute resources.[59] Soviet elites were therefore already well positioned to "capture" the state by appropriating its assets, which set a strong precedent for rent-seeking attitudes and behavior to prevail and, more importantly, to become the accepted norm for acquiring wealth and influence. Moreover, the continued practice of promoting personal ties over institution-building as a way to conduct "official" government business served not only to reinforce these tendencies among Russian elites, but also to enable them to actually succeed in realizing their own private interests over those of the state. In this regard, the predominance of informal networks and personal ties in post-Soviet Russia appear to be tearing away at the fabric of the state, rather than, as some have suggested, providing the foundations for state-building.[60]

Notes

1. See, for example, *Russian Economic Reform: Crossing the Threshold of Structural Change* (Washington, D.C.: World Bank, September 1992).

2. "Quota and Export Rules Cloud Outlook for Russian Industry," *Oil and Gas Journal* 89 (November 25, 1991): 47.

3. "Quota and Export Rules Cloud Outlook for Russian Industry," *Oil and Gas Journal* 89 (November 25, 1991): 47; Dale Gray, "Evaluation of Taxes and Revenues from the Energy Sector in the Baltics, Russia, and Other Former Soviet Union Countries," *IMF Working Paper* (March 1998): 5. This made Russia the world's third largest oil producer.

4. One only need recall the cry of the American revolutionaries—"no taxation without representation"—to grasp the link between society's economic contribution to the state and its political leverage. For a more sophisticated theoretical treatment of this link, see Douglas North and Barry Weingast, "Constitutions and Commitment: The Evolution of Institutions Governing Public Choice in Seventeenth-Century England," *The Journal of Economic History* 49 (1979): 803–833; and Robert Bates and Da-Hsing Donald Lien, "A Note on Taxation, Development, and Representative Government," *Politics and Society* 14 (1985): 53–70.

5. The term *rents* simply refers to "'the income derived from the gift of nature,'" or income earned without needing to engage in productive activity. See Hazem Belawi and Giacomo Luciani, eds., *Nation, State and Integration in the Arab World, Volume 2: The Rentier State* (London, U.K.: Croom Helm Ltd., 1987): 49.

6. Belawi and Luciani, eds., *Nation, State and Integration in the Arab World* (London, U.K.: Croom Helm, Ltd., 1987): 52.

7. Belawi and Luciani, 51.

8. For details, see Thane Gustafson, *Crisis Amid Plenty: The Politics of Soviet Energy Under Brezhnev and Gorbachev* (Princeton, N.J.: Princeton University Press, 1989).

9. Matthew Sagers, Valeriy A. Kryudkov, and Vladimir V. Shmat, "Resource Rent from the Oil and Gas Sector and the Russian Economy," *Post Soviet Geography,* vol. 36, no. 7 (1995): 389 and 395.

10. Mancur Olson, "Dictatorship, Democracy, and Development," *American Political Science Review,* vol. 87, no. 3 (September 1993): 567–577.

11. Steven L. Solnick, *Stealing the State: Control and Collapse in Soviet Institutions* (Cambridge, Mass.: Harvard University Press, 1998), especially Chapter 2.

12. Compare this situation to other post-Soviet states, such as those in Central Asia, wherein the collapse of the Soviet Union invigorated the state-building

process. See, for example Pauline Jones Luong, "The Future of Central Asian Statehood," *Central Asian Monitor*, no. 1 (January 1999).

13. Michael McFaul, "State Power, Institutional Change, and the Politics of Russian Privatization," *World Politics* 47 (January 1995): 210–243.

14. For more detail, refer to McFaul, "State Power, Institutional Change, and the Politics of Russian Privatization"; and Maxim Boycko, Andrei Shleifer, and Robert Vishny, *Privatizing Russia* (Cambridge, Mass.: MIT Press, 1995).

15. For an insider's account of these events, see Alfred Kokh, *Privatizasiya v Rossii: ekonomika i politika* (Moskva, 1998).

16. A full explanation for this policy choice is beyond the scope of this chapter. See Pauline Jones Luong and Erika Weinthal, "Domestic Determinants of the International Role in Oil and Gas Development: The Case of Central Asia," unpublished manuscript (1998): 32–33.

17. C. Locatelli, "The Reorganization of the Russian Hydrocarbons Industry: An Overview," *Energy Policy*, vol. 23, no. 9 (September 1995): 813.

18. Sagers, Kryudkov, and Shmat, "Resource Rent from the Oil and Gas Sector and the Russian Economy," 398.

19. Valery Kryukov and Arild Moe, "How the Industry Structure Is Changing in the Former USSR," *Oil and Gas Journal*, vol. 90, no. 20 (May 18, 1992): 2.

20. For more detail, see Virginie Coulloudon, "Privatization in Russia: Catalyst for the New Elite," *The Fletcher Forum of International Affairs*, vol. 22, no. 2 (Summer/Fall 1998): 43–56; and Juliet Johnson "Russia's Emerging Financial-Industrial Groups," *Post-Soviet Affairs*, vol. 13, no. 4 (1997): 333–365.

21. Peter Rutland, "Lost Opportunities: Energy and Politics in Russia," *NBR Analysis*, vol. 9, no. 5 (Seattle, Wash.: December 1997): 15.

22. *Transneft* is the state-owned holding company for all of Russia's oil pipeline networks.

23. *Pipeline News*, no. 28, part 2 (September 16, 1996). Prior to the reorganization of the energy sector, oil and gas continued to be produced, as it was under the Soviet period, based on state orders and sold at set prices. After 1993, state orders remained only for "required deliveries for the export market and for the needs of 'priority' domestic consumers—agriculture, the Far North and the military." See Sagers, et al., "Resource Rent from the Oil and Gas Sector and the Russian Economy," 400, 403.

24. Locatelli, "The Reorganization of the Russian Hydrocarbons Industry: An Overview," 818. The holding companies thus operate very similarly to their predecessor, the Soviet Oil and Gas Ministry, which performed the same role for production associations.

25. Disputes between central and regional authorities over jurisdiction with regard to "export tariffs, access to pipelines, and custom duties" have continued since 1991. See, for example, Lucian Pugliaresi, "Russia Grappling with Economic and Political Challenges," *Oil and Gas Journal* 91 (August 2, 1993): 31; and Bruce Kellison, "Siberian Crude: Moscow, Tyumen, and Political Decentralization," in Stephen Kotkin and David Wolff, editors, *Rediscovering Russia in Asia: Siberia and the Russian Far East* (Armonk, N.Y.: M.E. Sharpe, 1995).

26. James Watson, "Foreign Investment in Russia: The Case of the Oil Industry," *Europe-Asia Studies*, vol. 48, no. 3 (1996): 432; Sagers, et al., "Resource Rent

from the Oil and Gas Sector and the Russian Economy," 405. The 1990–1991 foreign investment laws and price liberalization did not apply to the oil and gas sector.

27. These two policies are interrelated, of course, since restricted exports kept domestic oil and gas prices artificially low by forcing producers to sell on the internal market.

28. Sagers, et al., "Resource Rent from the Oil and Gas Sector and the Russian Economy," 406. There were 30 of these "special exporters" in 1993, 18 in 1994, and 14 in 1995. Sagers, et al., 408.

29. For details, see Sagers, et al., "Resource Rent from the Oil and Gas Sector and the Russian Economy," 409.

30. Sagers, et al., 405.

31. Sagers, et al., 420–421.

32. *Energy and Politics*, part I (January 19, 1998).

33. Locatelli, "The Reorganization of the Russian Hydrocarbons Industry," 813.

34. Sagers, et al., "Resource Rent from the Oil and Gas Sector and the Russian Economy," 399.

35. "Doubt Voiced About Russian Privatization Move," *Oil and Gas Journal*, vol. 90, no. 46 (November 16, 1992): 1.

36. "Profile: Russia's New Energy Czar," *Oil and Gas Journal*, vol. 91, no. 5 (February 2, 1993).

37. Sagers, et al, "Resource Rent from the Oil and Gas Sector and the Russian Economy," 405.

38. Sagers, et al., 404.

39. Sagers, et al., 410.

40. Sagers, et al., 410.

41. *Energy and Politics* 5, part 1 (February 17, 1998).

42. "Russia OKs Partial Gas Co. Sale," *The Associated Press* (November 2, 1998).

43. Watson, "Foreign Investment in Russia: The Case of the Oil Industry," 434–438.

44. PSAs are known to attract the most foreign investment because they establish a long-term stable relationship with the host country and tend to offer foreign companies the greatest autonomy in their operations.

45. Watson, "Foreign Investment in Russia: The Case of the Oil Industry," 438–442.

46. Sagers, et al., 429.

47. See, for example, Kryukov and Moe, "How the Industry Structure Is Changing in the Former USSR," 3.

48. Locatelli, "The Reorganization of the Russian Hydrocarbons Industry," 819.

49. Sagers, et al., "Resource Rent from the Oil and Gas Sector and the Russian Economy," 420.

50. Sagers, et al., 407–408. See also Rutland, "Lost Opportunities," 20.

51. By some estimates, this practice has cost the government treasury "$10–15 billion a year." See Rutland, "Lost Opportunities," 18.

52. These elites, of course, are not entirely "new," but have their roots in the Soviet past. See McFaul, "State Power, Institutional Change, and the Politics of Russian Privatization."

53. For a more detailed description of this "social contract," see Peter Hauslohner, "Gorbachev's Social Contract," *Soviet Economy*, vol. 3, no. 1 (1987): 54–89.

54. See, for example, Adam Przeworski, *Democracy and the Market* (Cambridge, UK: Cambridge University Press, 1991); and David Held, *Models of Democracy* (Stanford, Calif.: Stanford University Press, 1987).

55. Pauline Jones Luong and Erika Weinthal, "Energizing the Post-Soviet State: Energy Development Strategies and Prospects for Democracy," unpublished manuscript, 47–50.

56. Margaret Levi, *Of Rule and Revenue* (Berkeley and Los Angeles, Calif.: University of California Press, 1987): 10.

57. Peter Evans, *Embedded Autonomy: States and Industrial Transformation* (Princeton, N.J.: Princeton University Press, 1995): 12.

58. I attribute this description to Stephen Holmes, presentation at the Annual Meeting of the American Association for the Advancement of Slavic Studies (AAASS), Seattle, Washington (November 1997).

59. Solnick, *Stealing the State: Control and Collapse in Soviet Institutions*; McFaul, "State Power, Institutional Change, and the Politics of Russian Privatization."

60. See Gerald M. Easter, "Personal Networks and Postrevolutionary State-building: Soviet Russia Reexamined," *World Politics* 48 (July 1996): 551–578.

2

Do the People Rule?
The Use of Referenda in Russia

MARK CLARENCE WALKER

Political leaders have used referenda for over two thousand years to fulfill their goals, and Russia's elites used these votes in the 1990s for strikingly similar purposes. The dictionary defines a referendum as the submission of a proposed public measure or actual statute to a direct popular vote;[1] its synonym *plebiscite* originates in the Roman *plebes*, or commoners, polled by Julius Caesar in order to subvert the decisions made by the Roman Senate. Often cast as an aspect of democratic politics, in reality the referendum can blur the line between democracy and authoritarianism depending on how it is used and manipulated by political leaders.

The referendum is arguably a tool of democracy because it allows the people's will to be expressed and thus grants some legitimacy to a political regime.[2] In fact, some have claimed that the referendum is a better measure of the people's will than the direct election of representatives in the form of parliaments and presidents.[3] The reality of how referenda have been used and what they reflect about Russian democracy, however, suggests something different. Russian President Boris Yeltsin and his use of the referendum have raised questions throughout his tenure about his commitment to democracy and the role the people actually play in Russian politics. Indeed, Yeltsin's use of the referendum and Russia's experience with it suggest that the people may not be as engaged in Russian democracy as one would expect.

Referenda grant legitimacy to individuals, interests, and institutions, and therefore may change the distribution of power between entities, but they may also increase tensions between competing political individuals, interests, and institutions. Referenda called to settle disputes between competing parties do not always resolve the issue. Nor do they necessarily serve as a democratic tool. Instead, they can function to enable elites to further their own interests, beneath the veneer of popular legitimacy. Though the intentions behind using the referendum vary, its ability to be manipulated has been a consistent factor in its popularity. The use of referenda in Russia is no exception to this rule.

In this chapter, I argue that referenda in the post-Soviet government reflect a democratization that has been led thus far by a political elite with little direction from the citizenry. Referendum topics have been concerned with the distribution of power between institutions and elites and not necessarily the welfare of the public as a whole. Moreover, citizen participation in initiating referenda in Russia has not increased over time. These observations suggest that Russia will continue to be led by the few for the few in the foreseeable future.

Referenda in Russia

The March 1991 Referendum in the Russian Republic on Instituting the Office of President

The history of referenda in Russia begins with the first and last referendum held in the Soviet Union. On March 17, 1991, Mikhail Gorbachev, general secretary of the Communist Party and president of the Union, called a referendum on the preservation of the Soviet federal state. Reform and secessionist groups in the republics were rallying for autonomy from the central Soviet authorities; the Baltic republics were pushing for nothing less than full independence. These groups had been encouraged by Gorbachev's tacit approval of the secession of Eastern Europe from the Soviet bloc in 1989. Gorbachev believed correctly that a majority of the Soviet people would want to stay in some sort of union even though many in certain republics would not. The Soviet republics responded in a variety of ways: by boycotting the vote, changing the question, holding counter or dueling referenda, or by simply adding another question to the ballot. The Russian republic, under the leadership of Boris Yeltsin, decided to add a question asking whether the Russian people wanted to institute the office of president for the republic.

In the Russian republic, the conflict was not simply center versus periphery but also Gorbachev versus Yeltsin. Yeltsin had been an ally of Gorbachev's in his push to reform until, in a meeting of the Central Committee, he openly criticized Ligachev, the CPSU's second in command, and Gorbachev himself for the slow pace of reform. In response, Gorbachev publicly chastised and humiliated Yeltsin and removed him as head of the Moscow Communist Party organization on November 11,

1987. But by the spring of 1990, Yeltsin had risen to chairman of the Russian republic's parliament and had gained popular recognition as opposition leader to Gorbachev and the center.

Yeltsin used the upcoming vote on the union referendum as an opportunity to hold a vote in the Russian republic on establishing the institution of the presidency. For Yeltsin, boycotting the referendum was too strong an action to take at the time, but introducing another question for the Russian people to answer was not. Yeltsin decided to add a question to the Russian republic ballot that would set the groundwork for an institution—a popularly elected Russian presidency—that would allow him to directly challenge the authority and legitimacy of Gorbachev. On January 25, the Presidium of the RSFSR Supreme Soviet agreed to hold the all-union referendum and recommended that the Russian Supreme Soviet consider additional questions. Yeltsin was then able to place his question on the ballot: "Do you consider it necessary to introduce the position of President of the RSFSR, elected by universal suffrage?"

In addition, the domino effect of referendum begetting referendum continued at the local level where anti-Yeltsin forces and others devised additional questions of their own on regional and city levels. Most of these questions were relatively benign; nevertheless, the precedent had been set for challenges to the sovereignty of the Russian republic through the referendum device. These challenges would multiply in just a few years.

The mandate to create the presidency in the March 17 Russian referendum was very clear. This referendum established the position of president of the Russian Soviet Federative Socialist Republic with the approval of 69.9 percent of the Russians voting (see Table 2.1). On June 12, Boris Yeltsin won the first popular election for president with 57.3 percent of the vote in a field of six candidates.[4] It was a considerable defeat for the Communist Party; the CPSU commented afterwards that its leaders had "finally lost authority."[5]

Referenda, Elite Bargaining, and the Distribution of Power Between Nascent Political Institutions. The addition of the question on whether to establish the Russian presidency in the March 1991 referendum may have been the single most important act in Soviet and Russian politics since the introduction of glasnost and its acceleration by the Chernobyl nuclear disaster in 1986. It extended a legitimacy to the popularly elected Russian presidency that, in turn, gave Yeltsin the authority to challenge the group of conservative Soviet forces that attempted a coup in August 1991. The Russian presidency has also been the only major institution to survive since the breakup of the USSR, having bested the old Congress of People's Deputies that met its violent end in October

TABLE 2.1   Results of the March 17, 1991, Referendum in Russia on Instituting
the Presidency

*Question: "Do you consider it necessary to introduce the position of President of the
RSFSR, elected by universal suffrage?"*

		percent of electorate	percent of vote
Total electorate	101,776,550	100.0	—
Total number of voters in the referendum	76, 425,110	75.1	100.0
Spoilt papers	1,633,683	1.6	2.1
Total number of valid votes in the referendum	74,791,327	73.5	97.9
"Yes" votes	53,385,175	52.5	69.9
"No" votes	21,406,152	21.0	28.0

SOURCES: *Izvestiya* (March 26, 1991): 2; Stephen White, Richard Rose, and Ian
McAllister, *How Russia Votes* (Chatham, N.J.: Chatham House, 1997): 76; Staff of
the Commission on Security and Cooperation in Europe, 1991, *Referendum in the
Soviet Union: A Compendium of Reports on the March 17, 1991 Referendum on the Future of the U.S.S.R.* (Washington, D.C.: U.S. Government Printing Office).

1993. This office has essentially been the only continuous, institutional
link to survive the transition period between the old Communist regime
in Russia and the nascent democratic one. If Gorbachev had not introduced the referendum device, it is probable that Yeltsin would have introduced the Russian presidency but perhaps not by popular vote and
perhaps not in time for the August 1991 coup attempt.

In short, there had been a shift in the distribution of power between institutions and elites in the Soviet Union, and it had happened as the result of a referendum. Yeltsin's use of the referendum to establish the institution of the Russian presidency gave him an unprecedented
platform—in June 1991 he became the first popularly elected leader of
Russia. The legitimacy of the General Secretary, the Politburo, and the
Central Committee of the Communist Party of the Soviet Union paled in
comparison. Moreover, the authority that these institutions claimed as
the vanguard of Communist ideology eroded over time when their mismanagement of the Soviet economy and nationalities issues became evident. Thus, the referendum played an important role in the transition
from Communist to democratic rule by conferring legitimacy where
none had existed before.

Conflicts in Russia and the Soviet Union that pitted the president versus legislatures, and the federal governments versus substate govern-

ments, were in essence elite conflicts over the distribution of power. Elites often sought to consolidate more power for their respective institutions in order to implement their goals over the objections of their opponents. An example of this was Yeltsin's creation of the Russian presidency in 1991, which gave him a platform from which to challenge Gorbachev. Elites also called referenda in the hope of maneuvering around their opponents. With his referendum on the union treaty, for example, Gorbachev aimed to preserve his own power and subvert the legitimacy of independence-minded republics. Moreover, elite goals that changed the distribution of power between nascent political institutions often had long-lasting effects upon the form of government of the newly established democratic state. Thus Russia developed a strong presidential government as a result of Yeltsin's battles with his opponents. During these conflicts, Yeltsin's use of the referendum device was central. Even though Gorbachev failed to keep the Soviet Union intact, he did attempt to use a referendum to legitimize a new union treaty among rebellious republics, which is another example of elite power exerting a strong influence on the character of political institutions and the distribution of power between them during periods of conflict.

Referenda have been used by executives and regional governments to increase their power, but have simultaneously increased tensions between the various individuals whose interests were at stake. For example, the March 1991 union treaty referendum and the republic autonomy referenda spawned increased tensions between participants.[6] All of the participants gained confidence coming out of the referendum voting: The hard-liners felt they had won the union treaty referendum; the republics felt as if their autonomy referenda had given them more freedom; and Gorbachev was confident enough to pursue ratification of a new union treaty, having won on the question he called. The result was that hard-liners felt empowered to attempt a "union-saving" coup against Gorbachev in August 1991. Similarly, the April 1993 Russian referenda (discussed below) and Yeltsin's dispute with the parliament in 1992 to 1993 raised questions among Muscovites about which side the armed forces might take in a civil war.[7] These referenda raised expectations and created a situation in which there would be definite winners and losers playing a zero-sum game.

Changing the distribution of power between elites and institutions in a transition period raises the specter of conflict. High expectations of success and misperceptions of the intentions of one's opponents are often the precursors to wars between states.[8] Misperceptions among domestic elites in competition over the distribution of power between nascent political institutions in transition suggest a very similar outcome. The April 1993 Russian referenda illustrate the strategic choices that domestic political actors face and show why conflict might arise when elites pursue their own goals. Though referenda are not the source of the conflict, they often exacerbate a situation and make conflict more likely.

Referenda and Elite Bargaining in Russia, 1992–1996. The subjects of the political debates between elites from 1992 to 1996 in the post-Soviet states can be reduced to two issues: economic liberalization and the continuing role of the Communist Party and its elites.[9] Economic liberalization here encompasses privatization of state resources. The most pronounced debate over the continued role of communism occurred in campaigns for elected office between two factions: the Communist and reform candidates. Communist candidates favored the citizenry hardest hit by economic liberalization by promoting socialist economic programs and a slowing of reform. Reform candidates attacked their Communist opponents for being associated with those Soviet Communists responsible for authoritarian regimes, the mass repression of people and ideas, and economic stagnation. Reform candidates themselves differed internally on how fast and how far economic liberalization plans should go; nevertheless, they remained united, apart from and against the Communists, no matter how fractured their ranks became.

In the early stages of the transition from communism, elite bargaining over policy often led to deadlock. Battles over policy became battles over the distribution of power between institutions, as elites attempted to consolidate the necessary power for their government body to implement goals regardless of the opposition. Presidents desired not only to concentrate power unto themselves, but also to dismantle the legislatures that opposed them. Regions within states not only created and strengthened regional governmental structures but also strived to become independent of the federal government. Both types of situations created a constitutional crisis in which the use of violence by military and security forces loomed as the only way to resolve the conflict. Elites began to utilize the referendum as a device not only to settle these disputes in their favor but also to ward off the threat of violence.

The threat of violence, nevertheless, played a central role in elite bargaining. Elites worried about which side the military would take if the policy dispute disintegrated into armed conflict.[10] Losing an armed conflict would allow the victors carte blanche in the revision of the institutions the losing elites represented. Moreover, the losing elites who survived the armed confrontation would be, at the very least, jailed under severe charges, such as treason. Elites who believed the military was on their side were more resolute in their position and pressed their agendas more aggressively than the ones who believed the military would not support them in a violent conflict with their opponents. Elites who believed they would not be supported by the military would develop strategies that attempted to avoid violent conflict.

When elites did not know which side the military would take, uncertainty confused the participants' strategies. Moreover, if elites on both sides of the conflict believed that they enjoyed the backing of the military, both sides might have displayed confidence. Such situations had a high probability of leading to violence, when each expected the other to capitulate but neither did. The Russian April 1993 referenda are an example of this type of misperception. Both President Yeltsin and Parliament Speaker Khasbulatov believed the military would support them, their institutions, and their referendum positions. Both called on factions within the military to support them against the other. As it turned out, the forces Yeltsin depended upon came through for him in the end and shelled the parliament into submission some months later.

Nevertheless, the Russian April 1993 referenda show what happens when legislatures decide to fight back. In some cases, legislatures can put up significant opposition to executives during a referendum campaign, can change the character of the questions, and challenge the interpretation of the votes. Often, in these situations, executives need the support of the military in order to overcome relatively strong legislatures.

The April 1993 Referenda in Russia

The August 1991 coup attempt against Gorbachev drained the old Communist system of its last ounce of legitimacy. The coup was thwarted by the heroic efforts of the newly elected president of Russia, Boris Yeltsin, who challenged the plotters to release Gorbachev from house arrest and end their unconstitutional maneuvers. In the end, a sufficient sector of the military complied with Yeltsin, and, after only a few days, the coup leaders quickly began to lose enthusiasm for their ill-conceived action.

Gorbachev had not realized the degree to which the system he had worked in and for all his life had been weakened. Directly after his return to Moscow, he addressed a session of the Russian parliament as if nothing had changed. Yeltsin, eager to punish Gorbachev for his dismissal and public humiliation years before, repeatedly embarrassed Gorbachev by cutting him off, taking his papers from him, and stating that his attachment to the old Communist system would have to end because both communism and the union were dead. Yeltsin's behavior was a public demonstration of what most people knew: Communism, in its monopolistic form, at least for now, was finished. Gorbachev grudgingly presided over the dismantling of the Soviet Union over the next few months until its official termination the night of December 25, 1991.

Yeltsin, on the other hand, was at the height of his power. He appointed Yegor Gaidar as his prime minister, who, with Yeltsin's full blessing, began a program of "shock therapy" based loosely on the economic transition program instituted in Poland. The most concrete aspect of this program, which would affect every Russian, was the allowance of the prices of goods to float to their natural level. Beginning in January 1992, the prices on basic foodstuffs rose to hyper-inflationary levels. For elderly pensioners, and for people on fixed wages, it was a disastrous turn of events.

The Russian Congress of People's Deputies soon began to criticize Gaidar and then Yeltsin for Gaidar's economic policy. Though they initially supported Yeltsin and his proposed economic policies, they soon decided that the reforms had been too extreme in concept and too quick in implementation. They claimed to speak for the people who were worst hit by these changes.

The Russian Congress of People's Deputies from 1992 to 1993 is a good example of a carryover institution whose representatives, and views, are increasingly remote from a polity and society in transition. The Congress had been elected under Gorbachev in 1990, and while the members were elected in multi-candidate races, these elections were not multiparty. Most members represented the old Communist Party, large state enterprises, and collectivized agriculture. Though executives can outrank such institutions, carryover institutions can present a major obstacle for a reform effort.

The disconnection between the Congress of People's Deputies and President Yeltsin on economic affairs was the beginning of the conflict between Yeltsin and the Congress. The Sixth Congress in November 1991 had voted to give Yeltsin extraordinary powers to institute reforms, but by the time the Seventh Congress of People's Deputies had convened in December 1992, it had reconsidered Yeltsin's powers. In 1992 the conflict between Yeltsin and the standing parliament—the Supreme Soviet—had reached the point where gridlock had taken hold of the policymaking process. To overcome the deadlock caused primarily by disagreement on economic issues, Yeltsin suggested calling referenda on whether Russia should be a presidential republic, whether a Constituent Assembly should adopt a new constitution, and whether land could be bought and sold. The first two referendum suggestions were explicitly meant to dismantle the Congress and replace it with a bicameral system. The Congress, in turn, passed constitutional amendments that curtailed Yeltsin's extra-constitutional powers. Ruslan Khasbulatov, chairman of the Supreme Soviet and the Congress of People's Deputies, made a compromise with Yeltsin to freeze the constitutional amendments in exchange for holding a nationwide referendum scheduled for April 11, 1993.

On March 7, Yeltsin revealed the questions he proposed for the April referendum: Should Russia be a presidential republic; should the supreme legislature take the form of a bicameral parliament rather than a congress; should the new constitution be adopted by a constituent assembly instead of the Congress; and should citizens be able to buy and sell land? At the time, a Yeltsin victory on these questions seemed doubtful.[11] The Eighth Extraordinary Congress of People's Deputies, held from March 10 to 13, reversed its earlier position by calling off the referendum and furthermore stripping Yeltsin of his extraordinary powers.

The stage was now set for a constitutional and political crisis. The deadlock between Yeltsin and the Congress had reached the point at which both sides resorted to shouting and making threats. On March 20 on nationwide television, Yeltsin announced the imposition of a "special regime" permitting him to rule by decree until April 25, when a referendum on a constitution, a vote of confidence in him, and on a law on new parliamentary elections would be held. The Congress appealed Yeltsin's action to the Constitutional Court while some informally called for his resignation. On March 23 the Constitutional Court ruled Yeltsin's decree unconstitutional without ever seeing the text of the document. On March 24, the decree was published by Yeltsin; the hard copy of the document called only for a "vote of confidence," not a referendum—which required congressional authorization—and omitted any mention of presidential rule, which undercut calls for Yeltsin's ouster. On March 26, the Ninth Congress of People's Deputies began with a debate over Yeltsin's impeachment. In the end, the vote to impeach Yeltsin lost by only 72 votes; Yeltsin had vowed to ignore the vote if it had passed.

The Wording of the April 1993 Russian Referenda.   The Congress decided instead to take action believed to be less volatile and indisputably legitimate—it decided to go ahead and call a referendum. The referendum, though, would be one that included questions it had worded with the goal of embarrassing and politically debilitating the president of Russia. On March 29, it decided to try to beat Yeltsin at his own game. The April 25 referendum contained the following questions:

1.   Do you trust the President of the Russian Federation, Boris Nikolaevich Yeltsin?
2.   Do you approve of the socioeconomic policies implemented by the President of the Russian Federation and the government of the Russian Federation since 1992?
3.   Do you consider it essential to hold pre-term elections for the presidency of the Russian Federation?

4. Do you consider it essential to hold pre-term elections for the People's Deputies of the Russian Federation?

The first three questions were clearly an attempt by the Congress to embarrass and derail Yeltsin; the wording of the referendum questions was adept. Note the use of the word "trust" in the first question. In the second question, Yeltsin's opponents in the Congress hoped to embarrass Yeltsin in two ways. First it was believed that his economic policy was unpopular, but to make sure it was perceived in such a way, they attached the phrase "and the government of the Russian Federation since 1992" as a clear reference and reminder of former Prime Minister Gaidar's unpopular shock-therapy initiatives. The third question was an obvious attempt to strip Yeltsin of his office halfway into his presidential term. To propose, as the fourth question, a vote on whether pre-term elections should also be held for the Congress was a gamble but probably a risk the deputies felt they could take in order to seem fair to the public. Furthermore, the Congress stipulated that approval of the questions required 50 percent of the eligible voters and not just 50 percent of those who voted; this was instituted in order to make it easier for Yeltsin to lose on the questions, especially the first two. If this congressional stipulation was upheld by the courts, then any vote that failed to garner 50 percent of the eligible voters, or electorate, would be technically invalid by law even if a majority of those voting approved it.

The tide began to turn against the Congress just before the vote. Yeltsin and his supporters had campaigned hard for positive results on the referendum. They simplified their stand by broadcasting to the public that they should vote, "Da, Da, Nyet, Da" or "Yes, Yes, No, Yes." At times it was thought that the insistence on a "No" vote for question three might end up confusing the public and so the rallying call was simplified even further to "Da, Da, Da, Da." Furthermore, Yeltsin won a clear victory when, on April 21, the Constitutional Court ruled that the Congress had been too stringent; only the last two questions needed to be approved by 50 percent of the electorate. Yeltsin's opponents began to fear that Yeltsin would "win" the referendum: the Socialist Workers' Party of Russia predicted on Thursday, April 22, that President Boris Yeltsin would win the support of the population, but only thanks to a massive brainwashing campaign on the eve of the referendum.[12] The last of the polls showed "no hopes" for the People's Deputies. Less than 15 percent of Russians supported the Congress of People's Deputies which left "no hopes for a political re-animation of this branch of authority," according to an opinion poll in six Russian regions conducted jointly by the Russian "Mneniye" sociological service, the British Gallup poll, and "Saatchi and Saatchi" company.[13]

The Interpretation and Consequences of the April 1993 Russian Referenda. The manipulation of the referendum device does not end with the vote. Referendum results must be interpreted and framed. Usually the referendum winners have the best opportunity to do this, but anyone may do so, including the referendum opponents. Common themes broached in a discussion of referendum results focus on whether or not a majority of the votes and/or electorate are represented in a vote tally, whether or not the turnout was adequate, and the exact meaning of a question's text. When referendum opponents have a platform, such as a legislature, from which to compete with referendum proponents on a vote's interpretation, the process of determining the results of a referendum and implementing its mandate become even more difficult.

Boris Yeltsin and his supporters heralded the results of the April referendum as a victory for the Russian president and his policies of reform (see Tables 2.2–2.5), but, in actions that spoke as loudly as their words over the next five months, a resolute group of Communists and nationalists showed that they did not. On May 5, 1993, the Central Election Committee released the final results of the referendum vote with the following numbers:

- Do you trust the President of the Russian Federation, Boris Nikolaevich Yeltsin?

  58.7 percent of those participating voted "Yes."
- Do you approve the socioeconomic policies implemented by the President of the Russian Federation and the government of the Russian Federation since 1992?

  53 percent of those participating voted "Yes."
- Do you consider it essential to hold pre-term elections for the presidency of the Russian Federation?

  49.5 percent of those participating voted "Yes."
- Do you consider it essential to hold pre-term elections for the People's Deputies of the Russian Federation?

  67.2 percent of those participating voted "Yes."
- Overall, approximately 64.2 percent of the Russian electorate took part in the referendum.[14]

From a Western point of view, Yeltsin had good reason to claim victory, having a majority of voters support both him and his policies. But the Russian voters before *perestroika* lived under a system that often produced near unanimous votes within governing bodies, an effect of the Communist principle of democratic centralism. Therefore, majoritarian

TABLE 2.2   Results of the April 25, 1993, Referendum in Russia on Confidence in President Yeltsin

		percent of electorate	*percent of vote*
Total electorate	107,310,374	100.0	—
Total number of voters in the referendum	68,869,947	64.2	100.0
Spoilt papers	1,468,868	1.4	2.1
Total number of valid votes in the referendum	67,401,079	62.8	97.9
"Yes" votes	40,405,811	37.7	58.7
"No" votes	26,995,268	25.2	39.2

SOURCES: *Rossiiskaya gazeta* (May 6, 1993): 1; Stephen White, Richard Rose, and Ian McAllister, *How Russia Votes* (Chatham, N.J.: Chatham House, 1997): 82.

TABLE 2.3   Results of the April 25, 1993, Referendum in Russia on Support for the Economic and Social Policies of President Yeltsin and the Government

		percent of electorate	*percent of vote*
Total electorate	107,310,374	100.0	—
Total number of voters in the referendum	68,759,866	64.1	100.0
Spoilt papers	1,642,883	1.5	2.4
Total number of valid votes in the referendum	67,116,983	62.5	97.6
"Yes" votes	36,476,202	34.0	53.0
"No" votes	30,640,781	28.6	44.6

SOURCES: *Rossiiskaya gazeta* (May 6, 1993): 1; Stephen White, Richard Rose, and Ian McAllister, *How Russia Votes* (Chatham, N.J.: Chatham House, 1997): 82.

rules that require no more than approximately 51 percent of the vote for victory seemed strange to the Russian population, and victories based upon no more than 60 percent of the vote could have been perceived as questionable. Irrespective of how the population at large felt, it soon became clear that Yeltsin's opponents did not respect his victory. Moreover, because the vote to call new elections for the Congress of People's Deputies fell short of the Constitutional Court mandate of 50 percent of the entire Russian electorate, Yeltsin's opponents in the Supreme Soviet

TABLE 2.4   Results of the April 25, 1993, Referendum in Russia on Whether
There Should Be Early Elections for President

		percent of electorate	*percent of vote*
Total electorate	107,310,374	100.0	—
Total number of voters in the referendum	68,762,529	64.1	100.0
Spoilt papers	2,316,247	2.2	3.4
Total number of valid votes in the referendum	66,446,282	61.9	96.6
"Yes" votes	34,027,310	31.7	49.5
"No" votes	32,418,972	30.2	47.1

SOURCES: *Rossiiskaya gazeta* (May 6, 1993): 1; Stephen White, Richard Rose, and
Ian McAllister, *How Russia Votes* (Chatham, N.J.: Chatham House, 1997): 82.

TABLE 2.5   Results of the April 25, 1993, Referendum in Russia on Whether
There Should Be Early Elections for the Congress of People's Deputies (Legislature)

		percent of electorate	*percent of vote*
Total electorate	107,310,374	100.0	—
Total number of voters in the referendum	68,832,060	64.2	100.0
Spoilt papers	1,887,258	1.8	2.7
Total number of valid votes in the referendum	66,944,802	62.4	97.3
"Yes" votes	46,232,197	43.1	67.2
"No" votes	20,712,605	19.3	30.1

SOURCES: *Rossiiskaya gazeta* (May 6, 1993): 1; Stephen White, Richard Rose, and
Ian McAllister, *How Russia Votes* (Chatham, N.J.: Chatham House, 1997): 82.

remained in power and became even more determined to resist Yeltsin's
moves.[15]

Ruslan Khasbulatov, the Supreme Soviet, and other key hard-liners
thwarted every attempt by Yeltsin to capitalize on his referendum victory. Khasbulatov blocked Yeltsin's effort to adopt a new constitution by
returning to his old argument that the current document should be
amended gradually one piece at a time, and he resisted Yeltsin's call for
new, multiparty elections for parliament in the fall of 1993. Inevitably,

tensions began to rise between the president and parliament.[16] Under Khasbulatov's guidance in the summer of 1993, the Supreme Soviet sought to thwart the tight budget restraints and voucher privatization program of the Yeltsin government's economic policy.[17] Moreover, Khasbulatov planned to submit constitutional amendments to the Congress of People's Deputies that would remove Yeltsin as head of the Security Council and take away his ability to sign international treaties.[18] It seemed as if Khasbulatov was attempting to bait President Yeltsin into a showdown that Khasbulatov believed he could win:[19]

> The most plausible purpose of this strategy was to provoke Yeltsin into dissolving the parliament . . . this action would result in [the] automatic impeachment of the president. Khasbulatov clearly expected to win this confrontation, believing that the armed forces would not side with Yeltsin, and that in any event, he would hesitate to use them against the parliament.
>
> . . . Speaking on September 18, Khasbulatov barely disguised his strategy. He argued that Yeltsin could not continue to be head of state because his judgment was impaired by alcoholism and that he was attempting to impose a "dictatorial, plutocratic regime." He also warned Yeltsin that any attempt to dissolve the parliament would immediately result in his ouster and urged the army to remain loyal to the constitution.[20]

The military, however, sided with Yeltsin in the end as the conflict escalated. On September 21, Yeltsin issued a set of decrees dissolving parliament and the powers of its deputies, and set a date for multiparty elections to a new legislative body in December. Khasbulatov and Aleksandr Rutskoi, the renegade former Russian vice president, refused a compromise—consisting of holding simultaneous elections for both president and parliament—and instead barricaded themselves along with supporters in the Russian parliamentary building, called the "White House." This was the same Russian parliament building that Yeltsin rallied to during the August 1991 coup attempt. At the time, his two staunchest supporters and resisters to the plotters were Khasbulatov and Rutskoi, the two men he now faced barricaded in the same building. Having armed themselves and their supporters, Khasbulatov and Rutskoi's forces instigated several clashes. After Khasbulatov and Rutskoi's forces ransacked the mayor's building and put the Ostankino television broadcasting center under siege, the military, at Yeltsin's behest, not only intervened at Ostankino but also took the battle to the White House in the heart of Moscow. The military bombarded the parliamentary building with artillery, stormed it, and took it with elite troops.

Afterwards, Yeltsin dismantled the old governing system and set up a presidential democracy with a weak parliament and no vice president.

Not only did he hold elections for the new legislative bodies in December 1993, but he also called a referendum to legitimize passage of a new constitution formally changing the government system. Even though he had centralized a vast degree of power in the executive, he also took care to give himself, the Russian president, the sole and unilateral means to call future referenda.

The December 1993 Russian Referendum on a New Constitution

The Timing of the December 1993 Referendum.   Coming directly on the heels of the victorious but tragic October conflict with the parliament, Yeltsin timed the new elections and the December referendum on a new Russian constitution to take advantage of the clear upper hand he held in the post-conflict political environment. He had been ruling by decree since his dissolution of parliament on September 21, 1993. Because he had won the referenda called in April 1993, he expected to win on the constitutional vote and to have a parliamentary majority to his liking.

Partisanship and a short amount of time marked the referendum campaign. The Central Electoral Commission was only created on September 29, and the specific commission in charge of providing organizational and financial support to the referendum was not formed until November 22. Yeltsin, threatening the political parties standing for election on November 26, stated that criticism of the draft constitution would be penalized by the withdrawal of their free airtime on television. The chairman of the Central Electoral Commission, Nikolai Ryabov, expressed his hope during a television interview that the constitutional referendum would pass. Moreover, it was suggested by First Deputy Prime Minister Shumeiko that the Communist Party and Nikolay Travkin's Democratic Party be banned from participating in the election because of their pronouncements asking the Russian public to vote down the draft constitution.[21]

The Russian polity, however, had seemingly been turned off by the infighting among the political elite. The Central Election Committee reported that the turnout for the referendum and election was 54.8 percent—down nearly 10 percent from the 64.2 percent turnout of the April 1993 referenda. In all, 56.6 percent of those voting supported the adoption of the new constitution by a referendum question that asked simply, "Do you accept the constitution of the Russian Federation?"[22] The constitution needed 50 percent of the electorate to participate and 50 percent of those voting in favor of the referendum for the constitution to be adopted (see Table 2.6).

The Interpretation and Consequences of the December 1993 Russian Referendum.   The consequences of the December 1993 referendum were

TABLE 2.6   Results of the December 12, 1993, Referendum in Russia on Approval of the Constitution of the Russian Federation

		percent of electorate	*percent of vote*
Total electorate	106,182,030	100.0	—
Total number of voters in the referendum	58,187,755	54.8	100.0
Spoilt papers	1,818,792	1.7	3.1
Total number of valid votes in the referendum	56,368,963	53.1	96.9
"Yes" votes	32,937,630	31.0	56.6
"No" votes	23,431,333	22.1	40.3

SOURCES: *Rossiiskie vesti* (December 25, 1993): 1; Stephen White, Richard Rose, and Ian McAllister, *How Russia Votes* (Chatham, N.J.: Chatham House, 1997): 99.

clear: Russia was now a presidential republic. The draft constitution, now essentially the first new constitution for Russia since the 1978 Soviet Brezhnev constitution, included elements of the French and American constitutions. The president now had the preponderance of the power with the ability to appoint the prime minister; the head of the Central Bank; the justices of Constitutional Court, Supreme Court, and High Court of Arbitration; the general procurator and the High Command of the armed forces. The president can also issue decrees, institute a state of emergency, and introduce martial law. As head of state, the president provides direction for both domestic and foreign policies. Directly elected by the electorate to a four-year term, the president cannot serve for more than two consecutive terms of office.[23]

The new Russian parliament is substantially weaker than its predecessor and the president. It is a bicameral legislature with a lower chamber entitled the State Duma and a higher chamber called the Federation Council. Though a president cannot dissolve the Federation Council, he or she may dissolve the State Duma and call for new elections if the lower chamber rejects the "prime minister three times, votes no-confidence in the government twice in three months, or votes no-confidence in the government after the prime minister has asked for a vote of confidence."[24] The parliament, on the other hand, cannot easily impeach the president. First, the Duma must form a commission to determine if the Supreme and Constitutional Courts should consider whether the president has committed a "grave" crime or act of treason. Second, the Supreme Court must rule and then the Constitutional Court must agree that such a crime or treason has been perpetrated by the president. Last, two-thirds of the Duma and then two-thirds of the Federation Council within three months of each other must vote to impeach the president in order for him to be removed. Moreover, with regard to the legislature, the Duma and Federation Council can only override a presidential veto if two-thirds of both chambers approve.[25]

After almost two years of conflict, the distribution of power between the executive and legislative branches of government in Russia was resolved with the use of a referendum approving a new constitution. The constitution approved by the December 1993 referendum remains to date the constitution of the Russian Federation. Russia, essentially now a presidential republic, has already been through one election cycle for president in 1996 and parliament in 1995.

The April 1993 referenda were, as with all the referenda discussed so far, initiated by the executive, but unlike any of the preceding cases, the legislature decided to fight back in earnest. In Russia, resistance by the Congress of People's Deputies before the 1993 votes took the form of refusing to hold the referenda, limiting the extraordinary constitutional powers of the Russian president, and finally imposing its own wording on the questions. Resistance afterwards took the form of refusing to allow new elections to be held for the Congress because of the supposed ambiguity of the results. In this case, the referenda made manifest, and seem to have exacerbated, a fundamental rift between Yeltsin and the Congress.

Referenda and Russia's Push for Democratization

By serving as a means, or forum, for the continued and perhaps increased elite conflict over constitutional issues, the referendum device may have slowed Russia's democratic transition. The evidence for this is the continued domination of referendum topics by the political elite: They still propose and call the majority of these votes on subjects that mostly concern their well-being with little regard for the welfare of the people. The public has been shut out of the process of proposing referenda and suggesting topics that relate more directly to their lives and interests because basic issues of governance have not yet been resolved.

If one breaks down Russia's referenda into those that have been held and into those that have just been proposed but not held, support for the above conclusions becomes evident. Table 2.7 charts the referenda that have been held. The political elite, represented by Boris Yeltsin and the parliament, proposed all of the votes that were held. Their subjects concerned the power of Yeltsin either vis-à-vis the Soviet center or the Russian parliament. The people initiated none of the referenda that were

TABLE 2.7 Referenda in Russia: Held

Question/Topic	Date held	Who proposed	percent turnout	percent YES
Presidency for Russia	Mar. 17, 1991	Yeltsin	75	70
Confidence in Yeltsin	Apr. 25, 1993	Yeltsin and parliament	64	59
Approve Yeltsin's economics	Apr. 25, 1993	Yeltsin and parliament	64	53
Early elections for president	Apr. 25, 1993	Yeltsin and parliament	64	50
Early elections for deputies	Apr. 25, 1993	Yeltsin and parliament	64	67
Approve Yeltsin's constitution	Dec. 12, 1993	Yeltsin	55	57

SOURCE: Mark Clarence Walker, "Vox Caesaris Vox Populi: Why and When Referendums Are Called in the Post-Soviet States and Their Effects" (Ph.D. diss., University of California, Berkeley, 1999): 229–276.

TABLE 2.8 Referenda in Russia: Proposed but Not Held

Question/Topic	Date proposed	Who proposed	Scientific reason not held
Preserve Russia	Feb. 1, 1991	Yeltsin	Fears about how autonomous republics would react
Elect president	Feb. 1, 1991	Yeltsin	None
Constitution, which includes private property, parliamentary versus presidential republic	Apr. 30, 1992	Yeltsin	Opposed by Sergei Filatov, first deputy chairman of the parliament, on 5/5/92
Constitution, which includes private property, parliamentary versus presidential republic	June 1, 1992	Democratic Russia—million signatures, and Yeltsin	Victim of stalemate between Yeltsin and parliament

(continues)

TABLE 2.8 *(continued)*   Referenda in Russia: Proposed but Not Held

Question/Topic	*Date proposed*	*Who proposed*	*Scientific reason not held*
Recall Yeltsin	July 31, 1992	The "Working Russia" movement of Viktor Anpilov	None
President versus Congress	Jan. 1, 1993	Yeltsin	Endless bickering between Yeltsin and legislature that led to modified questions
Early presidential elections	Jan. 1, 1995	An initiative group in spring 1995	The referendum law states that the president must approve the referendum to be called
Greater integration with Belarus	Oct. 3, 1995	Federation Council	It was suggested on 10/3/95; no date given for it to be held
Original question: "Do you believe that the activity of the government should be evaluated according to the people's standard of living?"†	Dec. 17, 1995	Congress of Russian Communities; they need 2 million signatures	The Moscow Electoral Commission voted 9–3 to reject the registration of the referendum questions on December 7
Merger with Belarus	Jan. 13, 1997	Yeltsin	None

SOURCE: Mark Clarence Walker, "Vox Caesaris Vox Populi: Why and When Referendums Are Called in the Post-Soviet States and Their Effects" (Ph.D. diss., University of California, Berkeley, 1999): 229–276.
† Here the word "government" means the presidential apparatus.

held. The only question directly related to the people's welfare was on Yeltsin's economic policies in April 1993. On the other hand, the people have proposed several referenda that have not been held (see Table 2.8). The subjects of these referenda, however, have been mostly concerned with the governance of Russia and not the general welfare of the people.

If Russia democratizes successfully, the need for the referendum device will diminish. The issues that encourage elites to use the referendum, like issues of governance and constitutional matters, will be resolved in a democratically consolidated regime. Though elite participation in politics may remain significant, civil society will begin to play an increasing role in Russian government. If Russia fails to consolidate democratically, it may need to continue the attempt to resolve basic constitutional issues. If that is the case, elites will be tempted to use referenda to achieve the goals they might otherwise have lost, and the Russian people may simply continue to play the role of legitimizers of elite actions instead of the masters of their own fates.

Notes

1. *The American Heritage Dictionary of the English Language*, 3d ed., s.v. "referendum."

2. Edward S. Herman and Noam Chomsky, *Manufacturing Consent: The Political Economy of the Mass Media* (New York, N.Y.: Pantheon Books, 1988).

3. Jean Jaques Rousseau, Karl Marx, and Friedrich Engels have preferred the institutions of direct democracy—of which the referendum is one—as opposed to the institutions of representative democracy like parliaments and presidents. Charles de Gaulle in post–World War II France advocated for referenda while strongly denouncing parliamentarism. Referenda have also been advocated by the American Progressive movement at the turn of the nineteenth century and by the late-twentieth-century conservative movement.

4. This figure is taken from the official results of the Russian 1991 presidential election published by the Central Electoral Committee in *Rossiyskaia gazeta* on June 20, 1991.

5. Center for the Preservation of Contemporary Documentation, 1991. Moscow: Fond 89, perechen' 22, document 81.

6. Staff of the Commission on Security and Cooperation in Europe, *Referendum in the Soviet Union: A Compendium of Reports on the March 17, 1991 Referendum on the Future of the U.S.S.R* (Washington, D.C.: U.S. Government Printing Office, 1991).

7. David Remnick, *Resurrection: The Struggle for a New Russia* (New York, NY: Random House, 1997): 49–50.

8. Geoffrey Blainey, *The Causes of War* (New York, N.Y.: Free Press, 1973).

9. Michael McFaul and Nikolai Petrov, *Russia: An Electoral History 1989–1996* (Washington, D.C.: Carnegie Endowment for International Peace, 1997).

10. Remnick, *Resurrection,* 49–50.

11. Moscow *Kuranty*, in Russian (March 10, 1993): 4. Foreign Broadcast Information Service, *Daily Report: Soviet Union* (March 11, 1993): 52; and (March 12, 1993): 3.

12. Moscow ITAR-TASS, in English (April 22, 1993). Foreign Broadcast Information Service, *Daily Report: Soviet Union* (April 23, 1993): 32.

13. Moscow ITAR-TASS, in English (April 23, 1993). Foreign Broadcast Information Service, *Daily Report: Soviet Union* (April 23, 1993): 33.

14. Staff of the Commission on Security and Cooperation in Europe, *Report on the April 25, 1993 Referendum in Russia* (Washington, D.C.: U.S. Government Printing Office, 1993).

15. Yitzhak M. Brundy, "Ruslan Khasbulatov, Aleksandr Rutskoi, and Intraelite Conflict in Postcommunist Russia, 1991–1994," in Timothy J. Colton and Robert C. Tucker, eds., *Patterns in Post-Soviet Leadership* (Oxford, Ohio: Westview Press, 1995): 93.

16. Mary McAuley, *Russia's Politics of Uncertainty* (New York, N.Y.: Cambridge University Press, 1997): 41.

17. Yitzhak M. Brundy, "Intraelite Conflict," 93.

18. Yitzhak M. Brundy, "Intraelite Conflict," 94.

19. Yitzhak M. Brundy, "Intraelite Conflict," 94.

20. Ruslan Khasbulatov, "Tol'ko v usloviiakh demokratii vozmozhny reformy dlia naroda," *Rossiiskaya gazeta* (September 21, 1993): 3–4.

21. Staff of the Commission on Security and Cooperation in Europe, *Russia's Parliamentary Election and Constitutional Referendum: December 12, 1993* (Washington, D.C.: U.S. Government Printing Office, 1994).

22. Staff of the Commission on Security and Cooperation in Europe, *Constitutional Referendum.*

23. Staff of the Commission on Security and Cooperation in Europe, *Constitutional Referendum.*

24. Staff of the Commission on Security and Cooperation in Europe, *Constitutional Referendum.*

25. Staff of the Commission on Security and Cooperation in Europe, *Constitutional Referendum.*

3

The Divided Russian Elite: How Russia's Transition Produced a Counter-Elite

VIRGINIE COULLOUDON

In August 1998, the Russian stock market collapsed, provoking a dramatic crash of the banking system and triggering an intensification of Russia's economic crisis, as well as upheaval in the executive branch, where Prime Minister Sergei Kirienko was fired in a tense political atmosphere.[1] Yet, during the year preceding the financial and institutional crisis of summer 1998, a significant number of Russian scholars and representatives of the elite had expressed faith in their country's economic stability. To be sure, elites in Moscow supplied far more positive pronouncements than those living in Russia's provincial cities. And elites in financial institutions expressed more confidence in their future than did the directors of industrial plants. But, even in the apparently wealthy capital of the Russian Federation, which had drained most of the country's financial resources, elite sentiments contradicted each other. It was easy to find politicians and industrial managers who were confident that the financial market was now boosting the rest of Russia's troubled economy. But it was equally easy to locate other politicians and industrial managers who claimed just the opposite and predicted an impending financial crash and a deep political-institutional crisis. What was most striking was that elites' opinions did not seem to correlate with either their political party affiliation or with the industrial sectors in which they worked.[2]

Russia's traditionally overpowerful executive branch and the undivided attention it pays to a small circle of wealthy "oligarchs" have led scholars to focus on key political figures and their clientele, in order to decipher political intrigues and their "clan logic." Until 1995, this scholarly debate focused mostly on the origins of Russia's new elite. To elaborate a typology of the post-Soviet Russian elite, many surveys have explored these politicians' geographical and educational backgrounds in order to explain the roots of elite alliances and networks. Others have focused on the links that tied Russian politicians to the former Soviet elite, known as the *nomenklatura*.[3] But the repeated conflicts that occurred between elite groups under Yeltsin's rule have raised additional questions; namely, what exactly divides the Russian elite and what holds members of any given elite group together?

The Russian press often focuses on three dividing lines that distinguish categories of elites: the line between monetarists and industrialists; that between liberals and conservatives; and the split between elites living in Moscow, or the "center," and those living outside Moscow, in the "periphery." These divides do provide an explanation of many political and institutional conflicts in today's Russia. What preliminary interviews have shown, however, is the existence of an additional dividing line— one less visible, but extremely deep-seated in elites' minds—that divides elites on the basis of their understanding of the role of power, in general, and their perception of the Russian state, more specifically.

These interviews suggest that two opposite elite spheres have been coexisting in Russia for over a decade, starting in 1988, when economic reforms were initiated under the regime of then Soviet president Mikhail Gorbachev. Ruled by different standards, as I will show below, these spheres divide elite individuals who have close ties to the state from those who have achieved their current elite positions without the backing of the state and have forged a different understanding of the role power should play in politics and economics. These two groups, emerging as the result of the transition process, have engendered a new dichotomy in Russia's political life. While scholars focusing on elites have repeatedly demonstrated that a systematic policy of elite-based patronage is an obstacle to democracy,[4] no one has studied another apparent conflict inherent in the transition process, namely, the antagonism between these two opposing elite groups.

Having focused extensively, if not exclusively, on the Russian president, Boris Yeltsin, and his team of federal government officials—in other words, on the executive branch—Western and Russian scholars have emphasized the growing arbitrariness of Yeltsin's regime. There is now a general tendency to consider the transition process a failure. However, this chapter seeks to highlight a different driving force in the transition, and to shed light on unknown actors, who have always existed behind the narrow political and economic oligarchy that dominates contemporary Russia. It examines the fundamental opposition between two different states of mind within the elite and shows that the way power and the state are perceived by the Russian elite should be considered a decisive factor in the way that elites form alliances or divide amongst themselves.

To articulate this particular reading of the antagonisms evident in Russia's political realm, I will discuss the mechanisms that have created two main elite groups (an elite, and a counter-elite) and will examine their respective values and attitudes toward the state and toward the economic reforms. I will show why these two groups have come to oppose each other, and will put Russia's elite political conflicts in the context of Russia's transition to democracy, arguing that the transition has served as a catalyst for the development of the counter-elite. But, before focusing on the values and behaviors of Russia's elite groups, we must briefly examine the events that led to the transition process and reflect upon the flaws and paradoxes of Yeltsin's regime, in order to understand how a background favorable to the rise of a counter-elite was created.

Elites and the Transition Process

It is generally thought that the turning points between Soviet and post-Soviet Russia are the August 1991 coup and the breakup of the Soviet Union in December 1991. These events were indeed the most important ones, from a geopolitical perspective. Yet, with respect to the transformation of the centrally planned economy, and therefore to the building of a new elite, one should instead consider the law on cooperatives, passed under Gorbachev's rule in 1988, as the first watershed.[5] It was then that the Soviet authorities allowed an embryonic private sector to develop. Shortly thereafter, the first decision to create a private banking system was adopted.

To develop a monetary system, the Kremlin had to create financial institutions. Under the Soviet regime, banks were linked to one or another industrial sector and were merely deposit banks. They were left untouched under the new system and kept working with the industrial corporations of the sector they had been linked to.[6] Created during the years 1989 to 1991, the majority of the private banks grew with the backing of the political leadership. As Joel Hellman has shown, these banks were of three different types. The first group, made up of banks set up by industrial corporations (former Soviet ministries), ministries of the autonomous republics, and regional production associations, continued to represent the interests of particular branches of industry. To this first group belonged Avtobank, a bank created by the Ministry of the Automobile Industry and the gigantic KamAZ automobile plant. One could find numerous similar examples.[7] The banks of this first group were supposed to meet the new economic requirements and help the industrial sectors finance themselves. A second group of banks was created by local leaders who were trying to regroup strategic enterprises in their regions.[8] The third group was composed of banks which benefited from the backing of the CPSU Central Committee, the Komsomol (Communist Youth Organization), the KGB (Committee for State Security), and the Foreign Trade Ministry. Prior to the 1998 crisis, banks belonging to this last group were among Russia's most powerful; some of them were even considered the instrument of the ruling oligarchy.[9] Whether they belonged to one or another category, these new financial institutions were headed by senior executives who had been co-opted from the state enterprises or the ministries.

Meanwhile, the former Soviet ministries, in charge of regulating industry, were transformed into private corporations with the aim of creating a different type of industrial apparatus. Both in the financial and industrial sectors, the authorities either co-opted new cadres or placed the former cadres at the head of the new companies. In either case, as the new economic institutions were established, they were staffed according to a state policy of patronage.[10]

The first paradox—or flaw—of the transition lies precisely in the development of a state policy of patronage and cronyism, where one would have expected instead to find competition and new rules of recruitment. In interviews, elite respondents who were close to Yeltsin during the first years of his presidency explained the persistence of patronage by emphasizing the Soviet legacy of a highly inefficient economy and a politically hostile environment, and therefore the necessity of relying on trusted individuals. When they acquired power after the collapse of the Soviet Union, members of Yeltsin's entourage created a new team disconnected from the traditional networks of the CPSU Politburo and Central Committee, but they did not break with the traditional rules of recruitment.

Co-optation of a loyal clientele was simultaneously developed on two different levels. On the one hand, in the political arena, by appointing regional governors, the Yeltsin team sought to rely on the executive branch as a vertical chain leading from the Kremlin down to the local level. On the other hand, on the financial side, lacking such developed financial structures, the state had no choice but to continue to back the creation of "private banks" by government institutions. This first flaw—developing a state policy of patronage in a liberal, marketizing economy—was thus inherent in the transition process and became aggravated under Yeltsin's regime. The government's policy of patronage became even more obvious on the eve of the 1996 presidential elections, at which point Russian and Western scholars, as well as Russian politicians, began to assert the idea that the country was ruled by an oligarchic regime.[11]

The second flaw of the transition period lies in Russian leaders' choice to impose democratic reforms by occasionally resorting to nondemocratic means. This was particularly true for Yeltsin, whose policy has often been interpreted as the implementation of an autocratic regime prior to shaping a democracy.[12] The politically hostile environment of the first years of Yeltsin's regime and the institutional vacuum left by the collapse of the Soviet state pushed Yeltsin's team to use Russia's traditional lack of a balance of power as a means for imposing democratization. In the process of democratization, therefore, Russia's new legislature was given far less power than the executive branch.

By taking personal responsibility for implementing a democratic regime, while occasionally resorting to force, Yeltsin gave the representatives of his personal team, as well as the executive branch, the right to rule the country in an arbitrary way. But this led to an unforeseen situation in which, on both the federal and local levels, members of the executive branch eventually developed their own quasi-absolute power and ceased to obey the center.[13] In addition to corruption, this abuse of power had another negative effect. Using the privilege of the all-powerful executive branch, members of the federal government as well as regional executives imposed their own reform policies, in whatever way they considered best, without consulting the president or the legislature. Soon, the vertical power structure of the executive branch was broken and the Kremlin could no longer rely on regional leaders to enforce its economic policy at the local level. Russian scholars have demonstrated that this fundamental misunderstanding and lack of balance between the executive and legislative branches inevitably leads to conflict, which in turn leads to an even more arbitrary implementation of state policy.[14]

Another specificity of the transition process lies in the composition of post-Soviet interest groups. Under the Soviet regime, various industrial lobbies—such as the energy sector or the military-industrial complex—competed for state subsidies. As soon as the Soviet ministries, which were at the core of the centralized economy, disappeared and cut state subsidies to industry, industrial managers and regional leaders tried to find other sources of funding and thus formed new interest groups. The industrial sector–related lobbies that had existed under the Soviet regime—what Suzanne Keller has called the "strategic elites"—evaporated, replaced by a more diversified set of elite networks.[15] These new elite groups were made of politicians, businessmen, industrial managers, and journalists, and formed a conglomeration of former Soviet *nomenklatura* and new Yeltsin-identified elites. They cut across industrial sectors and placed their combined power at the disposal of one or another top figure in Russian national politics, in the hope of accumulating

enough influence to gain access to the country's riches. As Mikhail Malyutin has put it, Russia thus developed "groups of authorities," but no
"elite" groups in the Western understanding of what an elite should be.[16]

This brings us to the fourth paradox of the transition period, one that
explains the rise of the counter-elite. While they were developing a new
regime, relying on a newly born oligarchy and reinforcing the role of the
state in the economy, government officials were also opening windows of
opportunity for non-*nomenklatura* and non-state elites. Beginning in 1988,
a different type of elite managed to grow rich and develop political careers without the backing of the state. As we will see below, this particular point—the lack of backing from the state—was instrumental in shaping a worldview among this counter-elite, one that is different from that
held by the state elite composed of bureaucrats and elite representatives
co-opted by Yeltsin and his entourage.

Without the backing of the state, members of the counter-elite were
forced to develop a deeper and more pragmatic understanding of the
Russian economy. They found a common language with many local institutions and, more importantly, a way to negotiate with local parliaments,
progressively shaping a new trend in the balance of power. In order to
survive, they avoided political confrontation and concentrated on more
fundamental problems. Since the beginning of the economic reforms,
they have adopted different values from those of the state elite—namely,
an enterprise-oriented culture and a marked preference for a policy of negotiation. In Robert Putnam's words, having developed horizontal relations of reciprocity, cooperation, and mutual trust, they are now closer to
building a civic community than is the state elite.[17] In sharp contrast to
this, the state elite has encouraged vertical patron-client relationships.

Both politicians and industrial managers emphasize the necessity of
building a coherent and loyal group in order to survive in the hostile environment of the transition period. But what holds the members of a particular group together? The Russian press has emphasized nepotism, notably at the level of ministries. In October 1997, one leading newspaper
disclosed that officials in the Railroad Ministry had signed commercial
contracts with private enterprises owned by their relatives. This huge organization was labeled the "Ministry of Wives and Sons."[18] This anecdo-
tal example seems, however, to be more an exception than the rule.

According to the respondents interviewed for this project, the main criteria for recruitment into a particular elite group remain shared values
and a similar career path during the years of transition. Even more revealing, however, is the role the state played—or did not play—in their
professional career. Indeed, the presence, or absence, of the state's support in the respondents' careers represents a profound divide that sepa-
rates them into two distinct elite groups. In short, the profile of each of

the two main elite groups is shaped precisely by their relationship to the state.

Elite Profiles and Relationship to the State

The main difference between members of the elite and the counter-elite—what I have labeled the "vertical" and "horizontal" elites—lies in the career path that they either chose or were forced to follow during the transition period.

Regarding the profiles of these elites, the "verticals"—the ruling elite—are the ones most familiar to scholars in the post-Soviet field. Members of the post-Soviet oligarchy, as well as many governors and industrial managers who rely on the backing of the state, are classic representatives of this "vertical" elite. Referring to Russia's elite groups, the media often cite three subgroups, all of which would be considered "verticals": the so-called "Government group" led by the prime minister in office, the "President's Group" led by former First Deputy Prime Minister Anatoli Chubais, and the "Moscow Group" led by Moscow Mayor Yuri Luzhkov.[19] These three "vertical" subgroups compete with each other for political influence, destabilizing the political and economic environment in the process. Although members of the "Government," the "President's," and the "Moscow" subgroups have different political agendas, they share an understanding of the state, which they perceive as being vertical and highly centralized.

These three subgroups represent the core of Russia's ruling elite. True, most of their leaders have made their career in the aftermath of the collapse of the Soviet Union. But they recruit exclusively through co-optation and patronage, a behavior that is in keeping with the Soviet pattern of recruitment.

Examples of co-optation by the state are numerous, but Vladimir Potanin's rise as the head of Oneksim Bank offers one of the most interesting pictures. On January 20, 1993, the Finance Ministry, then headed by Boris Fyodorov, decided to create a new bank to "increase Russia's hard currency reserves," to "stop capital flight," and to exert reliable control over the money supply.[20] Fyodorov wrote a letter to Central Bank chairman Viktor Gerashchenko, asking him to help with the granting of a license to the United Export Import Bank (Oneksim Bank). He then backed Potanin's appointment as the head of the new bank, notably because Potanin himself, as well as his father, had always been close to the circle of foreign trade executives, and because one could easily assume that he would immediately decipher the ins and outs of the financial sector, which was traditionally considered one of the most secret spheres of the Soviet and post-Soviet state.[21] In such a close environment, one had to be in the know before being recruited, whereas all the economists from the Soviet/Russian government, who had not dealt with exports, were considered to be strangers, members of the "outside" world.

At that time, two other banks, the Vneshtorgbank and the International Bank of Moscow (MMB), were authorized to manage the hard currency accounts of Russia's foreign trade organizations. Oneksim Bank progressively took control over most of their accounts and staff members. Potanin's bank was officially presented as a private establishment, although in fact, it already represented the interests of the state and, on a private level, those of some of the Foreign Trade Ministry's top executives. Shortly after it was created, it became the government's official agent in a number of financial deals.[22] It eventually became one of the most powerful private banks in Russia. Potanin, at its head, became known as one of the oligarchs, a member of Chubais's elite subgroup.

Beyond the boundaries of this "vertical" elite, however, another elite has emerged, using the numerous windows of opportunity provided by the transition period. Composed of self-made businessmen, industrial managers who are no longer "red directors," and governors who are not part of Yeltsin's team, this counter-elite has grown in membership since 1988, though it still lacks cohesiveness. What links this counter-elite together is the fact that they have developed without state backing.

Examining the composition of the "horizontal" counter-elite along these lines, one can highlight three different profiles, which reflect three different patterns of elite behavior: first, relative unknowns in the state structures or "outsiders" who used economic windows of opportunity during the transition to build up their economic power; second, elites abandoned by the state and forced to adapt to the new environment; and third, elites who became disillusioned with the state while occupying top positions in the government.

The first of these patterns of behavior—using windows of opportunity—describes businessmen who, in the years 1987–1988, transformed Gorbachev's law on cooperatives into an opportunity to open their own private enterprises, usually a company trading computers or specializing in barter. Perhaps one of the brightest representatives of this group is former biologist Kakha Bendukidze, who, in the late 1980s, managed to develop a cooperative set up on the premises of the chemical plant where he was employed. By the time of the 1998 financial crisis, Bendukidze owned about fifty enterprises; he had invested in the former military-industrial complex and bought two huge machine tool plants, Uralmash and Izhorskie Motory.

These newly born businessmen did not enjoy the support of the Komsomol, which at that time had a quasi-monopoly on cooperatives, known as Centers for Scientific-Technical Creativity of Youth, or NTTMs.[23] They claim this latter circumstance forced them to be more inventive and take advantage of loopholes in existing legislation in order to succeed. Later, these businessmen used a second window of opportunity, this time offered by the Yeltsin administration, to buy a considerable number of privatization vouchers and invest them into companies that they would eventually resell or restructure. Despite their successful development, they complain that the lack of support from the state, which favored a handful of privileged oligarchs, prevented them from investing in strategic companies, such as the telecommunication giant "Svyazinvest" or "Norilsk Nickel," Russia's main nickel producer.[24] They also emphasize that their status as outsiders led to their being constantly harassed by the tax police.[25] In retrospect, it appears that a certain recklessness was requisite to the development of private business without the blessing of the Party or Komsomol. This first pattern, therefore, describes the experience of only a few enterprising individuals with outstanding skills.

The second pattern—abandonment by the state and forced adaptation to a hostile environment—can be found mostly among industrial managers. When the Soviet economic system collapsed, central planning and centralized distribution suddenly vanished, and industrial managers were left in their previous positions without instructions from above. They were thus forced to be inventive in setting up new networks of suppliers and dealers, keeping their plant running, and selling their output.[26]

One illustration of this second profile can be found in Oleg Belonenko, former director of the KAMaz car production giant. Having been first at the head of the factory's Komsomol organization, then the number-two man in the KAMaz Communist Party organization, Belonenko decided not to open a private business in 1988 and concentrated instead on industrial management. The shock, he says, came in September 1993, when he lost his traditional customers, impoverished by three-digit inflation. What is interesting is how Belonenko describes the following years and the way he adapted. "I understood suddenly in 1993 what the market was," he told me. "Picture this. From my windows, I could see the huge lots where the newly produced cars were parked. And I could see endless lines of consumers waiting for days for the cars they had been expecting for so long. Suddenly, in September 1993, the lines disappeared and the lots were so packed there was no longer room to park the cars. I waited for the line to show up for a month, and then I understood: If I don't change the situation, I will not be able to pay salaries and keep the factory open. A different process had begun. I needed to elaborate an offensive strategy and to get used to marketing." Belonenko had previously attended theoretical marketing and management courses at the Management Academy of the Soviet Government, but he applied his knowledge only after he was forced to do so, then introducing new management and marketing techniques into the plant.

Such changes in behavior did not occur before the second or third year of Yeltsin's regime, after industrial managers had had a chance to change their mentalities and adapt their management methods to the new environment. Foreign investors and representatives of international financial organizations claimed that, at the time, they were unable to find a common language with these "red directors" and accused them of being unable to follow Western guidelines and implement any reform policy. But those industrialists, who eventually transformed themselves into competent businessmen, justify the delay by arguing that they needed time both to make their team efficient and to create horizontal links in a formerly centralized environment, where there was no industrial fabric and the only existing economic relationships were vertical.

The third profile of the "horizontal" counter-elite—growing disillusionment with the state while occupying a top position in the government—refers mostly to politicians. In their understanding, whereas "power" is an essential instrument to implement a reform policy, the "state" is only a synonym for Yeltsin's team and their abuses of power. Their main qualm about politicians in the "vertical" elite concerns the way reforms should be implemented. While most government and presidential administration officials of the "vertical" elite consider that politics should be the driving force of the reforms, representatives of the "horizontal" counter-elite reject the conventional top-down imposition of reform. Not surprisingly, they would argue for a lesser role of the state in the economy and for a systematic search for consensus within politics. On the regional level, these sentiments are easily found among governors disillusioned by federal policy, and who are now fundamentally questioning the role of the state in the economy.

Shared Values

Although Russia's endless elite power struggles reflect the absence of both political cohesiveness and a shared understanding of the public good, one can find interesting trends in the values that elites share. Differences between the "verticals" and the "horizontals" cross party lines and do not necessarily correlate with political views. To understand a given group's attitude toward reforms—and thus its composition—one should not focus on the usual typology, which takes mostly into consideration educational background and geographical and class origins. Instead, the main criteria that can be used to distinguish between the "vertical" and "horizontal" groups are found in the elites' worldviews and attitudes toward power and the reform process. These criteria were revealed in interviews in several ways.

One question concerning the respondents' experience in the Communist Youth Organization provides an interesting illustration of elites' worldviews. Most of the respondents—if not all—were Komsomol activists; they all went through the same experience. But what they recall as the most important part of that experience differs from one group to the other. Overall, two attitudes prevail. On the one hand, people who, from the very beginning of their adult life, had planned to follow a career among the ruling elite tried to enter one of the state's networks; they admit that the Komsomol offered them "useful connections for the future." On the other hand, those who achieved economic and political success without the backing of the state say that the Komsomol offered them an invaluable opportunity to develop personal initiative, and gave them their first experience in balancing budgets, organizing student construction brigades, and managing personnel. Although it is clear that what the Komsomol has brought to them are *both* connections and experience, the way respondents answer often reveals their personal worldview. The responses by elites in the first group thus reflect a hierarchical vision of the world, while those in the second group stress the centrality of horizontal integration with other individuals and social groups.

On other points, "vertical" and "horizontal" elites also differ fundamentally. Overall, members of the "vertical" subgroups believe that, at least during transition periods, politics, in particular the executive branch, is the only driving force capable of implementing reforms while avoiding social and economic disorder. Consequently, they believe that the state should regulate both the financial and industrial development of the country until democracy and a free market are secured. In their view, there is thus a temporary need for collusion between politics and economics. Additionally, members of the "vertical" elite are convinced that political reform of the economy and the society should take place within a short period of time, and many of them argue that the state should eventually withdraw from the economy. In the meantime, however, the perceived need for an all-powerful state—even for a short period of time—often leads to a polarized worldview, according to which members of the "vertical" group tend to consider those who disagree with their policy as "potential enemies." Agreement on this issue, in turn, often helps them self-identify and, therefore, shapes their political discourse and economic behavior. This is true for the three subgroups described above, including for most of the respondents of Chubais's group, who are often labeled "young reformers."

In opposition to the "vertical" elite, members of the "horizontal" counter-elite have developed different values, although they too share with the previous group a willingness to implement a free market and to maintain electoral democracy in Russia. But they differ substantially from the "verticals" in advocating a lesser role for the state in the economy, developing greater interaction—not collusion—between the industrial and political realms, and favoring a genuine balance of power between the executive and the legislative branches. Indeed, they express a lack of confidence in the executive's capacity to act as the agent of reform, and prefer the legislature as a source of reform policy. They also stress the importance of conflict resolution through negotiation. The "vertical" elite, by contrast, tends to favor the resolution of conflicts by force, using the tax police as a political tool in struggles for power.[27]

In terms of time frame, members of the "horizontal" group argue that reforms should be gradual, and most of them criticize the "shock therapy" policies implemented in 1992 by former Prime Minister Yegor Gaidar. It is true that this last point—preference given to a slower tempo of reform—is one of the main points articulated in the Communist Party's program; but members of the "horizontal" counter-elite disagree with the Communist idea of a centralized economy and state-subsidized industry. In their eyes, implementing "gradual reforms" means considering economics—not politics—as the driving force of the reforms and, more importantly, accepting initiatives from below. They believe that accepting initiatives either from regional governors or from businessmen and industrialists who volunteer to restructure state enterprises is the best way to unify the elite, to avoid frustration on the part of the non-state elite and, consequently, to avoid many economic and political conflicts.[28]

In the minds of Russia's elite, the disagreements presented above are considered fundamental. They cut across political affiliations and concern personal ethics. Asked whom they respect most in the political arena, several politicians-respondents provided an answer that—in the West—would be unusual: "Although I stand politically on the side of A, I definitely understand B better, and share B's worldview," several respondents said. Some even acknowledged that they privately advocate to vote for B, not necessarily for A, the leader of their own party.

The emphasis respondents spontaneously put on the importance of a shared worldview is symptomatic of a transition period, wherein individuals' values develop not always in accordance with political and economic programs. It is precisely in this gap between ethics and the political or economic realms (i.e., between one's preferred set of structural economic and political reforms, and the way those reforms are implemented) that often lies the source of political conflicts.

Power Struggles

The successive changes encountered in Russia's political and economic environments, as well as the evolution of values during the transition, complicate any analysis of ethics in today's Russia. As Sheila Puffer and Daniel McCarthy have shown in their study of business ethics in transitional Russia, "different ethical behaviors may prevail for the same individual, and certainly among individuals, even within the same group. There has been virtually no stable state for ethical principles for many people participating in Russian business. Instead, they have been pulled in many directions by competing forces, some of which prevailed at one time, while others took precedence on other occasions."[29] This ongoing evolution in the values of Russia's elite has contributed deeply to the apparent chaos in politics and business, and to the fuzziness of elite groups, which seem to form and to disappear according to short-term political or financial considerations.

To decipher the conflicts within the Russian elite, one must distinguish between two levels of conflict. The first level, "inter-elite conflicts," sets groups against each other along the lines of political parties, industrial sectors, or regional lobbies. Competition between governors and the federal authorities, as well as struggles for power and influence launched by elite groups close to the prime minister, the presidential administration, or the Moscow City government, are illustrations of "inter-elite conflicts." A second level of conflict seldom analyzed by the Russian media, the "intra-elite conflicts," occurs within a given group. All influential politicians, businessmen, or industrial managers experience these kinds of conflicts; they all are thrown into competition not only with other officials, but also within their own ranks.

This means that elite representatives may react more or less aggressively depending on the level of conflict they are involved in. Some may focus on gaining enough clout within their group before beginning any struggle for influence outside their group; others may choose the opposite tactic and seek the backing of the all-powerful state leaders before reaffirming their power within their own group. In each case, the given affiliation of the individual with either the "vertical" or the "horizontal" elite group might explain his tactical—and, therefore, temporary—moves in the struggle for power.

Analysis of the behavior of Russia's regional political elites, particularly the governors, reveals the distinction between "vertical" and "horizontal" elite groups. Within their territories, most of the governors belonging to the "vertical" group resort to traditional instruments of power and, often, to arbitrariness.[30] They employ the rhetoric of anticorruption campaigns, they control the local media, notably the local television channels, and foster the formation of local oligarchies loyal to them.[31] On the level of "inter-elite" competition, being independent—or not—from the center depends less on the individual governor's mentality than it does on the economic potential of the region. Not surprisingly, the administrative regions bordering war-torn countries (as in Stavropol, where the flow of refugees from Chechnya and Daghestan rises daily) and economically poor areas (for example, the Bryansk administrative region) tend to seek protection either from the center or from a powerful political figure, and thus tend to fall into the "vertical" elite category. The language used by some of the local bosses in these areas is rather significant. In March 1999, in a desperate attempt to find resources for his constituency, the head of the Krasnaya Gora district (in the Bryansk region), I. Kirchenko, turned to Belarus president Aleksandr Lukashenka and urged him to take his district under his "patronage."[32]

In opposition to the Kremlin's tendency to strengthen political hierarchy throughout the country, other governors have developed a more consensus-oriented behavior. Although none of them has so far acknowledged the existence of any "horizontal" counter-elite, they have a radically different state of mind and a different attitude toward power. These governors no longer entertain any illusions about the current decision-making process. Most of them believe that the only way to implement reforms in their own region is to gain political clout and to bypass the vertical chain of power imposed by the Kremlin. To do so, they need to create a new lever of influence beyond the boundaries of both the existing legal institutions and the "informal institutions" that represent the influential clans close to the prime minister's office, the presidential administration, or the Moscow City Government. Paradoxically enough, the summer 1998 crisis worked as a catalyst for this group of governors, who understood that they needed to come together and get organized in order to defend their interests. In the same way that businessmen lacking Komsomol support used windows of opportunity to open cooperatives in the years 1988 to 1989, some of Russia's governors are now ready to use the windows of opportunity offered by the 1999 parliamentary and the 2000 presidential elections to increase their power, while rejecting the backing of the federal state.

In this respect, the political campaigns of Luzhkov's "Fatherland" and Samara Governor Konstantin Titov's "Russia's Voice," two political blocs bringing together governors of the Russian Federation, are revealing.[33] Although Luzhkov announced in April 1999 that the two blocs planned to merge,[34] the differences in the leaders' discourse and in their perception of how Russia's federative system should be reformed amount to disagreements that conform to the divide between the "vertical" and "horizontal" elite positions.

Whereas, for instance, Luzhkov states that Russia needs a "strong and effective executive authority" and advocates for a reduction of the number of the regions from eighty-nine to an undefined "more manageable" number,[35] the thirty governors of the "Russia's Voice" bloc argue that the Russian Federation is too monolithic and far too hierarchical. Instead of reducing the number of regions, its members advocate upholding the diversity of political and economic status among the regions that exists within the Federation, depending on the regions' geographical or economic specificity.[36]

Here again, while both the "vertical" and "horizontal" groups support the need for reforms, the difference between the two groups lies in the way they believe these reforms should be implemented and in their understanding of the role of the state. In an interview with the daily newspaper *Nezavisimaya Gazeta*, Titov stressed that both he and Luzhkov wanted to resurrect Russia, the difference being that he wanted to work through federalism, while the Moscow mayor would, he said, use "other methods."[37]

Unlike Luzhkov's "Fatherland" organization, where strict party discipline is imposed from above, "Russia's Voice" seeks to give its members maximum autonomy, leaving only the role of informal leader to its initiator Titov, who insists that the movement should be devoid of ideological dogmas.[38] This "horizontal" organizational principle is of central importance to Russia's Voice members, who consider themselves betrayed when the media depicts the movement as "Titov's bloc."[39] Even if it is not acknowledged consciously, personalizing the movement in that way reduces its significance to that of a mere political toy in the hands of a single ambitious politician. Fidelity to the movement's "horizontal" philosophy is fundamental for the governors precisely because the only "glue" holding their bloc together is psychological and lies in their attitude toward power. Just as mistrust toward the state was an instrumental force in bringing them together, mutual trust and power sharing is necessary to keep them together as a bloc.

There is little doubt that representatives of the "horizontal" counter-elite, whose power has grown at a distance from the state, also create their own clientele and try to lobby the executive branch both at the federal and regional levels. Although different values separate the two elites, one group is not inherently more democratic than the other. Consequently, to simply replace the "vertical" ruling elite with the "horizontal" counter-elite would not speed the process of transition; the counter-elite, as they share many attributes with the ruling elite, would doubtless embrace the "vertical" group's characteristics should they find themselves in power. The alternative to today's political regime, from which the ruling elite tends to exclude the non-state elite, cannot possibly be one that would merely ensure the replacement of individuals, as Russian authorities often claim. Rather than limiting oneself to co-opting a handful of outsiders to join the executive branch, thus diluting the values of the counter-elite into the ones of the "vertical" elite, one should use the very existence of this "horizontal" group, composed of men of different values and experience, as a wedge to shape a different balance of power. Taking their "horizontal" methods of management and reform programs into consideration, taking into account initiatives from below, while engaging in a constructive dialogue, one could push for substantial changes in the current vertical structure of the all-powerful executive office. This would doubtless favor a genuine balance of power and encourage the development of a civil society.

Notes

1. On August 17, 1998, the Russian government and the Central Bank in a joint statement issued a number of new policies, which effectively constituted a devaluation of the ruble. This created a panic in the Russian stock market. A ninety-day moratorium was also announced on payments for financial credits, received from Russian nonresidents, on the payment of insurance on credits insured by the mortgage of securities. See Intercon (August 17, 1999) quoted on Internet Securities at [http://www.securities.com].

2. This chapter is based on the findings of sixty preliminary interviews, conducted between March and December 1998, in Moscow and Yekaterinburg, in the Urals. These interviews were part of a research project, entitled "The Elite and Patronage in Russia," based at the Davis Center for Russian Studies, Harvard University. The author is grateful to the Smith Richardson Foundation for its support.

3. See, for example, Olga Kryshtanovskaya, "From Soviet Nomenklatura to Russian Elite," *Europe-Asia Studies,* 48 (July 1996): 711–734 and "Nomenklatura nashego vremeni," *Obshchaya Gazeta* (January 23–29, 1997); Yuri Burtin, *Novyj stroy. O nomenklaturnom kapitalizme: stat'i, dialog, interv'yu* (Moscow: seriya mezhdu proshlim i budushchim, 1995).

4. See, for example, Donald N. Jensen, "How Russia Is Ruled," in Peter Rutland, ed., *Business and the State in Russia* (Boulder, Colo.: Westview Press, forthcoming 1999). The article can also be read on the Web at [http://www.rferl.org/nca/special/ruwhorules/index.html].

5. The authorization was given by presidential decree. A year later, in 1988, the Supreme Soviet (Parliament) passed the law on cooperatives. See A. Jones, W. Moskoff, *Ko-ops. The Rebirth of Entrepreneurship in the Soviet Union* (Bloomington & Indianapolis, Ind.: Indiana University Press, 1991).

6. This was the case with Agroprombank (agro-industrial sector), Vneshtorg-bank (foreign trade), Mezhregionbank (regions of the Russian Federation), Russia's Promstroibank (industrial investment bank), Saint Petersburg's Prom-stroibank (Saint Petersburg), and Sberbank (savings bank). Agroprombank subsequently acquired stakes in 16 commercial banks, and Promstroibank did the same with 15 other banks. For a detailed history of the first years of Russia's banking system, see Joel Hellman, *Breaking the Bank: Bureaucrats and the Creation of Markets in a Transitional Economy*, Columbia University Ph.D. diss., 1993, in particular Part 2, Chapter 2, 126–186.

7. For example, the State Supply Committee (Gossnab) created Commercial bank for Wholesale Transactions (Tokobank) with the participation of its local branches, and the Ministry of Petrochemical Industry created the Commercial bank for the Development of the Petrochemical Industry (Neftekhimbank). State enterprises and industrial associations also created their own banking structures. This was the case with Aeroflot (AeroflotBank), Energomash (Energomashbank), and AvtoVAZ (AvtoVAZBank).

8. The Komi Republic created SyktyvkarBank and the Republic of Bashkortostan (Bashkirya) founded Vostok Bank. In some cases, banks were created directly by regional enterprises. This was the case with Stolichny Bank, which was created by several Moscow-based construction firms.

9. Created between 1989 and 1991, these banks are Menatep, Most-Group, Kredobank, Mosbiznesbank, and Inkombank.

10. On the rules of patronage under both the Soviet and Yeltsin's regimes, see M. N. Afanasyev, *Klientelizm i rossiyskaya gosudarstvennost'* (Moscow: Tsentr konstitutsionnykh issledovaniy moskovskogo obshchestvennogo nauchnogo fonda, 1997).

11. Thomas Graham was one of the first Western scholars who focused on this "clan logic"; see "The New Russian Regime," translated in *Nezavisimaya Gazeta* (November 23, 1995). On March 18, 1998, then Deputy Prime Minister Boris Nemtsov held a roundtable meeting entitled "Russia's Future: Democracy and Oligarchy." See his article in *Nezavisimaya Gazeta* (March 17, 1998). For an interesting and complex overview of Russia's current elite and oligarchy, see Peter Rutland, who demonstrates that "Russia's elite is primarily a continuation of the more dynamic and adaptable fragments of the old Soviet elite" in "After August: Elite Consolidation, Institutional Decay and Political Stability in Russia" (unpublished paper, 1998). Anders Åslund develops the opposite point of view and considers that there was no oligarchy under Yeltsin's regime in "The Myth of Oligarchy," *Moscow Times* (January 29, 1998).

12. Russian scholars Igor Klyamkin and Lilya Shevtsova compared the Yeltsin regime to an "elective monarchy," in which the president has "absolute powers," in the article "Eta vsesil'naya bessil'naya vlast'," *Nezavisimaya Gazeta* (June 24, 1998).

13. As Joel Hellman has shown, leaders in postcommunist countries tend to insulate the state, favor arbitrage opportunities, and implement partial economic reforms "that generate concentrated rents for themselves, while imposing high costs on the rest of the society." Joel S. Hellman, "Winners Take All: The Politics of

Partial Reform in Postcommunist Transitions," *World Politics,* vol. 50, no. 2 (1998): 203–234.

14. A. Dmitriev, E. Stepanov, A. Chumikov, "Rossijskij sotsium v 1995 godu: Konfliktologicheskaya ekspertiza," *Sotsiologicheskie Issledovaniya* (January 1996): 6–23.

15. For a definition of "strategic elites," see Suzanne Keller, *Beyond the Ruling Class: Strategic Elites in Modern Society* (New Brunswick, NJ: Transaction, 1991). In his book on lobbying mechanisms, Vladimir Lepekhin argues that by the 1970s "branch clans" had come to dominate industrial sectors and that networks spanned economic, party, and police organizations. He adds that these "monopolies" were already "beyond the control of even the Politburo" and "increasingly usurped both power and property." Vladimir Lepekhin, *Lobbizm: analiz deyatel'nosti lobbistskikh grupp v kontekste obshchepoliticheskoy situatsii v Rossii. Problema zakonodatel'nogo regulirovaniya lobbizma: proekt zakona "O regulirovanii lobbistskoy deyatel'nosti v federal'nykh organakh gosudarstvennoy vlasti"* (Moscow: Fond IQ, 1995). For a sector-related analysis of Russia's lobbies, see the four volumes edited by Klaus Segbers and Stephan De Spiegeleire, *Post-Soviet Puzzles: Mapping the Political Economy of the Former Soviet Union* (Baden-Baden: Nomos, 1996). More specifically on the regional elites, see Philip Hanson, *Regions, Local Power and Economic Change in Russia* (London: Russian and CIS Program, Royal Institute of International Affairs, 1994) and Talgat Minnibaev, *Politicheskaya kar'era provintsialov* (Kazan: Tatarskoe knizhnoe izd., 1991).

16. Mikhail Malyutin, "Authority Groups: Stabilisers and Chaots," in Klaus Segbers, Stephan Spiegeleire, eds., *Post-Soviet Puzzles,* vol. 3 (Baden-Baden: Nomos, 1996): 155–159. In the same volume see the article by Yakov Pappe, wherein he argues that, unlike in Western countries, the Russian elite is not considered exemplary by the society; "Russian Economic Elite: A Group Portrait Anno 1994," Segbers and Spiegeleire, 39. In the same spirit, see also the editorial by a member of the Academy of Sciences, Zhan Toshchenko, "Kak zhe nazvat' tekh, kto pravit nami?" *Nezavisimaya Gazeta* (December 31, 1998) available on Internet Securities at [http://www.securities.com].

17. Robert D. Putnam, Robert Leonardi, Rafaella Y. Nanetti, *Making Democracy Work: Civic Traditions in Modern Italy* (Princeton, N.J.: Princeton University Press, 1993).

18. Aleksei Kirikov, "Ministerstvo Zhen, synovey i plemyannikov," *Izvestiya* (October 24, 1997): 1.

19. When Chernomyrdin was in power, the "Government group" was composed of his supporters. At the beginning of 1999, this group was made up of representatives of Yevgeny Primakov's entourage. By the time this article was written, it was not clear whether Prime Minister Sergei Stepashin would develop his own group or would enlarge the "President's Group," to which he was believed to belong. Former First Deputy Prime Minister Anatoli Chubais is now chairman of Russia's electric power monopoly, UES. Moscow Mayor Yuri Luzhkov is a prominent contender for the 2000 presidential elections.

20. Extracts from a letter sent by then Finance Minister Boris Fyodorov to Central Bank Chairman Viktor Gerashchenko. Yaroslav Skvortsov, Mikhail Loginov, "Skromnoe obayanie Oneksim Banka," *Kommersant Daily* (November 16, 1995).

The article also emphasizes that Deputy Foreign Trade Minister Oleg Davydov backed Fyodorov's request and asked Valery Khokhlov, chairman of the board of the International Bank for Economic Cooperation (MBES), to give some of the bank's real estate to Oneksim Bank. Oneksim Bank—a short name for *Obedinennyj Eksportno-Importnyj Bank*—got its license from the Central Bank on April 20, 1993.

21. Potanin's father, Oleg, was Soviet economic representative in Indonesia in the late 1950s. He then headed the "Vostokintorg" foreign trade association. After graduating from MGIMO (Moscow State Institute of International Relations) in 1983, Vladimir worked eight years in the Foreign Trade Ministry before creating, in 1991, "Interros," then a simple import-export trading company.

22. In 1995, it became the Bank of the State Committee for Bankruptcy and Privatization. It was also authorized by the federal government to manage the funds allocated for the reconstruction of the war-torn breakaway republic of Chechnya.

23. The Komsomol has invested huge amounts of money in these private cooperatives. In 1988, for example, in the Urals city of Sverdlovsk (now Yekaterinburg), the Komsomol helped open 30 cooperatives in the Kirov district alone, investing up to 11 million rubles. Author's interview with Russian sociologist and former Sverdlovsk Komsomol activist Igor Savelev (Yekaterinburg, June 30, 1998).

24. In November 1995, during the government program known as the "loans-for-shares" privatization, Oneksim Bank acquired a 38 percent stake (with the majority of votes) in Norilsk Nickel in return for a $170.1 million loan. In July 1997, after a hotly contested auction, Oneksim Bank took control of Svyazinvest. Virginie Coulloudon, "Privatization in Russia: Catalyst for the Elite," *The Fletcher Forum of World Affairs*, vol. 22, no. 2 (Summer/Fall 1998): 43–56.

25. Author's interviews with chairman of the "Bioprocess" holding company, Kakha Bendukidze (Investment Forum, Harvard Kennedy School of Government, January 11, 1998, and Moscow, March 20, 1998), and with Grigory Tomchin, president of the "All-Russia Association of Privatized and Private Enterprises" (Moscow, March 28, 1998).

26. Oleg Belonenko eventually joined Bendukidze's team with Uralmash. Author's interview with Belonenko (Yekaterinburg, June 26,1998).

27. In April 1996, the newspaper *Kommersant Daily* published several articles denouncing the pressure exerted by the tax police, which leads not only to tax evasion but also to abuses of power on the part of the authorities. In November 1998, the tax police ordered the Balakovsky nuclear plant to stop functioning until it paid its debts to the tax inspection. *Moskovskie Novosti,* no. 45 (November 15–22, 1998): 8. In July 1998, in an attempt to get its debts back, the government suddenly closed down several buildings and sanatoriums belonging to the gas monopoly Gazprom. See, for example, Irina Granik, Aleksandr Malyutin, "Neulovimy Rem," *Kommersant Vlast'*, no. 26 (July 14, 1998): 19–23; and Maksim Buylov, "Gazprom osvobozhdaet nomera," *Den'gi,* no. 28 (July 29, 1998): 9–12.

28. Author's interviews with Grigori Tomchin (Moscow, March 23, 1998) and with Vladimir Lopukhin, former fuel and energy minister, 1991–1992 (Moscow, July 10, 1998). Together with Kakha Bendukidze, they offered the government to help with the restructuring of the Railroad Ministry. They claim that, after having

first accepted, Chubais suddenly rejected the program. They both believe that the real reason for this brusque refusal lies in the fact that they are "outsiders" to the state elite.

29. Sheila M. Puffer, Daniel J. McCarthy, "Business Ethics in a Transforming Economy: Applying the Integrative Social Contracts Theory to Russia," in B. Kumar and H. Steinmann, eds., *Ethics in International Management* (Berlin and New York: de Gruyter, 1998). On the evolution of the Russians' mentality and ethics during the transition, see also Igor Dubov, ed., *Mental'nost' rossiyan* (Moscow: Image-Contact, 1997).

30. For the traditional instruments of power under the Soviet regime, see Mikhail Heller, *Cogs in the Wheel: The Formation of the Soviet Man* (New York, N.Y.: Alfred A. Knopf, Inc., 1988).

31. Sverdlovsk Governor Eduard Rossel is one example of a "vertical"-type governor, eager to maintain the vertical chain of the executive power from the Kremlin down to his region in the Urals and using his network to retain control over the region. During the fall of 1998, he pressured the head of the Yekaterinburg subsidiary of VGTRK, the second federal TV channel, to leave so that he could replace him with one of his own men. See Natalya Mints, "Creation of National Television Network Causes Scandal in Yekaterinburg," *EWI Russian Regional Report*, vol. 4, no. 6 (February 18, 1999). In defiance of the elementary rules of the free market, Rossel also issued a decree forbidding shareholders in strategic regional enterprises to fire their directors without his consent. *Izvestiya* (February 16, 1999), cited by *EWI Russian Regional Report*, vol. 4, no. 6 (February 18, 1999).

32. The Russian way to put it is *vzyat' shefstvo nad rayonom*. A. Kornya, "A. Lukashenko vzyal shefstvo nad Krasnoi Goroi," *Bryanskie Izvestiya* (February 24, 1999): 1, reprinted in Internet Securities at [http://www.securities.com].

33. These two political blocs appeared early in 1999, at the eve of the December 1999 legislative and June 2000 presidential campaigns. "Fatherland" is the political bloc of Moscow's Mayor Luzhkov, and "Russia's Voice" is led by Samara Governor Konstantin Titov.

34. Luzhkov's "Fatherland" held its second congress in the city of Yaroslavl on April 24, 1999, convening 800 delegates. This alliance with "Russia's Voice" is part of Luzhov's electoral strategy to gain the confidence of the provinces, where the wealthy capital Moscow is often perceived with resentment. *Kommersant Daily* (April 27, 1999).

35. These two points are clearly developed in the "Fatherland" program. See *Kommersant Daily* (February 27, 1999) quoted in *EWI Russian Regional Report*, vol. 4, no. 8 (March 4, 1999).

36. Interview with Samara Governor Konstantin Titov, *Nezavisimaya Gazeta* (February 26, 1999): 1 and 6. See also interview with Ingushetiya President Ruslan Aushev in *EWI Russian Regional Report*, vol. 4, no. 9 (March 11, 1999). In this interview, Aushev emphasizes, "We are not only a federative state, but also a multinational one as well, and the regions differ according to their national characteristics. Smolensk and Tula are still suffering from the accident of Chernobyl. Therefore, the conditions of their agreement with the center should be different. I represent a people who have been deported; therefore, in our treaty there should

be a point about people's full rehabilitation. The Maritime Territory (Vladivostok) should wring out its economic independence, otherwise it cannot survive. Obviously it must be given greater autonomy to conduct its own foreign economic policy. The same is true for Yakutiya (Sakha). Some regions should be declared off-shore zones. Thus, each region should make an agreement with the center based on its geographic, national, or other characteristics."

37. *Nezavisimaya Gazeta* (February 26, 1999): 1 and 6.

38. In the words of Titov, who is chairman of the organizing committee of Russia's Voice, he and his colleagues in the Federation Council, the upper house of the parliament, no longer entertain any illusions about political parties being able to produce appropriate legislative acts. He decided to create this bloc to gather governors beyond the party lines. Vladimir Korsunsky, "Gubernatory v pokhode," *Izvestiya* (February 26, 1999): 4. See also *Nezavisimaya Gazeta* (February 19, 1999).

39. According to the daily newspaper *Vremya-MN*, this has already created tensions within the movement. Kemerovo Governor Aman Tuleev said he was not part of any "Titov's bloc" and would rather work in an organization led by Prime Minister Yevgeny Primakov. See *Vremya-MN* (February 23, 1999): 2; and *Trud* (March 5, 1999): 2.

PART II

The State:
Weak Institutions and
Crumbling Capacity

4

Is the Russian State Coping with Organized Crime and Corruption?

LOUISE SHELLEY

In August 1998, the ruble and the Russian banking system collapsed. The market for short-term Russian treasury notes (GKOs), which had financed the operations of the Russian government through extremely high interest rates, crashed when the GKOs were declared almost worthless. The government of Russia announced that it was unable to meet its debt payments. The International Monetary Fund stepped in with an aid package of over four billion dollars, much of which, according to American regulators, was taken out of the country before it was able to serve its intended function: to stabilize the ruble.[1]

The financial collapse of the Russian state in August 1998 glaringly revealed that the Russian state was not coping with organized crime or corruption. Until that moment, many believed that these problems were peripheral issues complicating the Russian transition. Now it is believed that the widespread incidence of corruption and crime has been derailing the larger processes of democratization and free market reform all along, and that it is undermining the very capacity of the state to function. The losses of billions of dollars of the IMF bailout over the course of a few days, precipitated by the collapse of the GKO pyramid market and the insider cronyism of the Russian banks, raised alarms and convinced many that corruption and organized crime should be issues central to economic analysis.

The Russian financial collapse not only revealed the weaknesses of Russian institutions but also contained important lessons for world markets, as rich hedge funds and banks suffered enormous losses.[2] International financial institutions lost billions because corruption, crony capitalism, and the failure to collect taxes had depleted the Russian treasury and undermined state capacity. The Russian government continued to borrow more money to compensate for the theft of state resources and the failure of its infrastructural reforms to raise revenue. Russia's high level of indebtedness and its inability to meet its international obligations will undermine Russian development for the foreseeable future.

Before August 1998, many Westerners believed that Russia was making a peaceful and steady transition to democracy, developing institutions capable of running a free market. They ignored the warning signs, including audits by the Chamber of Accounts, the miners' strikes over nonpayment of wages, and the numerous and consistent reports from the Parliament and the Ministry of Interior documenting the departure of billions of dollars monthly from Russia. Their failure to anticipate the August collapse was based on an improper understanding of the inability of the centralized Russian state to control currency flows, promote equitable privatization, collect revenues, or promote a transition from the socialist economy.

The Soviet Union collapsed, a weak and corrupt state. The demands on the new Russian state only increased with the demands of the transition. But the state's capacity to administer its affairs did not increase; rather, its momentum toward collapse was perpetuated and exacerbated in the post-Soviet period by corruption. Corrupt activities acquired even more significant proportions with the demise of the Communist Party, the privatization of state-held property, and the entry of Russia into the global economy.

The Russian state could not curb the rise of corruption or organized crime because the state was simultaneously privatized and stolen. The state functions of order maintenance, delivery of social and medical services, and guarantee of contracts were assumed by private groups, some of them showing the profile of organized crime.[3] The state was hampered in the reconstruction of its depleted infrastructure as systemic corruption siphoned off money needed to rebuild Soviet industry. Officials charged with overseeing the reconstruction of Soviet infrastructure pocketed such large quantities of revenue from loans for shipyard construction that projects were not adequately completed. Consequently, the domestic economic situation worsened and the indebtedness increased. Soon the capacity to repay debts evaporated as the end products proved to lack the necessary competitive edge to succeed on international markets.

The stealing of the Russian state refers not only to the physical assets of the state and the values of the society, including its commitment to democratization, but also to the functions of the state appropriated by corrupt governmental officials for their personal gain.[4] The militia failed to police the streets and prevent crime; military personnel were more concerned with appropriating stockpiles of arms than defending the state; and health care officials confiscated medical supplies before they reached the sick. Police and members of the military sold their arms and nuclear materials to crime groups rather than fulfilling their roles to protect citizens and the state.[5]

The dire picture of the incapacity of Russian institutions to deal with the concomitant problems of organized crime and corruption should not obscure the fact that many members of state institutions, the legislature and the government, have been trying to combat these problems. Although the will for concerted national effort might be difficult for those outside the country to detect, Russia cannot be characterized as completely apathetic or unwilling to curb the corruption and crime evident in its governing bodies. Sources show that many individuals are actively trying to stop the misappropriation of state resources and fight the armed criminals who are a potent force in many regions of the country, particularly Siberia and the Far East.[6]

Analyzing the Problem

The problem of combating organized crime and corruption evokes the image of investigators, prosecutors, and police. While the threat of penalties and incarceration might discourage future crimes from being committed, it does not prevent organized unlawful activities from becoming deeply rooted in Russia's transitional economic system.

The institutions needed to address the problem of organized crime and corruption might best be found outside the legal or law enforcement arena, whose coercive—rather than preventive—measures often fail to provide an integrated approach to the task of restructuring a society.[7] Bureaucracy, conflict-of-interest-laws, and supervisory agencies, such as auditors, must provide accountability and transparency to function with authority and trust. As democratic systems of government have shown, an anticorruption governmental strategy should emphasize the importance of a system of checks and balances. Financial oversight and accountability, distribution of power among branches of government, and an independent media are prerequisites for good governance. In other words, "democracy and free markets are not necessarily a cure for corruption. A shift from authoritarian to democratic rule does not necessarily reduce payoffs."[8]

In a period of massive redistribution of property, such as that which followed the end of socialism, primacy must be given to ensuring an equitable share for all citizens, and legal norms establishing and protecting property rights must be implemented. Effective regulation of the distribution of multilateral and foreign loans is needed to ensure the reconstruction of industry. None of these tasks were accomplished by the Russian government.[9] Nor were these approaches advocated by the foreign governments and multilateral organizations providing massive amounts of aid and loans to Russia in the 1990s.

Instead, many economic advisers favored rapid privatization and deregulation, despite Russia's highly criminalized environment, without careful consideration of the consequences. Disregarding historical examples to the contrary, many naïvely believed that crime and corruption, clearly evident under the Communist system, would diminish with a deregulated market economy. None of the advisers to Russia heeded recent lessons of privatization in other countries. They did not draw a parallel from the situation in Mexico in the 1980s, where the privatization of state property enriched the oligarchy, many of whom operated in the legitimate and illegitimate arena simultaneously. Nor did they make a comparison with New York City, where the Cosa Nostra acquired its monopoly over the garbage industry in the 1950s, when city garbage collection was privatized without any safeguards over which businesspeople would acquire this function. Instead, advisers relied on privatization and deregulation to cure the ills of the Russian economy, when in reality these became mechanisms that allowed a criminalized elite and organized crime to gain even greater control.

The rise of organized crime and corruption, therefore, should not be blamed solely on the ineffective law enforcement agencies of the post-Soviet period. The preconditions for this problem, as will be discussed below, lie in the Soviet era.[10] But the problem was exacerbated by Western aid policies that did not make anticorruption and anti–organized crime strategies a central part of their development and privatization agendas. Crime-fighting strategies focused too narrowly on police training and passage of laws when they should have emphasized systemic approaches to preventing problems.

The desire by the West to support reformers rather than overall processes of reform meant that the West did not practice what it preached. Instead of focusing on larger issues of implementing good governance, many Western countries and international financial institutions dealt with a small clique around the Yeltsin government and engaged the new oligarchy, or the newly rich and powerful business moguls who dominated banking, the media, and Russia's natural resources, and were key Yeltsin advisers. They bypassed Parliament, supported a constitution that personalized power in the president, and failed to encourage and support the development of regulatory institutions. Moreover, the IMF undermined the separation of powers by instructing the Yeltsin government to veto certain laws passed by the Duma.

Western analysts who equated the rise of oligarchs with the robber baron era of capitalism ironically helped a few ambitious individuals to consolidate enormous financial empires. In the process, those successful entrepreneurs violated the privatization rights of the ordinary citizens when they denied them their rightful stake in the enterprises and apartments where they had worked and lived for decades.[11] With such concentration of wealth, these new financial giants could buy up newspapers and television stations, thereby muzzling the media that had been liberated during the Gorbachev era.[12] Without a free press or an active civil society, no external forces remained to counteract the further criminalization of the state and the economy.

By focusing on quantitative indicators of economic performance and privatization, Western advisers failed to see the reality that lay beneath the surface. The transition to a democracy and free market was doomed as those guiding economic and political policies failed to see that crime and corruption were capable of derailing the transition to a market economy and a democratic society.

The pervasive corruption and the rise and penetration of organized crime into the state and the economy cannot be explained solely by the failure to create institutions and norms. The answers should be sought in the legacy of the Soviet system and the flawed process of transition. Central to this problem is the fact that "law enforcement agencies also suffer at the mercy of the lingering ideological prejudices of Soviet jurisprudence."[13] The inability of law enforcement agencies to effect reconstruction was compounded from the beginning by the corrupt legacy of the Soviet period.

Accountability in the Soviet Period

The USSR has been referred to as "the corrupt society."[14] Yet one must examine this label and the ways it was used internally. For although corruption was pervasive, the USSR was not without a modicum of accountability. Accusations of corruption were often used as a weapon to eliminate political opponents. While these charges did not fall uniformly across the society or the political elite, those in positions of authority knew that they were vulnerable to serious allegations of misconduct and abuse of authority.[15] This threat of prosecution, therefore, set some limits on the appropriation of state property and discouraged visible displays of wealth. Also, it ensured that embezzled resources were accumulated within the country, rather than sent to offshore bank accounts.

To ensure accountability during the Soviet period, erring Party officials were subject to Party discipline and periodic campaigns were waged against corruption. Even though Party officials often enjoyed immunity from prosecution because law enforcement agencies had to obtain Party permission before pursuing errant personnel, some investigations still went through and were made public. These campaigns against corruption, particularly those launched under Andropov (CPSU General Secretary from 1982 to 1984), deprived many individuals of their senior positions; some were even incarcerated.[16] Details of their misconduct and sanctions were published in Party journals. While many in the Party felt that their position of power provided them with unlimited privileges, for some, this accusatory process represented Party discipline, a method of accountability, and a check on their behavior.

In retrospect, those examining Soviet tolerance for corruption might judge the system harshly and evaluate the measures taken against economic crime and financial misconduct as insignificant or meager. But many Russian officials attempting to combat corruption during the current years of transition voice regret that the albeit minimal controls of the Soviet era died along with the USSR. Russian data for the decade from 1986 to 1996 show a marked decline in the registered number of offenses for embezzlement by officials (down 33 percent), bribery (down 17 percent), and misuse of official position (down 33 percent). While the reports of crimes decreased in number, the actions taken against offenders shrank even more, suggesting that the government failed to act against major offenses during this crucial period of redistribution of state property. Those sentenced for the crime of official embezzlement declined ten times. Whereas in 1986, 26,507 persons were convicted of this offense, in 1994 the number was 2,747. Convictions for bribery went down three times in the same time period.[17] This downward trend was reversed, at least temporarily, after Evgenii Primakov became prime minister in 1998.

With the collapse of the Communist Party toward the close of the Soviet era, Party discipline disappeared. Nothing replaced it. Much of the privatization and theft of the state was perpetrated by the *nomenklatura,* the Party elite, who were suddenly freed from any responsibility for their actions. The existing moral vacuum was exacerbated by a lack of institutional controls.

Not only did Party officials jettison any pretense of building the Soviet state, but the idea that Russia should be reconstructed enjoyed little popularity. Unlike Estonia, and to a lesser extent Lithuania, which had large constituencies for nation-building, Russia inherited a collapsed social and economic order. The energy and desire to build an accountable government did not emerge. Rather, those in positions of power saw this transitional period as a moment to seize all available state assets, whether they were Russia's rich natural resources, the ships of the commercial fleet, or the liquid assets of the state. The foreign aid designated for rebuilding the country was systematically appropriated with no thought to the economic and social consequences for the impoverished citizenry, the state, or its future.

All engaged in this grab for property—labeled *prihkavtizatsiya*, a play on the word for privatization—secure that they would face no consequences. Indeed, since Russia became a state at the end of 1991, no significant trials have been held for either high-level officials or organized crime figures. Media exposés revealed organized economic crimes of massive proportions, but almost all remained unpunished, despite well-documented journalistic reports.[18] The only way the law enforcement apparatus could achieve results was through cooperation with their foreign counterparts, who had difficulty investigating complex criminality they did not understand. The results of this collaboration, as will be discussed later, were limited.

Privatization of the State

The primary force exacerbating corruption was the division of state property. This process, which began in the Gorbachev era, accelerated after the collapse of the USSR. Privatization of state assets occurred on a mass scale. Within a short period of time, the USSR changed from total state ownership to large-scale private ownership. By the mid-1990s, the proportion of the Russian economy owned by the state was less than that in Mexico and Italy, countries with long traditions of state-controlled economies. In a few years, Russia privatized 15,000 industrial firms and tens of thousands of shops. A greater percentage of Russian output was produced in the private sector than in parts of Western Europe,[19] where countries have stronger legal protections and safeguards within the private sector.

To place this phenomenal redistribution of property in perspective, the equality achieved after seventy years of Soviet rule was eradicated within a few years of its collapse. By fall 1998, 40 percent of the Russian population lived below the poverty line, a figure reminiscent of the pre-revolutionary period. A small elite possessed almost all the wealth, and a new secure middle class failed to emerge.[20]

Measures and institutions established to address organized crime and corruption traditionally begin, not with the police, but with the division of property. John Locke defined property as a bulwark against authoritarianism, but in the USSR in the early 1990s, little was done to protect citizens' property rights. Instead, the property rights of the majority of the citizens were violated, as the process of property redistribution became distorted by corruption and organized crime.

Voucher privatization, auctions, and enterprise privatization were originally intended to help citizens acquire property ownership, which would then give them a stake in the future society. Each Russian received vouchers worth a few dollars to trade in for shares of the privatizing state. But this exchange did not bring the intended outcome. Instead, most vouchers earned citizens an immediate bonus of under ten dollars and were acquired by large investors, including Western firms, allowing *them* to obtain a sizable share of Russia's valuable assets for a pittance. For example, First Boston acquired 17 million of the 144 million vouchers distributed by the Russian state and subsequently became a major player in the Russian economy.[21] With murky laws guiding privatization, no legal action could challenge this massive consolidation of Russian property in foreign hands, an objective that was very far from the intentions of the designers of voucher privatization.[22]

The enforcers of organized crime barred ordinary citizens from auctions of factories and other enterprises by means of physical force. Managers acquired the controlling packet of shares in their enterprises—often a prelude to stripping enterprises of their assets—and then shut them down.[23]

Meanwhile, no laws monitored the registration or advertising of share funds; millions of citizens consequently lost their life savings in pyramid schemes. MMM was the most notorious of these schemes, which induced the investment of money with promises of high rates of return. More and more citizens were sucked in after the first investors were richly compensated. By the time that the MMM fund collapsed, 10 to 12 million citizens had invested. In June 1994, a decree was issued "On the Protection of Interests of Investors"[24] that provided only a cursory response to the problem, mandating the registration of all publicly offered securities and the establishment of a financial threshold for joint stock companies. But the decree underscored an enormous loophole when it presented the following qualification: "[J]oint stock companies created as a result of privatization of state and municipal enterprises are exempt from this requirement."[25] This loophole did little to facilitate the intended aims of the privatization process.

MMM was only the most infamous of the many pyramid schemes that were set up throughout the country. Reports on 984 such companies were compiled by the Ministry of Interior, and criminal cases were initiated against 600.[26] Only a few of these cases have led to convictions.

Through this mechanism of pyramid schemes, many of which operated with the tacit consent or outright collusion of regional leaders, much of the Russian citizenry lost its life savings. This was a major mechanism by which property was redistributed away from the ordinary citizenry to the new financial elite.[27]

A decree against fraud in the privatization process was introduced late in 1993, after a significant share of Russian property had already been privatized. This presidential decree, intended to promote transparency, required directors of newly privatized companies to publish shareholder registers detailing the quantity of shares owned by individual investors. The decree also required firms to register the company's charter capital, categories of shares, dividends, share transactions, stock splits, and consolidations. Yet no legal mechanisms ensured compliance with this decree. The decree also had no provisions to protect enterprises from managers who sold output at reduced prices to companies they owned, reducing potential profit for shareholders.

All this was possible because, until 1997, no criminal code defined the criminal offenses of a market economy. No enforcement agencies had the capacity to investigate or prosecute complex economic offenses. Laws creating the voucher program did not prevent the hijacking of the secondary market in vouchers by organized crime, voracious robber barons, or greedy Western investors searching for high returns. No mechanisms ensured that vouchers, the prime means to redistribute assets to citizens, would effect an equitable redistribution of property. Rapid privatization was promoted in hopes that the transition to capitalism would be irreversible.[28] Those designing the program failed to understand that the corruption and distortions of the Soviet period would be institutionalized in the newly privatized state if safeguards were not placed over the privatization process.

These domestic conditions were sufficient to ensure the redistribution of state property to crony capitalists, bureaucrats, and members of organized crime. But the distortions of this reallocation process were exacerbated by the foreign aid process. Foreign assistance programs to promote privatization paid no attention to the endemic corruption and organized crime of the incipient market economy.[29] Intent on making the transition from communism to capitalism permanent, assistance programs facilitated privatization but established no anticorruption safeguards. They only worked to ensure that property was transferred from state to private hands as rapidly as possible. Institutions to oversee the division of property, such as the St. Petersburg Privatization Committee, became the most corrupt of institutions.

Hundreds of millions of dollars intended to assist in the privatization process were funneled through the organizations established by Anatolii Chubais, who served both as deputy prime minister and Yeltsin's chief of staff. Chubais and his associates, the so-called reformers, were not held to the same accountability standards as those that AID and the World Bank applied to other contractors.[30]

The failure to grant most citizens a fair share of the former Soviet state undermined all chances for profound social, political, and legal reform. A citizenry without a financial stake in the future could not protect itself.

Both public and private law enforcement could be bought or influenced by the new propertied elite. This result occurred because the newly rich understood that they could gain more by violating legal norms than observing them.

Crime and Corruption

In the post-Soviet period, every form of crime has increased. This includes the offenses that are a threat to daily life, the serious organized crimes that affect all sectors of the economy, and the pervasive corruption. Between 1986 and 1996, despite the reduced capacity of the law enforcement apparatus to act against crime, the recorded offenses doubled. The national total increased from 1.3 million in 1986 to 2.6 million in 1996. The most serious increases in crime were in the categories of premeditated murder, premeditated assault, armed robbery, and theft.[31] Many of these offenses, particularly those in the category of premeditated homicide, are closely linked to the rise in organized crime.

The available data for organized crime groups are equally alarming and reveal the maturation and endurance of the crime groups. The number of crimes, the number of crime groups, the number of groups with more than ten members, and the number of groups in existence for more than one to five years increased annually between 1989 and 1995.[32] By the mid-1990s, organized crime had penetrated into every sector of the economy. It inhibited the development of entrepreneurship. The presence of organized crime was most noted in commerce and trade, in particular the shuttle trade from Italy, China, and Turkey, and in the transport and banking sectors.[33] Its control over illicit trade in drugs, human beings, and arms was nearly complete.

Emphasis on the gangster side of organized crime obscured the deleterious role of the oligarchs, many of whom acquired their property through illegal means. The loans-for-shares deal, in which Russia's leading banks obtained significant shares of Russia's mineral and industrial wealth in exchange for financial loans, resulted in the transfer of many valuable state assets to the oligarchs at bargain-basement prices. These arrangements—like many other privatizations of major Russian companies, such as the telecommunications giant Sviazinvest—represented the worst of insider trading. The Russian Chamber of Accounts has found serious legal violations in these transfers of state property.

The oligarchs' control over the banking sector is the most criminal part of the equation. The Ministry of Internal Affairs (MVD) acknowledged in 1993 that 400 banks are under the control of organized crime.[34] The intersection of organized crime and the oligarchs in the banking sector provided ample opportunities for embezzlement of funds, tax evasion, and money laundering. Assistance money and foreign and multilateral credits for infrastructure projects were diverted from the Central Bank to designated commercial banks where trusted individuals would transfer money offshore.

Hundreds of millions, if not billions, of dollars were stripped from the national treasury by those with supervisory authority. The most notorious example is the Golden ADA case, in which diamonds and other valuables, such as historical coins, were shipped by the planeload to California for sale. This sale, authorized by top-level officials of the Ministry of Finance and other high-level officials, resulted in losses to the treasury estimated at one-half billion dollars.[35] The Russian government was slow to respond to requests for assistance from American prosecutors because the responsible officials were close associates of President Yeltsin. Only with the waning of Yeltsin's power was Yevgeny Bychkov, the former head of Roskom Dragmet (the Russian Committee of Precious Metals), arrested in February 1999 for his alleged role in the diversion of diamonds.

The intense centralization of the Russian government positioned officials in Moscow to siphon off resources intended for the provinces. They were able to do this with foreign infrastructure loans and state budget money. For example, audits by the Chamber of Accounts revealed that the money budgeted for the restructuring of the gold industry was diverted to renovate historical buildings in Moscow. All this was possible because no adequate accounting and monitoring system existed in the Central Bank or the Ministry of Finance. The result was that Russia's hope for a strong economic future—a healthy gold industry that would help the state obtain foreign currency—was cannibalized for a Moscow facelift. Corruption at the center jeopardized economic growth in the regions. Veniamin Sokolov, an auditor of the Chamber of Accounts, described the diversion of funds: "In the cases where large sums of money are supposedly sent out to far distant regions, most of the money disappears not en route to the region; it disappears in Moscow itself."[36]

Diversion of money for large infrastructure projects has utilized the same methods as those used during the New Economic Policy (NEP) years, 1921 to 1928, which allowed private enterprise to operate and foreign investment to occur in many regions of Russia. The scenario is as follows. First, large-scale projects are developed on the regional level. Then, emissaries for powerful ministries force regional plant or industrial leaders to sign agreements that give Moscow-based individuals or companies the exclusive right to represent them. Finally, aid resources or international loans, which are transferred to Russia from abroad for these projects, can be siphoned off through the Central Bank before the money ever reaches the provinces. This method of forcing local figures to sign exclusive agreements with Moscow facilitators is not new. The same strategy was used by Russians to fleece Western businessmen in the 1920s.

The decentralization of the Russian economy has transferred some resources to the regions, and the regions in turn have been less willing to send their revenues to the central government. Economic policies to decentralize the Russian economy have made corruption more sophisticated at the regional level, providing more money to divert from federal programs and local revenues. This problem is epitomized in the Russian Far East, which receives one of the largest shares of central government subsidies. In this situation, Moscow no longer serves as an intermediary for the export of capital. Officials and organized crime figures on the regional level have established direct links abroad and developed more complicated mechanisms to enrich themselves and to cover their illicit and semi-illicit activities. Money now flows directly from many regions to offshore bank accounts throughout the world.

Developing Laws and Legal Institutions

After the collapse of the USSR, Russia confronted an unprecedented rise in all forms of crime commission. The laws needed to regulate a market economy had not yet been developed, and the law enforcement apparatus was weakened both by internal corruption and competition from the private sector.

Laws

A major problem arose with the strategy of legal reform, which undertook a fragmentary rather than a coordinated approach. Many Russian lawyers wanted an integrated legal approach, but the foreign legal assistance provided by specialists from different branches of the law focused on the reform needs in their particular area. Thus, the systemic approaches, which would safeguard the emergent market economy against criminal encroachment, were never developed. Consequently, the civil laws needed to foster trust in a market economy were developed apart from the regulatory mechanisms. The criminal code prohibiting offenses against a market economy never considered the regulatory or civil mechanisms.

Stock and commodities markets and the institutions to facilitate privatization were often created in advance of any mechanisms to enforce violations of legal norms. This chaos created a wild capitalism unable to take advantage of decades of Western experience in regulation. Privatization efforts proceeded without an institutional perspective. Such a perspective, defined by the economics school of Douglas North, argues that to achieve economic growth, institutions and legal norms must be in place.[37] In post-Soviet Russia, however, economic change preceded the needed framework, contributing to poor economic growth.

The failure to establish legal guidelines more rapidly can be explained by several factors: the antagonisms between the Parliament and the presidential administration, the problems of corruption and criminalization of both houses of the Russian Parliament (the Duma and Federation Council) and some of the presidential advisers, and the absence of a clear vision of what was needed in the legal process.

The most important step in the fight against organized crime and corruption was the adoption of a new criminal code. The final version represented a compromise, negotiated by the vice president of the Academy of Sciences, between alternative versions presented by the presidential administration and those who worked closely with the Duma Committee on State Security. The latter represented more of the ministries' interests. Negotiations over this draft were protracted, in part, because of the conflict between Yeltsin's supporters and the Duma. Also contributing to its slow formulation was the endemic problem of corruption among those in power who did not want their profitable activities in the new market economy to be defined as crimes.

The absence of such laws enhanced the possibility of stealing more from the state during the transition. Ultimately, after years of discussion, the new Criminal Code was signed by Yeltsin just before his reelection and went into effect on January 1, 1997. For the first time in Russia, the law (Chapter Seven of the Code) recognized crimes committed by organized groups and allowed for prosecutions, not only of those who committed the crime but also of those who directed it.[38]

No law on corruption has been enacted. In November 1997, the Duma passed a weak anticorruption law, called the Law on the Fight with Corruption.[39] Although it poses little threat to those in power, it still has not proceeded past the Federation Council and the presidential administration. A separate law on organized crime is pending. The strict provisions of the Organized Crime Law on Detention of Suspects conflict with legal guarantees in the Constitution. A law on money laundering, recently passed on the third reading by the Duma, has stalled at the level of the Federation Council. It is doubtful that this draft will become law.

The absence of a unified framework to address the complicated problems of organized crime, corruption, and money laundering have left many holes in Russia's legal framework. Sophisticated criminals are well aware of these gaps and exploit them. Therefore, the institutions set up to fight crime can often investigate only elements of an offense and not all its diverse dimensions.

The absence of a law on corruption implies that only bribery is now a punishable offense. Such a narrow legal definition restricts conceptualization of the problem and the strategies to deal with its far-reaching manifestations. Many widespread actions that should be considered corrupt in Russia are not made illegal in the criminal code. These include the participation of government officials in commercial operations from which they obtain profits; the use of official positions to move money into favored banking institutions in order to receive personal profits for oneself, friends, and family members; the provision of benefits by officials to commercial firms in exchange for personal gain; and the placement of government funds and other resources in selected banks and investment funds.[40]

Finally, in the absence of conflict-of-interest laws, many individuals simultaneously run the industries and the efforts to privatize them. Without adequate safeguards on the declaration of assets by officials and their family members, and with inadequate enforcement mechanisms for individuals who provide false asset declarations, the government can do little to ensure the integrity of its officials.

Legal Institutions

A variety of institutions, ranging from new regulatory institutions to specialized units within the police, such as the regional police administration responsible for dealing with organized crime (RUOP), have been designated to address organized crime and corruption. Among the most notable new institutions are the Chamber of Accounts and the tax police. Also, the Central Bank's responsibilities have been updated to include monitoring money laundering and illicit financial flows. The impact of these underfunded and often poorly trained institutions is quite limited. Compounding the general difficulties are the significant problems of corruption and the political pressures applied to ensure that no action is taken against favored oligarchs and high-ranking officials.

Demoralized by the low pay and the insecurity of their work in state law enforcement bodies, numerous law enforcement personnel in Russia are leaving or have left for the private sector.[41] Many are lured by larger salaries. Some law enforcement officials enjoy the benefits of both worlds—retaining their government positions while simultaneously working in the private security sector.

The new private enforcement bodies, usually staffed and run by former MVD and KGB personnel, often work directly or are managed by organized crime groups. Firms are forced to contract for their services or face extortion by organized crime groups. But many businesses are forced to resort to the private sector because they can no longer rely on the weakened and corrupted state sector.

The traditional institutions set up to fight crime and corruption are the Ministry of Internal Affairs and the Procuracy. Criminalization of the police is a very significant problem. In 1993, Russian police officials reported that 13,000 Internal Affairs employees (out of a total workforce of over one million) were directly collaborating with organized criminal groups and many more were accepting bribes.[42] A survey conducted outside Irkutsk in 1998, in one of the two labor camps where former law enforcement and government officials are incarcerated, revealed that the majority of inmates had worked for the police, which is a branch of the Ministry of Internal Affairs.[43] While former officials in the Procuracy, the judiciary, or the customs service were most often convicted of offenses related to their positions, police personnel were most likely to be incarcerated for ordinary crimes, such as assault and theft. Less than a third of former police had committed job-related offenses, such as bribery and abuse of power. In contrast, the majority of former procurators, as well as the preponderance of customs (86 percent) and judicial (89 percent) personnel, were convicted of bribery and abuse of power. The offenses of police personnel differed little from the criminals they were policing. Those outside policing were more often convicted of corruption.[44]

Examination of the corruption data from the survey reveals that the majority were driven to engage in corruption by financial reasons (61.7 percent), while the security of their families (12.1 percent), feelings of obligation for previous services (14.2 percent), and familial relations (10.6 percent) provided a much smaller portion of the explanations for this conduct. Almost 40 percent of those who had worked in the police force and had received bribes acknowledged that they were on the regular payroll of criminal organizations, while less than one-sixth of those in other parts of the legal system acknowledged such relationships. Those who were convicted did not see themselves as exceptional, because over 40 percent of those surveyed stated that chance circumstances had led to their arrest on bribery charges.

The survey also provides surprising evidence of the internationalization of corruption. Most corrupt and criminal links were with individuals in their region, or over 65 percent, yet over 27 percent had contacts with officials from other regions and ethnic groups, and over 18 percent with representatives of other countries.

RUOP, the division of the police established in the late 1980s to combat organized crime, has had limited success.[45] In some parts of the country, RUOP remains a key institution in the fight against organized crime, particularly against the violent banditry activities in Eastern Siberia and in the border areas with China and Mongolia. But in other areas, it is a partner of the crime groups. This is particularly true in the Russian Far East, where the police and the crime units join forces with crime groups and serve as political and economic instruments designed to attack enemies rather than address the deeply rooted problems of systematic unlawful behavior.[46]

The failure of RUOP to penetrate organized crime groups and initiate successful investigations is only partly its own fault. Significant interference by crime groups and their political protectors has given most criminals immunity from prosecution. Despite provisions against money laundering and organized crime in the new criminal code, high-level cases are not reaching the courts.

In early 1999, Prime Minister Primakov began a campaign against high-level corruption, which made possible the initiation of some major investigations against officials of the Yeltsin government and its oligarch protectors. According to the Russian interior minister, 18,000 officials were detained in Russia in 1998. In twelve regions in Russia, those detained held high positions, such as deputy governor.[47] Yet oligarchs and ministers at the national level have yet to be touched. The forced resignation of Procurator General Yuri Skuratov in February 1999, initiated by President Yeltsin, occurred almost immediately after the state's leading law enforcement official moved against Boris Berezovsky, an oligarch closely allied with Yeltsin.[48] In a rare moment of independence, the upper house of Parliament defied Yeltsin and refused to accept Skuratov's resignation because of his actions against the oligarchs.

The new bodies designed to address organized crime and corruption have had little effect until now. Political ambition to address the problem has been low. Furthermore, irrational policies that established exorbitant and unrealistic rates of taxation, and the absence of coordination among the tax police, Federal Security Bureau (FSB), and the Central Bank in the monitoring of problems of capital flight and money laundering, have provided the criminals and the corrupt officials ample opportunities to raid the treasury and move money overseas.[49]

Cooperation with foreign law enforcers, particularly from the United States, has yielded results in a variety of cases. But efforts by officials overseas to address the globalization of Russian organized crime have been stymied by the corruption of Russian law enforcement personnel who have often failed to respond to foreign requests. For instance, the Swiss failed to successfully prosecute a Russian crime boss because Russian authorities did not provide assistance. Furthermore, American law enforcement efforts to prosecute individuals in the previously cited Golden ADA case have been frustrated by Russian government officials' failure to answer their requests for legal documents, presumably because they concern off-limits, high-level officials. Moreover, the infiltration of organized crime into policing structures has resulted in the misuse of Interpol by Russian crime groups who are trying to strike at their Russian enemies abroad. In a noted case in the Netherlands, some suspect that Russian crime figures used the Dutch branch of Interpol to strike at one of their enemies. Law enforcement authorities in the Netherlands have been unable to solve the half dozen contract murders of Russians committed on their territory.

The Chamber of Accounts has conducted some of the most hard-hitting investigations of corruption. The Duma introduced the Chamber of Accounts in 1994, despite presidential resistance, including a presidential veto, which was overcome by sufficient votes in the lower house. A supervisory body created to monitor state assets, the Chamber of Accounts was discredited by its opponents as a tool of the Communists. Its members represent a variety of political positions, from the ultra-nationalist Zhirinovsky to the liberal Yabloko party. At the present time, the body brings benefits twenty times its costs to the state, but it remains underfunded.[50]

The Chamber of Accounts has undertaken investigations of high-level corruption and has referred cases to the prosecutor general, but only a few have been initiated. Many of the over 150 cases referred to the state prosecutor by the Chamber of Accounts involve very serious accusations, including the wholesale appropriation of the Russian commercial fleet, the loans-for-shares schemes, and illegal privatization of major Russian industries, such as Norilsk Nickel. Why the prosecutor general has failed to act is not known, but the deterrent might be pressure from the presidential administration and other powerful individuals. Prosecution of sophisticated economic crime is also hindered by a lack of knowledge about the mechanisms of international finance and money laundering.

The Central Bank, which has had the authority to prevent money laundering, has been a leading institution in moving money out of the country. The Chamber of Accounts refused to accept the financial report of the Central Bank in 1997, because it could not trust the Bank's data. Designated personnel of the oligarchs at the Central Bank oversee the financing of transactions in particular sectors of the economy. Money is diverted through an established route. It is channeled from the Central Bank to Sberbank, the large state savings bank, or other selected institutions, and then shifted to accounts overseas. By this method, funds designated for the construction of much-needed infrastructure projects are diverted. In this way, needed projects financed by multilateral organizations and foreign aid cannot succeed because too much has been lost through planned corruption.

A major investigation was launched by the Interior Ministry and the Chamber of Accounts after the collapse of the IMF aid package in August 1998.[51] Early in 1999, the former director of the Central Bank admitted, during the course of the investigation, that billions had been moved offshore to a Jersey-based company named Financial Management Company Limited. He claimed that the money had been moved from the Central Bank in order to evade Russia's creditors.[52] Aid money from various other sources has also been moved offshore after transfer to the Central Bank.

Finally, the tax police have been among the most corrupt of state law enforcement bodies. To ensure that the personnel of this body do not move against the oligarchs, their front men, who manage their offshore companies, are appointed as advisers to the tax police. Therefore, on the chance that any investigation might be mounted against them, these advisers have access to inside information from the law enforcement body.

The institutions to fight organized crime and corruption have failed to meet the challenge because they are themselves corrupted and, in the case of the police, highly criminalized. Even if the institutions could be reformed, Russia would still not be able to combat these problems because corruption at the top of the government frustrates actions by those below. Meaningful institutional reform can occur only when the leadership seeks good government and facilitates this process in subordinate institutions.

Conclusion

In Russia today, street crime, organized crime, and corruption have demoralized the citizenry and exacerbated the economic situation. Billions have been embezzled and moved offshore, depleting the funds needed to rebuild the economy, provide citizens a living wage, or ensure a social safety net. By undermining projects intended to rebuild its infrastructure, Russia has merely added to its burden of debt without improving the finances of its citizens.

Crime and corruption in Russia are more than a transitional problem during its transformation from a socialist to a market economy. They preclude the possibility of the success of this transition. The implication that so much of the top leadership is involved in illegal activity undermines the future welfare of emergent institutions.

The rule of law is central. Reform of law and law enforcement is crucial to a democratic transition. But internal reform is useless if the institutions are denied the autonomy they need to operate according to the law. During the Soviet era, the Communist Party regularly intervened in the administration of justice, but the demise of communism has not brought judicial independence. The terms of state ideology no longer justify interference in administrative activities, but a destructive interference continues where it serves the financial and political interests of the new elite and the oligarchs.

The Soviet Union collapsed, in part, because of endemic corruption. But corruption merely accelerated economic decline in the 1990s with the privatization of state properties and the availability of international aid monies. Russian indebtedness mounted. Concrete projects to revive the economy were not realized because of large-scale diversion of funds by high-level officials.

The costs and implications of this corruption and crime are increasingly being recognized within the Russian and the international financial community. The endemic corruption that contributed to the Soviet Union's collapse has been globalized. The most glaring illustration of this is the movement of Russia's treasury offshore to hide state assets from creditors. With this maneuver, the state deprived itself of the resources needed to pay its citizens salaries and social welfare benefits. Yet the consequences were also felt by Russia's creditors, including the International Monetary Fund, when Russia defaulted on its loans. The tragedy of Russia's precipitous decline has alerted the financial community, scholars, and officials, both inside and outside of Russia, to recognize the international costs of organized crime and corruption.

Notes

1. New York Times Service, "Rubin Wary About Russia," *International Herald Tribune* (March 20–21, 1999): 4.

2. Steven Mufson and David Hoffman, "Russian Crash Shows Risks of Globalization, Speculators Ignored Economy's Realities," *The Washington Post* (November 8, 1998): A1 and A34.

3. For a fuller discussion of this, see Louise I. Shelley, "Stealing the Russian State," *Demokratizatsiya*, vol. 5, no. 4 (fall 1997): 482–491.

4. Vladimir Brovkin, "Fragmentation of Authority and Privatization of the State," *Demokratizatsiya*, vol. 6, no. 3 (summer 1998): 504–517.

5. A senior instructor at the military academy reported on the enormous losses and profits made in stealing military equipment in A.I. Dolgova, ed., *Organizovannaia prestupnost'*, vol. 2 (Moscow: Kriminologicheskaia Assotsiatsiia, 1993): 86–93.

6. A.L. Repetskaya, *Bor'ba s organizovannoi prestupnost'iu v Aziatsko-Tikhookeanskom regione: problemy organizatsii i vzaimodeistviia* (Irkutsk: Irkutski tsentr izucheniia organizovannoi prestupnosti, 1998).

7. For a discussion of an integrated strategy, see Keith Henderson, "Corruption: What Can Be Done About It? A Practitioner's Perspective Through a Russian Lens," *Demokratizatsiya*, vol. 6, no. 4 (fall 1998): 681–691.

8. Susan Rose-Ackerman, "Democracy and 'Grand' Corruption," *International Social Science Journal*, vol. 48, no. 3 (September 1996).

9. A.I. Dolgova, ed., *Organizovannaia prestupnost'*, 78–79.

10. For a discussion of corruption in the Soviet era, see Alena V. Ledeneva, *Russia's Economy of Favours: Blat, Networking and Informal Exchange* (Cambridge: Cambridge University Press, 1998): 42–47.

11. For a fuller discussion, see Louise I. Shelley, "Privatization and Crime: The Post-Soviet Experience," *Journal of Contemporary Criminal Justice*, vol. 2, no. 4 (December 1995): 244–256.

12. Elizabeth Tucker, "The Russian Media's Time of Troubles," *Demokratizatsiya*, vol. 4, no. 3 (summer 1996): 422–438.

13. Yuriy A. Voronin, "The Emerging Criminal State: Economic and Political Aspects of Organized Crime in Russia," in Phil Williams, ed., *Russian Organized Crime: The New Threat* (London, U.K.: Frank Cass, 1997): 59.

14. Konstantin Simis, *USSR: The Corrupt Society* (New York, N.Y.: Simon and Schuster, 1982).

15. For a discussion on the limits of Party privilege, see Robert Sharlet, "The Communist Party and the Administration of Justice in the USSR," in Donald B. Barry, F.J.M. Feldbrugge, George Ginsburgs, and Peter Maggs, eds., *Soviet Law After Stalin*, vol. 3 (Alphen aan den Rijn: Sijthoff and Noordhoff, 1979): 321–392, and Louise Shelley, "Party Members and the Courts: Exploitation of Privilege," in D.A. Loeber, Donald B. Barry, F.J.M. Feldbrugge, George Ginsburgs, P.B. Maggs, eds., *Ruling Communist Parties and Their Status Under Law* (Dordrecht: Martinus Nijhoff, 1986): 76–90.

16. Yuri Feofanov and Donald D. Barry, *Politics and Justice in Russia: Major Trials of the Post-Stalin Era* (Armonk, N.Y.: M.E. Sharpe, 1996): 86–100.

17. V.V. Luneev, *Prestupnost' XX veka* (Moscow: Norma, 1997): 77–78.

18. N.V. Globus, *Ekonomicheskie Prestupniki* (Minsk: Literatura, 1996), which popularizes many of these cases that were reported but largely went unprosecuted.

19. Andrei Schleifer, "Foreword," in Joseph R. Blasi, Maya Kroumova, and Douglas Kruse, eds., *Kremlin Capitalism: Privatizing the Russian Economy* (Ithaca, N.Y.: Cornell University Press, 1997): x.

20. Edgar L. Feige, "Underground Activity and Institutional Change: Productive, Protective, and Predatory Behavior in Transition Economies," in *Transforming Post-Communist Political Economies* (Washington, D.C.: National Research Council, 1997): 32.

21. R. Stevenson, "An American in Moscow," *The New York Times* (September 20, 1994): D4.

22. David Ellerman, "Transitional Heresies of a Devil's Advocate," Internal Paper of World Bank (January 27, 1999).

23. S.A. Alekseeva, "Problemy bor'by s organizovannoi prestupnost'iu v sfere privatizatsii gosudarstvennoi i munitsipal'noi sobstvennosti," *Aktuanl'nye problemy teorii i praktiki bor'by s organizovannoi prestupnost'iu v Rossii* (Moscow: Moskovskii institut MVD, 1994): 198.

24. I.I. Osipov, "Rossiiskie finansovye piramidy: sposoby vyiavleniia i programma kompentsatsii vkladchikam," in V.I. Popov, et al., eds., *Tenevaia ekonomika i organizovannaia prestupnost' Materialy nauchno-prakticheskoi konferentsii* (Moscow: Moskovskii institut MVD, June 9–10, 1998): 158–159.

25. Scott Horton and Mikheil Saakashvili, "Stage Is Set for the Russian Securities Market," *CIS Law Notes* (February 1995): 7.

26. Osipov, *Tenevaia ekonomika i organizovannaia prestupnost' Materialy nauchno-prakticheskoi konferentsii* (June 9–10, 1998): 162.

27. Svetlana Glinkina, lectures, "Russian and Ukrainian Perspectives on Organized Crime," Center for the Study of Transnational Crime and Corruption, American University (November 12, 1998).

28. For a discussion of the logic of the irreversibility argument despite the public negative reactions to privatization, see Victor M. Sergeyev, *The Wild East: Crime and Lawlessness in Postcommunist Russia* (Armonk, N.Y.: M.E. Sharpe, 1998): 180.

29. Janine Wedel, "Clique-Run Organizations and U.S. Economic Aid: An Institutional Analysis," *Demokratizatsiya*, vol. 4, no. 4 (fall 1996): 571–602.

30. Wedel, *Demokratizatsiya*, 571–602.

31. Luneev, *Prestupnost' XX veka*, 94–95.

32. Luneev, *Prestupnost' XX veka*, 306.

33. S.S. Butenin and S.N. Frolov, "Deiatel'nost' federalnykh organov nalogovoi politsii po bor'be s korruptsiei i organizovannoi prestupnost'iu," in A.I. Dolgova and S.V. D"iakov, eds., *Organizovannaia Prestupnost'*, vol. 3 (Moscow: Kriminologicheskaia Assotsiatsiia, 1996): 176.

34. *Sostoianie pravoporiadka v Rossii i rezultaty raboty organov vnutrennykh del v 1993 godu* (Moscow: MVD RF, 1994): 11.

35. David E. Kaplan and Christian Caryl, "The Looting of Russia," *US News and World Report* (August 3, 1998): 26–40.

36. Veniamin Sokolov, "Privatization, Corruption, and Reform in Present Day Russia," *Demokratizatsiya*, vol. 6, no. 4 (fall 1998): 669.

37. North explains that the difference between the Czech and the Russian experiences in auctioning property existed because of the difference in legal norms and culture; Douglass C. North, "Understanding Economic Change," in Joan M. Nelson, Charles Tilly, and Lee Walker, eds., *Transforming Postcommunist Political Economies* (Washington, D.C.: National Academy Press, 1997): 13–18.

38. The English translation of the 1996 Russian Federation Criminal Code appeared in *Foreign Broadcast Information Service Supplement* (August 15, 1996).

39. Fond Indem, "Rossiia i korruptsiia: kto kogo" (Moscow, 1998), paper presented at National and International Approaches to Improving Integrity and Transparency in Government, Organized by the OECD and the OSCE, Paris (July 15–16, 1998): 32.

40. Indem, "Rossiia i korruptsiia: kto kogo," 32.

41. "MVD Personnel Chief Astapkin Discusses Militia, Crime," *FBIS Daily Report* (October 13, 1994): 47–48.

42. Louise I. Shelley, *Policing Soviet Society: The Evolution of State Control* (London and New York: Routledge, 1996): 198.

43. The survey was conducted in a Russian labor camp outside Irkutsk by the organized crime study center funded by a Department of Justice grant to American University. The author of this article helped develop the survey with the Irkutsk Center. It was administered to ensure confidentiality to the 500 inmates of the labor camp and there was a 60 percent response rate. Judging by the hand-

written comments submitted with the survey, the inmates felt that they could answer the questions with anonymity.

44. Gilles Favarel-Garrigues, "La politique soviétique de lutte contre les infractions économiques à travers les archives du Comité du Parti de la région de Sverdlovsk (1965–1982)," *Revue d'études comparatives Est-Ouest* 2 (June 1997): 183.

45. Dmitry Pavlov, Maksim Varvydin, and Mikhail Mikhaylin, "Vladimir Rushaylo Took the Floor," *Kommersant-Daily* (October 22, 1996), taken from FBIS on World Wide Web.

46. "Reports on Far East Press," *Organized Crime Watch-Russia*, vol. 1, no. 1 (January 1999): 6–10; and vol. 1, no. 2 (February 1999): 6–8.

47. "18,000 Officials Arrested in 1998 for Corruption," Itar-Tass (February 10, 1999).

48. Celestine Bohlen, "Raiding Offices, Russia Builds Its Case Against a Tycoon," *The New York Times* (February 4, 1999): A3.

49. V.M. Esipov, "Finansovo-kreditnaia sfera: voprosy preodeleniia kriminalnykh iavlenii," in A.I. Dolgova and S.V. D"iakov, eds., *Organizovannaia Prestupnost'*, vol. 3 (Moscow: Kriminologicheskaia Assotsiatsiia, 1996): 186–187.

50. Indem, "Rossia i korruptsiia: kto kogo," 49.

51. Andrew Jack, "Moscow Mystery of Missing $4.8 Billion," *Financial Times* (January 11, 1999): 3.

52. Michael R. Gordon, "Dispute over Cash Reserves Hits Russia's Central Bank," *The New York Times* (February 13, 1999): A3.

5

State Dysfunctionality, Institutional Decay, and the Russian Military

EVA BUSZA

We're looking at the full collapse of the armed forces and the liquidation of the country's defense capabilities . . . they don't fly, they don't sail, they don't train.

—*Former Russian Defense Minister General Igor Rodionov*[1]

One of the casualties of the collapse of the Soviet Union has been the Russian state. The powerful Soviet state has been replaced by a dysfunctional Russian state: one characterized by ineffective institutions.[2] While there are many signs of state dysfunctionality—the perpetual and dramatic changes in economic policy, volatility in the distribution of power among political factions, and the absence of a stable and effective governing system that could mediate political struggles—perhaps the most dangerous development has been the state leadership's loss of ability to use the armed forces to promote state goals. Such a change is of vital importance for it translates into an immediate decline of state power in both the domestic and international arenas.

In Russia, this particular dimension of state dysfunctionality has been reflected in three phenomena: the material deterioration of the armed forces, the emergence of a set of new destructive forms of soldier involvement in the state, and the growing inability of the civilian leadership to control soldier behavior.

This chapter will address these issues. The chapter begins with a discussion of the state of the Russian armed forces today. It analyzes the factors that contributed to the deterioration of the armed forces. It then describes new negative forms of soldier involvement in the state, arguing that they are symptomatic of the particular form of state-building occurring in Russia today, one characterized by the establishment of weak and dysfunctional state institutions.[3] The chapter then discusses how recent changes in soldier behavior may affect Russian democratic development and international stability. It concludes by examining the future potential for domestic and international actors to reverse these destructive processes.

The State of the Russian Armed Forces at the End of the 1990s

In the mid-1980s, the strength, structure, and resources of the Soviet armed forces secured the country its superpower status. According to Western estimates, 5,300,000 people were under arms.[4] Defense expenditure as a percentage of gross domestic product (GDP) was about 16 percent.[5] The Gorbachev cuts and the dissolution of the Soviet empire left the new Russian army with a force half its previous size: 2,030,000 soldiers under arms.[6] According to data provided by Alexei Arbatov, by 1994 the defense budget had fallen to 5.6 percent of gross national product (GNP). It then declined further to 3.5 percent of GNP in 1996.[7]

The end of the Cold War, the breakup of the Soviet Union, and changes in Russian assessments of current and future threats to its security justified a significant decline in the size and strength of the armed forces. Reformers in the General Staff came out with a program that covered a seven-year period up to the year 2000. The proposal called for reducing armed force levels to 1.5 million people by the end of 1995. It suggested changes for streamlining the military and increasing its cost effectiveness.

Over the next few years, reductions certainly occurred. Russian military expenditure fell 7 percent to 10 percent of GNP and active soldiers were reduced to an estimated 1.5 million.[8] Divisions were disbanded. The trouble was that the changes failed to follow a comprehensive blueprint, with the end result that new units were ill equipped, understaffed, and poorly trained, and lacked specific combat missions.

Russian specialists estimate that today most branches of the armed forces are staffed well below their full capacity.[9] According to estimates made by the International Institute for Strategic Studies, in 1998 the majority of units were manned at only 20 to 50 percent.[10] Irrational cuts have demoralized the soldiers, indicated by telling pathological behaviors. According to the Russian Defense Ministry, in the first eleven months of 1998, 800 servicemen were killed or died off-duty and 350 suicides were reported.[11]

The situation has reached grave proportions. At the beginning of 1999, an influential military journal, *Nezavisimoe Voennoe Obozrenie*, printed the findings of an internal analysis report conducted by the Russian General

Staff. Given the limited funds available for defense spending, the report advised that the Russian army be cut by half immediately, from 1.2 million to 550,000–600,000, in order to avoid "tragic disintegration within the next few years."[12]

As a consequence of this deterioration, the armed forces can no longer perform the basic functions that the Russian leadership has assigned to them: providing internal and external security.[13] The poor performance of the Russian military in the Chechen war only too clearly highlighted this fact. The Russian units were poorly trained and lacked leadership. The quality and quantity of conscripts was severely reduced by frequent incidences of draft dodging.[14] According to one estimate, only one of every six military units in the ground forces was at full strength in terms of combat tasks. The actual personnel strengths of more than 70 percent of the units were less than what is necessary for sufficient combat readiness even in peacetime.[15] Many units and their commanders simply refused to fight on the grounds that they were ill prepared for the assault.[16]

Empire Legacies, Dysfunctional States, and the Armed Forces

Why have we seen such incredible deterioration of the armed forces in Russia? The simplest answer—and the one most frequently offered in scholarly analyses and in newspaper articles—is the lack of resources resulting from economic decline. Russian leaders simply have not been able to afford to put into place needed structural changes that would make the military an efficient and obedient agent of the state. However, economic decline only provides a partial explanation.

Russian economic growth in the first years of the transition was negative. According to some estimates, the annual percentage change in GDP averaged minus 18.5 and minus 14.9 percent in 1992 and 1993, respectively.[17] The government budget was progressively cut in order to help control inflation. The armed forces were forced to absorb a large percentage of the cuts. But lack of resources did not have to translate into a lack of reform strategy. While the magnitude of the needed cuts certainly made the task a difficult one, some attempts might have been made to establish and then follow a realistic military reform program in the early years of the transition. But this did not occur because the actors who were in a position to enact change (i.e., the executive) initially did not prioritize military reform. Then, once the leadership decided to pursue reform measures, it failed to establish institutionalized mechanisms that would facilitate civilian involvement in oversight and enforcement of military reform proposals.

The initial lack of civilian elite concern with military affairs was reflected in a lack of initiative in actually creating a Russian armed force and providing it with a mission.[18] It was not until May 1992, five months after the formation of the new Russian state, that a Russian Ministry of Defense was created. From August 1991 to the spring of the following year, Russian soldiers were formally under the control of the Council of Heads of State of the Commonwealth of Independent States, but in actual fact existed as an autonomous entity without direct ministerial oversight. On May 7, 1992, President Yeltsin declared the formal creation of the Russian armed forces.[19] It was not until a full year later that Russian soldiers were given a military doctrine to follow.[20]

In the early months preceding the actual formation of the Russian army, the question of who would exercise control over the military was actively debated in Parliament. A number of draft laws were introduced but failed to pass. At the time of the actual creation of the Russian armed forces, the president seized the initiative and announced the formation of a new Russian presidential consulting body on issues of defense, security, and foreign policy: the Russian Security Council.[21] Its mandate was to deal with various issues including the future organization of the armed forces, the need to strengthen the borders of Russia, and policy toward various "hot spots" erupting on the territory of the former Soviet Union. It convened irregularly at the request of the president, and its recommendations were to serve as a basis for presidential decrees.[22] At that time the president also issued a declaration and decree outlining the priorities of the Russian armed forces. What was particularly notable about this document was that, with the exception of the last paragraph, there was no mention of mechanisms through which legislative oversight would be maintained. The last paragraph simply stated that attempts would be made to strengthen legislative mechanisms that provided civilians with oversight and input into defense policymaking.[23] This policy was problematic because there were no existing legislative mechanisms that could be bolstered.

The lack of priority that the Russian elite gave to reconstructing the Russian armed forces, and its failure to put into place institutionalized mechanisms of legislative regulation, can be explained in part by the legacies of the Soviet empire and in part by Yeltsin's strategy to ensure his immediate political survival.

The majority of Russian parliamentarians also initially seemed uninterested in considering the implications of empire collapse for the Russian military, both in terms of how this would affect the structure of the armed forces and how the military's mission would change. They did not seem to be concerned that benign neglect of the army could lead to a situation where military officers might mobilize as a group and challenge civilian authority. This early complacency stemmed from the experience of civil-military relations under communism, a regime in which the military was under the control of the Communist Party and insubordination was extremely rare. Soviet military norms had dictated that the armed forces were an instrument of the state and of the Communist Party: Their mission was to obey civilian orders. Most deputies seemed to assume this norm would persist, regardless of the elimination of Communist Party control over the Russian polity.

While President Yeltsin seemed to share the view that it was unlikely that the military would become a dangerous autonomous political force, he recognized at an early date the potential value of turning the military into a partisan force that would support him in intra-elite conflicts.[24] Taking advantage of the parliament's initial lack of interest in the military, he began to work toward co-opting the latter. He adopted two main strategies in an attempt to turn the military into a loyalist force that would stand behind him in periods of domestic upheaval.

First, he tried to foster military "goodwill" by allowing military elites to make many of the important decisions about how to institute reform. This was problematic because the military leadership—with the exception of a small minority of democratically inclined officers who soon either left or were dismissed—had little interest in sweeping reforms.[25] Many high-ranking officers were dismayed by the collapse of the Soviet empire, the entity they had been trained to protect.[26] The military elite's strategy of dealing with the political and economic turmoil was to try to preserve the key missions of the Russian forces and resist major force cuts. When reductions in the defense budget finally forced soldiers to adopt reforms, they tended to shy away from making the most cost-effective cuts: trimming the command structure and firing high-ranking officers.

Second, President Yeltsin began to replace the collapsed mechanisms of Communist civilian control over the army with a system that relied on two informal mechanisms for building partisan support and enforcing presidential authority. He began by forming a network of loyal supporters within the highest ranks of the military. Following precedents set by Gorbachev, he frequently exercised his presidential prerogative to dismiss officers who had adopted political positions contrary to his own, claiming that they were violating army "neutrality." However, as his critics were quick to point out, Yeltsin repeatedly promoted those who actively supported his own political views.[27]

The second informal mechanism that Yeltsin adopted in order to increase his presidential authority was to strengthen Russia's internal security, or paramilitary, forces.[28] Analysts have argued that his intent was to use the security forces to monitor and counterbalance the armed forces.[29] According to calculations made by Richard Staar, by 1995 the total number of troops in the various paramilitary forces was 1.1 million, whereas the forces subordinated to the Ministry of Defense totaled 1.9 million.[30] A different estimate was provided by Army General Makhmut Gareyev, who calculated that, in 1996, the size of the paramilitary forces numbered 2 million, while the regular armed forces under the command of the Ministry of Defense numbered 1.5 million.[31]

By relying on informal levers rather than a formalized set of mechanisms of control that were integrated into democratic institutions, Yeltsin began to strengthen his own personal control over the armed forces. At the same time, in adopting this strategy he was able to minimize the potential influence that his political opponents might have. A more formal system would have given other actors in the political arena easier access and more opportunities to influence the military hierarchy, which could have reduced the president's personal influence and power over the armed forces.

When it became clear to the Russian Supreme Soviet that the president was slowly monopolizing control over the armed forces, deputies quickly began the attempt to reassert their own control through a series of legislative initiatives on military policy.[32] Throughout 1993, parliamentarians authored a number of documents, including the laws "On Defense," "On Universal Military Duty and Service," "On the Status of Military Servicemen," "On the Defense Budget," and "On Martial Law." These laws, in conjunction with the existing constitution, began to provide the basis for a well-functioning system of civilian control that balanced authority between the executive and legislative branches of government.[33] However, while these laws provided a good starting point, a couple of difficulties surfaced. First, when actual crises arose, it became clear that the initial division of labor specified by the legislation gave rise to overlapping competencies without any legislative means for deciding where authority finally resided. In the context of a severe power struggle between the executive and legislative branches, this attribute could—and did—lead to policy paralysis. Second, while the rights and obligations of the various branches of government and the armed forces were outlined in these laws, little progress was made in creating institutional mechanisms that would provide a follow-up on policy decrees and ensure the actual implementation of the laws.

Tensions between the president and the parliament intensified through 1992 and into the spring of 1993. In March 1993, the parliament threatened to impeach the president. Yeltsin responded by threatening to suspend the parliament. A compromise agreement—between Rhuslan Khasbulatov, the leader of the parliament, and Yeltsin—to hold a referendum on a new Russian constitution in April 1993, and to hold general elections in November, temporarily defused the crisis. However, by the second half of September 1993, the executive-legislative struggle had once again reached crisis levels. On September 21, Yeltsin issued a decree dissolving the Russian Supreme Soviet and the Congress of People's Deputies. He announced that new elections to the parliament would be held in December. In the interim period all governing authority was to be transferred to the president and his government.[34] The parliamentary opposition responded by electing Vice President Rutskoi to the post of president, appointing a shadow cabinet, and occupying the legislature, known as the "White House." Suddenly, the country had two presidents, and the armed forces were faced with a situation in which *they* had to decide who was the legitimate authority. Meanwhile, both the parliamentary opposition and Yeltsin began to make frantic appeals to the armed forces to take their side.[35] Some soldiers and officers joined the opposition forces in the White House.[36] On October 3, led by retired General Aleksandr Makashov, the armed opposition tried to seize the Moscow mayor's office and the television tower, Ostankino. On the morning of October 4, President Yeltsin ordered the Defense Ministry to send military units to storm the White House. Significant evidence suggests that there was much military resistance to Yeltsin's order. Eventually, General Grachev, whose own initial behavior during this crisis remains murky, was able to lead a contingent composed of elite military units and palace guard divisions in an assault on the White House.[37] By evening, the remaining parliamentary opposition forces and their armed supporters had surrendered.[38]

Following the ambiguous role played by military officers during the stand-off between the parliament and the president in October 1993, neither Russian civilians nor the military elite could ignore the deepening crisis within the armed ranks. News of officers without food and shelter hit the headlines.[39] Disaffection was reflected in rising incidents of draft dodging and desertion. Increasingly military officers began to take the podium, entering the domestic political arena and sometimes implicitly, sometimes explicitly, threatening to play the military card.

These developments forced Russian policymaking elites to reevaluate the state of the army, and many legislators in the new Russian Duma authored reform proposals and began to pressure the military to make necessary changes. However, they quickly found that their efforts were thwarted by the absence of institutional mechanisms of civilian control that would have provided them with the authority and means to oversee the military and implement a reform plan. The system codified in the new Russian constitution of December 1993 bolstered the trends set in the first years of the transition by once again providing little basis for legislative involvement.[40] Instead the Constitution gave virtually complete power to the president, who continued to develop the informal channels of control that he had established in the early years of the transition.

The emerging governance structure has had several important ramifications for the armed forces. First, policy has tended to be crisis oriented, providing scant opportunity for resolving long-standing problems, including the reform of the armed forces. Throughout 1995 and 1996, the military elite continued to make cuts in a haphazard fashion, disregarding the declared policy aims of the government. One good illustration of this phenomenon was the elite's decision in June 1995 to extend compulsory military service from 18 to 24 months and abolish a number of exemptions that had previously existed.[41] Another good example can be seen in the development of policy regarding reductions within elite paratroop divisions. In the fall of 1996, Defense Minister Rodionov announced a plan that would reduce five divisions to three and place the remaining divisions under the command of existing military district commands. This plan aimed at cutting costs by reducing the replication of the existing command structure. After much opposition from General Lebed, then national security council secretary, as well as from the paratroop leadership, the presidential administration negotiated a compromise that retained five divisions and, instead of reducing the number of the more costly senior rank positions, made the cuts from within the lower ranks.[42] This outcome contradicted two stated civilian reform goals: to cut costs and create smaller but better-manned units.

Second, policymaking has been very informal and often relies on telephone calls between the president, prime minister, and defense minister. When crises arise, the president's security advisers coordinate ad hoc inter-ministry committees that strive to reach a consensus on a policy proposal that could then be adopted by Yeltsin.[43] Such patterns of policymaking not only restrict input into the policymaking process but also rely heavily on personalities. In both cases, such characteristics did not promote the development of democratic processes and stable institutional mechanisms. Moreover, they tend to be very sensitive to, and can even be paralyzed by, changes in the government and presidential staff.

Third, this type of policymaking system is weak in providing oversight mechanisms to ensure that policy is actually executed. It is particularly vulnerable to favoritism and corrupt practices. Some insight into the extent of corruption in the Defense Ministry was provided by a report made to the Duma by Lev Rokhlin, chairman of the State Duma Defense Committee, in 1996.[44] Among other incidents, the report detailed how some high-ranking officers had used money from the sale of government-owned military property to buy themselves Mercedes 500 SELs, and how other military officials had skimmed off the profits from a military contract signed with the Lithuanian firm "Selma." One of the most notable examples of corrupt activity discussed in the report was the illegal investment of large sums of money sent to military units by the

Defense Ministry. High-ranking officers temporarily diverted this money, invested it, and then pocketed the profits. A year or even more later, they would forward "the principal" to the units.[45]

Finally, not only has the existing system prevented the adoption of a comprehensive reform program and thwarted the establishment of an institutional mechanism of civilian control, but also it has directly effected changes in soldier behavior. As discussed below, some of the changes in military behavior challenge the development of democracy in Russia and the integrity of the Russian state. They may also pose a potential threat to international peace and stability.

Soldier Behavior, Democratic Governance, and International Stability

In order to cope with the deterioration of their organization, the new economic hardships in which they find themselves, and the pressures from a series of domestic political actors who have encouraged increased military involvement in the domestic political arena, soldiers have adopted a series of new roles that are undermining the ability of state officials to direct and implement policy in both the domestic and foreign arenas.

In the domestic arena, public involvement of military officers in partisan politics has increased. There is some institutional precedence for such behavior. Under communism, soldiers were encouraged to be members of the Communist Party, and they always appeared at political rallies in their uniforms. However, whereas "politicization" in a Communist regime reflected a narrow sphere of military autonomy, in a pluralistic political system this measure indicates exactly the opposite: the narrowing of civilian authority over military activity. "Politicization" in the context of a pluralistic political system translates into opportunities for military partisanship. Such opportunities provide the basis for the establishment of an autonomous political role for the armed forces.

At the time of the creation of the Russian army, discussion arose among the civilian elite on the subject of military involvement in running for office or engaging in other political acts, such as campaigning for officials, testifying in front of parliamentary committees, or making public policy statements. In fact, in late July 1992, an executive order was issued that prohibited all but the Defense Minister and his deputies from making public policy statements. This was followed by official proclamations that officers who were going to engage in politics were obliged to take a leave of absence or quit the army.[46] However, these declarations were rarely enforced. Measures were not taken to prevent officers from running for elected offices, and servicemen continued to be appointed to various executive posts. Moreover, no effective legislation was adopted to prevent officers from becoming engaged in partisan political activities within the barracks. The few cases of action taken to restrict soldier political activity tended to be presidential initiatives that, rather than being applied across-the-board to all officers who were involved in political activity, selectively targeted opponents and critics of the president. Supporters of the president, on the other hand, were rewarded with promotions and publicly praised.[47]

Military officers who ran for political office not only were able to supplement their income with an extra salary but also could gain from the many fringe benefits, both material and status-oriented, that accrued to government and legislative representatives. Thus, both civilian inaction to prevent the military from becoming involved in government and indications that soldiers who did become allied with various civilian factions could gain certain material benefits from their involvement created incentives for expanded military participation in politics.

Equally if not more important, has been a series of new roles and behavior that are a direct consequence of the economic cutbacks and the ill-conceived reform program. In response to lack of funding from Moscow, many commanders are being forced to rely on themselves to feed, clothe, and house their soldiers. Some units have resorted to business—both legal and illegal.[48] Others have forged ties with local authorities who have helped them ensure the survival of their men by providing them with food, shelter, electricity, and fuel. In order to supplement their low wages that, in some cases, have yet to be paid by the Ministry of Defense, soldiers have begun to moonlight. Some have hired out their services to local enterprises, various security forces, and the growing number of private armies, many of which are Mafia-run.[49]

Perhaps the most ominous development has been the dramatic rise in military involvement in crime and corruption since the late 1980s. President Yeltsin noted the severity of the problem, stating that crime, particularly organized crime, was a "direct threat to Russia's strategic interests and national security."[50] According to Defense Ministry statistics, in the first 11 months of 1998, reported crimes in the armed forces totaled 10,500. This was up from 10,000 in the previous year.[51]

Russian armed force involvement in criminal activity is far-reaching and ranges from narcotics to prostitution and gambling, from financial fraud to illegal dumping of toxic wastes. One particularly disturbing reported activity, which is especially damaging to the state-building process, is armed forces' involvement in theft and illegal sale of weapons, ammunition, and equipment.[52] The severity of this problem was underlined in a recent study conducted by the U.S. Air Force Institute for National Security Studies. It concluded that "Russian military and security organizations are the primary sources for the flourishing illegal weapons trade within and outside of the FSU." It further emphasized the importance of the links between military criminals and criminal organizations working within the Russian civil sector.[53]

The real increase in weapon theft dates back to the end of the Soviet era. Thefts rose 50 percent between 1989 and 1990. In 1992 thefts at weapons depots totaled 3,923 cases. By the next year they had risen to 6,430.[54] While civilians are frequently involved in the thefts (sometimes colluding with military guards and at other times simply attacking weapons depots), many instances of armed force personnel being the actual sellers of the stolen property have been reported.[55] Many of these weapons are purchased in various "hot spots" around the former Soviet Union (e.g., Tadjikistan and Nagorno-Karabakh). According to a 1996 Ministry of Internal Affairs (MVD) report, more than 5,000 illegally held firearms were confiscated in the North Caucasus, while MVD agents in the Leningrad and Pskov regions seized more than 7,000 smuggled weapons.[56]

Some of the more recent customers of stolen Russian weapons were the Chechens. According to an investigation carried out by Russian presidential advisers, the Chechens purchased arms from Russian military officers even after the Russian invasion in December 1994. These sales took two forms. The first category of transaction was the individual-to-individual sales where Chechen fighters bought weapons and munitions from the Russian soldiers they were supposed to be fighting. The second category was more organized and involved larger volumes of weapons. One incident reported to be under investigation was the attempted sale of a large quantity of plastic explosives, grenade launchers, and ammunition by the 104th Guards Airborne Division paratroopers to the Chechens in May 1995.[57]

Changes in military behavior and roles have implications not only for domestic governance but also for Russia's role in the international arena. In foreign policymaking, as a consequence of lack of direction from civilians or even strategic ignorance, the military seems to have increased its ability to influence decisions. This is particularly true in the case of conflicts in the former Soviet republics. For example, during the negotiations over the withdrawal of troops from Lithuania, Russian military authorities took steps to curtail the ability of civilians in the Russian Foreign Ministry to affect the direction of policy. They drew up an agreement on a timetable for troop withdrawal and sent it to the Foreign Ministry two days before it was due to be signed. This left civilian authorities little time to make amendments.[58] In negotiations over various "hot spots," like Abkhazia, Georgia, Tadjikistan, and Moldova, Russian military leaders played a very important part in negotiating cease-fires and peacekeeping operations. At one point Foreign Minister Kozyrev complained:

"Wholesale transfers of arms are taking place in the Transcaucasus and Moldova. . . . Under what agreement is this effected, I would like to ask . . . ? Why are the military deciding the most important political issues?"[59]

Information about the conduct of Russian military units in conflict zones reveals a further development: Particular armed force units chose to support different sides in the local conflicts regardless of the declared official Moscow policy, whether a commitment to neutrality or to the support of one particular side. The behavior of the Fourteenth Army in Moldova is illustrative of what happens, and can happen, when military units act independently of Moscow policy. After Moldova had established itself as an independent state, Russian policymakers made an international commitment to remain neutral and respect the territory and sovereignty of the former Soviet republic. In 1992 a section of the country east of the Dniestr River (the Transdniestr), which was heavily populated by ethnic Russians, claimed its right to secession and appealed to Russia for support. The Russian Foreign Ministry, in accordance with Russian official policy, denied all requests for help. In the meantime, the Fourteenth Army stationed in Moldova, under the command of Lieutenant General Gennadi Iakovlev, decided to act on its own initiative and support the Dniestr militia forces that were now fighting Moldovan troops. Eventually Yeltsin was able to regain control of the situation by sending General Lebed to restore discipline in the Fourteenth Army. By July 1992 an agreement was signed between Yeltsin and Moldovan President Snegur, authorizing the stationing of Russian peacekeeping troops. This incident illustrates an important point, namely, that from April to July 1992, Russian military officers acted in defiance of Russian international commitments.[60]

On balance, the new roles and behaviors adopted by Russian military officers are disturbing because they threaten the integrity of the Russian state and serve as an impediment to democratic consolidation. The implications of an expanded role for the military elite in partisan politics is perhaps most difficult to assess. Some commentators have downplayed the importance of this development. They argue that these officers are acting in their own interests and should not be seen as the reflection of a general politicization of the armed forces as an institution. They also point to the fact that military alliances with a number of different parties dilute the threat of one group's ability to play the military card. As a final point, they argue that military voting patterns reflect social voting preferences, and so the likelihood of mobilizing the military as a voting bloc is weak.[61]

It is instructive to note that traditionally democratic states have not allowed officers on active duty to hold political offices. When a soldier puts on a uniform and goes to the podium, she or he is making a political statement, indicating affiliation with—or even representation of—a powerful institution. This sets a dangerous precedent, for it helps to legitimize the idea that the military has a role to play in domestic politics. As historical experience has shown, military involvement in politics is, in the long run, incompatible with democracy.

The new roles that soldiers have been forced to adopt as a consequence of economic hardship have other negative ramifications for the domestic arena. One can anticipate a number of scenarios in which soldiers who depend on local authorities for maintaining their units or moonlight for private enterprises could find their loyalties divided. What would happen if a region decided to separate and federal forces were sent in to quash the rebellion? Where would the loyalty of the local forces reside? Under these conditions, a localized regional civil war appears quite possible.

A recent episode illustrates some of these new dynamics. Last November in the Far Eastern Military District, the stock company Khabarovskenergo threatened to shut off the electric supply to locally stationed military units. The local commander ordered armored personnel carriers to encircle the electric power stations and prevent such action from being taken. The situation was defused by the intervention of the regional governor, Victor Ishaev, who negotiated a settlement of the dispute.[62]

The increasing involvement of the armed forces in criminal activities is a particularly grave challenge to the integrity of the state. One analyst who has done work on comparative state collapse writes: "Probably the ultimate danger sign is when the center loses control over its own state agents, who begin to operate on their own account. Officials exact payments for their own pockets, and law and order is consistently broken by the agents of law and order, the policy and army units becoming gangs and brigands."[63] Highlighting this problem, President Yeltsin stated that "corruption in the organs of power and administration is literally eating away the body of the Russian state from top to bottom."[64]

The expanded role of the military in foreign policy decisions and the increasing frequency of military insubordination are particularly detrimental to Russia's role in the international arena. First, they hamper the ability of the state to articulate and follow a unified foreign policy. A particularly good illustration of this disunity can be found by looking at Russian negotiations during the Chechen crisis, where the policies declared by Defense Minister Grachev, chief negotiator General Lebed, President Yeltsin, and the Foreign Ministry were frequently at odds with each other.[65] Second, expanded military involvement and insubordination undermine the civilian leadership's ability to control an important sphere of foreign policymaking. This lack of civilian control ultimately challenges the democratic development of a state and its security. The illegal sale of weapons by Russian soldiers to Chechens provides a good example of how military insubordination and corruption threaten the very integrity of the Russian state.

The Russian leadership's failure to ensure domestic compliance with its international commitments also raises some important questions regarding the prospect for the Russian state to be a reliable participant in international treaties. In practical terms, it suggests that the international community may have to help Russia adhere to its international commitments. This may require negotiating very different types of international agreements: agreements that provide intrusive international involvement in creating domestic compliance mechanisms. Negotiating such multilateral agreements will be very difficult. As Russian resistance to many of the Nunn-Lugar proposals has shown, state officials are reluctant to agree to arrangements that they perceive as challenging existing sovereignty norms.[66] Unfortunately, failure to take such steps might mean that no force will be available to stop Russian domestic political actors from destabilizing the international system by engaging in various activities, such as selling nuclear materials to nonnuclear states in violation of international agreements.

Reversing State Dysfunctionality: Domestic and International Actors and the Future Prospects for Reform of the Armed Forces

In order to begin to eliminate some of the problems that have emerged as a consequence of the dysfunctional operation of Russia's security apparatus, it is absolutely essential that further disintegration of the armed forces be halted. This can be achieved by a four-step process. First, domestic actors who are in a position to enact change must be supportive of a comprehensive military reform program. Second, a realistic plan for streamlining and downsizing the armed forces must be adopted. Third, domestic actors must be willing to take measures to couple army reform with the institutionalizing of civil-military relations. This includes developing permanent, transparent, and institutionalized channels through which civilian and military expertise can be exchanged and used to develop policy, and establishing robust mechanisms for overseeing and monitoring military behavior. It also entails developing a transparent and just system of rewards and punishments that work to support the implementation of state policy. Finally, the jurisdictional boundaries and hierarchy of authority among and between civilian and military elites must be clarified.

The power to effect these changes lies primarily in the hands of Russian domestic actors. Recently there have been some positive signals that serious initiatives are finally being undertaken by Russian civilian and military elites along all four fronts. After mid-1997, a number of new initiatives directed at comprehensive military reform were announced by President Yeltsin and Defense Minister Sergeev. In July 1997, Yeltsin ordered by presidential decree a program that outlined the development of the armed forces until the year 2005.[67] The program sets out a two-stage process. In the first stage, from 1997 to 2000, the tasks of the armed forces will be specified, their structure and composition streamlined, and parallel and duplicating structures removed. Force size will be reduced by 700,000 to 1.2 million. The aim of the second stage of military reform is to supply the army and the navy with the latest weapons and hardware in order to further help streamline their structures. According to the plan, by April 2005, the Russian armed forces will consist entirely of professional and contract soldiers.

In late 1998 and early 1999, Defense Minister Sergeev announced further changes. By the end of 1999, the armed forces were to consist of four main branches: air, land, sea, and nuclear forces. The nuclear forces that had been subordinated to the various branches of the armed forces were to be brought under one strategic command, following the model of the U.S. Strategic Command. The previously existing eight military districts were to be merged into six.

The emergence of this plan, and evidence of continued commitment to it by domestic actors, provides some grounds for optimism. First, its articulation and continued development throughout the August 1998 economic crisis suggests that both President Yeltsin and Prime Minister Primakov were finally prioritizing military reform. Second, the proposal does not shy away from making difficult decisions, particularly streamlining the command structures. Third, there is concrete evidence that progress has been made toward actually implementing some of the proposals: the strategic rocket forces, space commands, and antiaircraft missile units have been merged into one service, as have air force and air defense units. Similarly, as of December 1, 1998, the number of military districts had been reduced to seven by the merging of the Siberian and Transbaikal districts into a new Siberian Military District. The planned merger of the Urals and Volga Military Districts seems to be well under way.[68]

A second source of optimism can be found in the renewed discussions about the need for strengthening civilian control of the armed forces and some evidence that progress has been made by the Finance Ministry to gain greater leverage over the Defense Ministry's allocation of defense monies.[69] Many analysts argue that control over defense spending is one of the most effective instruments for implementing civilian control over the armed forces.

There do, however, continue to be important grounds for concern. First, the existing reform program suffers from two central problems that have plagued previous projects: unrealistic calculations of costs and ambiguity. The apparent calculation of the cost of the proposed reforms does not seem to be commensurate with the financial resources available to the armed forces. The Russian General Staff has tried to make calculations about the relationship between expenditure on the armed forces as a percent of GDP and the size of the armed forces that can be maintained. In 1996 they made a set of projections for the year 2000, arguing that even if Russia's GDP grew at 20 percent per year (taking 1994 as their base year), by allocating 5 percent GDP to supporting the army, Russia could support a well-equipped army of at most 650,000–750,000 soldiers.[70] In view of these figures, the most recent claims of the Russian Defense Ministry—that the minimum requirements for the functioning of an army of 1.2 million soldiers can be met on the basis of a projected budget of 3.5 percent of a GDP that has significantly shrunk since 1994— seem unrealistic.[71]

Second, the reform plan is ambiguous. The plan announces that military districts will be given the status of operational commands of the entire forces under arms in the Russian Federation. In other words, the General Staff will supervise the activities not only of units subordinated to the General Staff, but also forces subordinated to the MVD and the numerous security branches of the former KGB that are currently subject to separate chains of command within each district. The means by which this coordination is to occur is not specified. A similar problem that does not yet seem to have been worked out is the relationship between the district strategic operational commands and the proposed central nuclear command, or for that matter the air, land, and sea commands.

In addition to doing little to specify jurisdictional boundaries or establish a clear chain of command among the various branches of the armed forces, the current proposals do not make much headway on developing regular paths for communication between civilian and military elites and providing a network of regulatory structures.

To date, international actors and institutions have been only marginally involved in influencing the process of Russian military reform. The key initiatives have included a set of military-to-military exchange programs, workshops on civil-military relations, and retraining programs for Russian officers.[72] These initiatives have been important, for they have not only provided seriously lacking financial resources, but also— and perhaps even more important—an infusion of new ideas about how to restructure state institutions. Nevertheless, the example of how Europe and the United States have been able to pressure the East European states through NATO to restructure more quickly their armies, and develop civil-military institutions that are integrated into evolving democratic systems, illustrates that there may be potential for much larger international institution involvement in affecting the evolution of Russian coercive structures. However, this would require the lowering of many political barriers that have been erected gradually since the end of the Cold War.

An important measure of a state's health is the health of its armed forces. As the discussion above has suggested, the state of the armed forces, the nature of civilian control, and the new roles and behaviors of soldiers in Russia today do not provoke optimism about the future development of Russian democracy, the future of a healthy Russian state, or the continued stability of the international system.

Notes

1. Quoted in Chris Bird, "Generals Predict Reforms Will Destroy the Military," *The Moscow Times* (July 7, 1997).

2. It is clear that no one archetype of a dysfunctional state exists. Dysfunctionality is a matter of degree. One end of the spectrum of dysfunctionality is easy to demarcate: extreme disintegration. It takes the form of civil war or revolution. The other end of the spectrum is much more difficult to identify. The problem lies in distinguishing between weak states (i.e., those whose capacity is heavily circumscribed) and ineffectual states. It is easy to see how the distinction blurs when one tries to identify the point at which the spheres of a state's purview become so limited that it becomes completely ineffectual. The concept of state dysfunctionality is made even more difficult by the fact that breakdown need not strike all state structures at the same time. Other terms used by scholars to categorize such states include "quasi," "nascent," "pseudo," or collapsed states. See Robert Jackson, "Quasi-States, Dual Regimes, and Neoclassical Theory: International Jurisprudence and the Third World," *International Organization*, vol. 41, no. 1 (1987): 528; and William Zartman, ed., *Collapsed States: The Disintegration and Restoration of Legitimate Authority* (Boulder, Colo.: Lynne Rienner Publishers, 1995).

3. For other proponents of this view see Deborah Yarsike Ball and Celeste Wallander, "Interests, Institutions, and Involuntary Defection: The Effects of Russian Civil-Military Relations on International Security Cooperation," Program on New Approaches to Russian Security, Conference Working Paper (Cambridge, Mass.: Davis Center for Russian Studies, Harvard University, 1998) and Stephen Blank, "Who's Minding the State? The Failure of Russian Security Policy," *Problems of Post-Communism* 45 (1998): 3–11. Ball and Wallander argue that Russian military behavior has undermined processes of policy evaluation and implementation within the state, undermining Russia's ability to act as a coherent state in the international system. Blank has noted that pervasive "deinstitutionalization" of the Russian state has extended to military institutions and is giving rise to state failure.

4. This number includes not only the five branches of troops (army, navy, air force, air defense, strategic nuclear forces) under the direction of the Ministry of Defense but also forces of the KGB/Border Guards, Ministry of Interior, and Railway and Construction troops.

5. *The Military Balance* 1998/1999 (London, U.K.: Oxford University Press, 1998): 296.

6. *The Military Balance* 1993/1994 (London, UK: Oxford University Press, 1993): 98–106.

7. Alexei Arbatov, "Military Reform in Russia: Dilemmas, Obstacles, and Prospects," *International Security* 22 (Winter 1998): 83–135. Estimates of Russian military expenditure vary for this period. For other indexes see *The Military Balance* 1995/1996 (London, U.K.: Oxford University Press, 1996): 112–113.

8. *The Military Balance* 1995/1996 (London, U.K.: Oxford University Press, 1996): 112–113.

9. Dmitri Trenin, quoted in Christopher Bluth, "Turmoil Looms for the Russian Military," *Jane's Intelligence Review,* vol. 8, no. 10 (1996). Retrieved from Lexis-Nexis.

10. *Military Balance* 1998/1999 (London: Oxford University Press, 1998): 112.

11. "More Woes for Russia's Military," *Jane's Intelligence Review* 11 (1999): 1. Retrieved from Lexis-Nexis.

12. "Russian Armed Forces Should Be Cut 50 pct," *Reuters Weekly* (February 10, 1999).

13. The 1993 Russian military doctrine specifies that the military's role is to protect the state from internal as well as external aggressors. "Osnovnie polozheniia voennoi doktriny Rossiskoi Federatsii," *Krasnaia Zvezda* (November 19, 1993): 3–4. In the "1997 Concept of Security," Yeltsin revoked the principle that the military had a role to play in preserving internal order by stating that it should not be used against civilians or for the attainment of internal political goals. This assertion was made a little murky, however, by following statements which envision that the military may be used in conjunction with other troops or organs of the Russian Federation against "unlawful armed formations posing a threat to Russia's national interests." From "Russian Federation National Security Blueprint," *Rossiyskaia Gazeta* (December 26, 1997); trans. in *FBIS Central Eurasia* (December 30, 1997). Clearly, the definition of an "unlawful armed formation" becomes the central factor in specifying limits on the military's policing functions. News that troops in the Moscow area were being put on alert to suppress domestic protests during the October 7, 1998, crisis suggested that the leadership had reverted once again to assigning the military both an internal and external role; Oleg Odnonlenko, "Nemoshchnyi Kulak," *Segodnia* (October 3, 1998): 1, 2.

14. For a discussion of conscription problems see Lt. Col. Vladimir G. Mukhin and Lt. Col. Aleksandr N. Ovchinnikov, "Armed Forces Manpower Shortage Threatens Country's Security: Politicians May Come to Understand This Too Late," *Nezavisimoe Voyennoe Obozrenie* (February 3, 1996): 3; trans. in *FBIS Daily Report* (March 3, 1996).

15. Boris Jelezov, *Defense Budgeting and Civilian Control of the Military in the Russian Federation* (Alexandria, Va.: Center for Naval Analysis, October 1997): 59.

16. For a good discussion of the Chechen war and the Russian military see Anatol Lieven, *Chechnya: Tombstone of Russian Power* (New Haven: Yale University Press, 1998) and Robert Barylski, *The Soldier in Russian Politics* (New Brunswick, NJ: Transactions Publishers, 1998): chapter 12.

17. "Russia Foresees GDP Narrowing by Five Percent in 1994 Versus Twelve Percent in 1993," *Journal of Commerce* (January 3, 1994).

18. It was only after a number of former Soviet states announced their intention to create their own armies, perhaps most importantly the Ukrainians, that Russian leaders reluctantly began to take steps to create their own defense structures.

19. "Ukaz Prezidenta Rossiiskoi Federatsii: o Sozdanii Vooruzhennykh Sil Rossiiskoi Federatsii," *Krasnaia Zvezda* (May 9, 1992): 1.

20. For the text of the military doctrine, see "Osnovnie polozheniia," *Krasnaia Zvezda* (November 19, 1993).

21. The council had five permanent members: the Russian President, Vice President, Prime Minister, the First Deputy Chairman of the Russian Supreme Soviet, and the Secretary of the Russian Security Council.

22. For a discussion of the formation and role of the Russian Security Council see *Current Digest of the Post-Soviet Press* XLIV 28 (August 28, 1992): 1–5, and Sergei Karkhanin, "Vosmaia Versiia," *Rossiskie Vesti* (August 13, 1992): 2.

23. For text, see "Zaiavlenie Prezidiuma," *Krasnaia Zvezda* (April 15, 1992): 2.

24. Yeltsin had learned this lesson during his power struggle with Gorbachev following the 1991 coup. In mid-December both men appealed to high-ranking military officials to support their position on the future of the Soviet Union and Russia. In this instance, the military threw their support behind Yeltsin. See William Odom, *The Collapse of the Soviet Military* (New Haven, Conn.: Yale University Press, 1998): 354–355.

25. Key reformers in the military included Vladimir Lopatin, V. Martirosian, and Vladimir Smirnov.

26. Dismay at the collapse of the Soviet Union was particularly evident in the views expressed by a number of officers at an All-Army Officers Assembly held in January 1992. For an account, see "Vsearmeiskoe Ofitserskoe Sobranie: Strastnyi Prizyv K Blagorazumiiu Politikov," *Krasnaia Zvezda* (January 21, 1992): 1–3.

27. The first indications that Yeltsin would use promotions as a tool to consolidate political allies in the military and secure his control, as opposed to supporting processes that would encourage the granting of promotions as a reward for excellence and achievement in the military profession, were in the immediate aftermath of the attempted coup in August 1991. Officers supportive of Yeltsin were promoted: most notably Commander-in-Chief of the Air Force, Marshal of Aviation Yevgenii Shaposhnikov, and Colonel General Pavel Grachev. The 1997 dismissal of Defense Minister Rodionov and replacement with Igor Sergeev were a continuation of the practice started in the early years of the reconstruction of the Russian state.

28. He increasingly focused on this policy toward the end of 1992 when his conflicts with the parliament intensified. Evidence that the security services had only provided lukewarm support for President Yeltsin during his struggle with the parliament in the fall of 1993 and in the December elections led Yeltsin to re-

structure the security apparatus in such a way as to increase his control over the various services. See J. Michael Waller, *The Secret Empire: The KGB in Russia Today* (Boulder, Colo.: Westview Press, 1994). The new paramilitary apparatus was composed of the Federal Counter-Intelligence Service (FSK), the Federal Agency for Government Communications and Information (FAPSI), the Main Guard Directorate, Border Forces, the External Intelligence Service (SVR), the MVD, and a set of security organizations tied to state enterprises, nuclear power plants, and the transportation, agriculture, and ecological sectors.

29. Lieven, 286–288.

30. Richard Staar, *The New Military in Russia: Ten Myths That Shape the Image* (Annapolis, Md.: Naval Institute Press, 1992).

31. Barylski, 433. For an excellent discussion of the early evolution of paramilitary structures, see Waller.

32. The Russian Supreme Soviet Committee for Defense and State Security headed by Sergei Stepashin came to life and increasingly began to challenge policy being made in the Russian Security Council. See Fel'gengauer, "Sergei Stepashin. Poslednii Tsentrist Verkhovnogo Soveta," *Segodnia* (May 18, 1993): 2.

33. They gave the legislature the right to approve legislation on defense issues, military policy, regulations, and doctrine. The president was given the right to make high-level military appointments but the parliament had veto power.

34. See "Ukaz Prezidenta Rossiiskoi Federatsii o Poetapnoi Konstitutsionnoi Reforme v Rossiiskoi Federatsii," *Krasnaia Zvezda* (September 23, 1993): 1.

35. Rutskoi and Khasbulatov announced that they would raise officer salaries, improve living conditions, cease troop withdrawal from the Baltics, allow servicemen to carry weapons at all times and use them in self-defense, sentence to death murderers of military personnel, and pay military consultants abroad in foreign currency. Shadow Defense Minister Achalov ordered Russian troops around Moscow to take up defensive positions around the White House while Defense Minister Grachev ordered them to stay in the barracks. See Alexander Rahr, "'Power Ministries' Support Yeltsin," *RFE/RL Research Report*, vol. 2, no. 40 (October 8, 1993): 10.

36. It is unclear how many soldiers joined the opposition in the White House. Based on available information, Taylor estimates that no more than 100–200 officers joined Achalov. See Brian Taylor, "Russian Civil-Military Relations After the October Uprising," *Survival*, vol. 36, no. 1: 10.

37. Defense Minister Grachev had meteorically risen through the ranks following his support of Yeltsin during the August 1991 coup. While Grachev had shown his initial support for Yeltsin through a well-timed joint appearance in Pushkin Square on September 22, 1993, as the crisis reached its climax on the evening of October 3 and early October 4 there were many rumors circulating about Grachev's reluctance to order troops to take the White House. At a pivotal Security Council meeting that night he had reportedly stated that he would not attack while crowds remained outside the parliament building. See Taylor, "Russian Civil-Military Relations," 11–12; Pavel Fel'gengauer, "Army's Role: Less Than Certain," *Moscow Times* (October 12, 1993): 1–2; and Fel'gengauer, "Armiia Vse-Taki Sdelala Svoe Delo," *Segodnia* 5 (October 5, 1993): 1.

38. For a more detailed discussion of the October 1993 events, see Taylor, "Russian Civil-Military Relations."

39. A 1993 report made by the Soldier's Mothers' Union, a group promoting respect for soldiers' rights, stating that four naval conscripts had died of starvation on Russki Island off Vladivostok, drew a great deal of public attention. An investigation by the Defense Ministry into the "hunger problem" found that other naval conscripts serving in the unit were 20–70 pounds underweight after having been fed a diet of potatoes and porridge for many months. See Sonni Efron, "Russian Army's No. 1 Enemy May Be Hunger," *Los Angeles Times* (July 28, 1995): Sec. 1A: 5; and Serge Schmemann, "Russia's Military: A Shriveled and Volatile Legacy," *The New York Times* (November 28, 1993): 1.

40. According to the new Russian Constitution, the Duma's control was limited to its right to adopt federal laws (these include laws on national security), to ratify international treaties and agreements, and oversee the current status and security of Russian borders. The Duma was also to be involved in the adoption of measures to ensure domestic stability and was to be engaged in the discussion of various issues including the federal budget. The power that it had previously employed to approve presidential appointments or dismissals of high-ranking military officers was removed. Even its control over the military through the defense budget was curtailed by the government's use of sequestration. For the text of the Constitution, see [http://coral.bucknell.edu.departments/russian/const/constit.html].

41. There had been a growing consensus among civilian leaders reflected in reform proposals that Russia needed to move from a conscript to a professional army. In response to budget cuts and changes in the composition of the army resulting from the departure of many junior and middle-level officers, the armed forces pressured the government to increase the number of conscripts. The civilian decision to comply with military requests by extending conscription service was in complete contradiction to their initially stated goals.

42. Lieven, chapter 8.

43. See Pavel Fel'gengauer, "The Theory and Practice of Reaching a 'Consensus' in Moscow: An Outsider's Estimation of the Russian National Strategic Decision-Making Bureaucracy." Paper presented at a meeting sponsored by the Department of National Security Affairs of the Naval Postgraduate School, Monterey, Calif. (November 14–17, 1994).

44. For a discussion of the report, see Colonel Andrei Orlov, "Military Mafia. Manuscript Found at General Staff. Why Have the 'Thieves in Uniform' Been Top Secret for Many Years?" *Sovetskaia Rossiia* (July 11, 1996): 5; trans in *FBIS Daily Report* (July 11, 1996).

45. Between 1992 and 1994, officials estimated that there were at least 100 incidents of this type of diversion. By 1994 to 1996 the quantity of "arrears" was judged to total hundreds of millions of rubles. See Orlov, 5.

46. General Armii Pavel Grachev, "Kto Khochet Zanimat'sia Politikoi Pust' Snimet Pogony," *Krasnaia Zvezda* (September 1, 1992): 1–2.

47. For a good discussion of how the military "vetted" military candidates for the 1995 parliamentary elections, see Barylski, chapter 5.

48. For example, a number of air force units have been engaging in private commerce: transporting commercial cargo and weapons during service hours and using military planes and fuel. Alexander Zhilin, "Has Russia's Air Force Become Privatized?" *Moscow News* 14 (April 10, 1997).

49. For a discussion of military involvement in "violent entrepreneurship" (i.e., private protection providers), see Vadim Volkov, "Who Is Strong When the State Is Weak: Violent Entrepreneurship in Post-Communist Russia," unpublished manuscript (St. Petersburg: The European University at St. Petersburg).

50. Rensselaer W. Lee III, "The Organized Crime Morass in the Former Soviet Union," *Demokratizatsiya*, vol. 2, no. 3 (1994): 392–412.

51. See "More woe for Russia's military." These figures should be approached with a degree of caution. In actual fact it is very difficult to assess the volume of crime in Russia let alone armed force involvement in crime. This is a consequence of two key problems. The first stems from the fact that reports only surface when perpetrators are caught. It is very difficult to assign a probability estimate of the number of crimes that go undetected. Russian Minister of Internal Affairs Erin estimated that the total number of crimes was twice as large as the reported number. The second problem results from the fact that it is in the interest of "crime-fighting" branches to exaggerate the reports of criminality: Their organizational interests (mission, size, and budget allocations) are dependent on state officials' assessment of the severity of the crime problem. See Graham H. Turbiville, "Weapons Proliferation and Organized Crime: The Russian Military and Security Force Dimension," *INSS Occasional Paper* No. 10 (Colorado: USAF Institute for National Security Studies, U.S. Air Force Academy, June 1996): 5.

52. This chapter does not discuss armed force involvement in illegal arms trading via their links with state weapon export companies like Rosvooruzhenie, Izhmash, and Rosvertol. There have been many allegations that officials in these companies are violating both national and international export control regulations. Reports suggest that many proceeds from the transactions go into private hands. See Aleksandr Minkin, "The Goats Want to Guard the Cabbage—It Is a Business They Love," *Moskovskie Komsomolets* (April 21, 1995); trans. in JPRS-UMA-95-020: 74–80; and Turbiville.

53. Turbiville, 14–24.

54. Lee, 396.

55. For a good summary of some of the more publicized incidents of military officers and security officials being caught selling weapons, equipment, and munitions, see Turbiville. Also see Doug Clarke, "Military Main Source of Criminals' Weapons," *OMRI Daily Digest* 68 (April 5, 1995): part 1; Svetlana Glushko, "Oruzhe Voruyiot i Soldati i Ofitseri i Kommersanti," *Rossiskie Vesti* (October 9, 1996): 3; Vladimir Il'in, "Prishlos' Podnimat'Istrbiteli, ili Vseobshchee Razoruzhenie Naroda?" *Pravda* 5 (January 12, 1996); John Lepingwell, "Military Corruption Increasing?" *Radio Free Europe/Radio Liberty Report* (September 27 1993): 185; and G.N. Nosov, "Army: Everything's for Sale," *Moscow News* (August 26 to September 1, 1994): 1, 3.

56. Vladimir Gondusove, TASS 1718 GMT (March 29, 1990) in FBIS-SOV-90-062; Yekaterina Glebova and A. Mikadze, "Munitioneers," *Moscow News* 51 (De-

cember 20–27, 1991): 6; "Raport: MVD o Sebe i Prestupnoi Srede," *Rossiyskie Vesti* (February 20, 1997): 1–4.

57. Doug Clarke, "Military Main Source of Criminals' Weapons," *OMRI Daily Digest* 68, part 1 (April 5, 1995); Robert Orttung, "More Revelations About the Beginning of the Chechen War," *OMRI Daily Digest* 28, part I (February 8, 1995); Yurii Smolin, "Otkuda v Chechnie Patroni?" *Argumenty i Fakty* 32 (1995): 7; and Turbiville.

58. John Lough, "The Place of the 'Near Abroad' in Russian Foreign Policy," *RFE/RL Research Report*, vol. 2, no. 11 (March 12, 1993): 21–29; Vladimir Ermolin, "Parlamentskii Komitet B'et Trevogu," *Krasnaia Zvezda* (October 28, 1992): 1.

59. Cited in Neil Malcolm, "Russian Foreign Policy Decision-Making," in Peter Shearman, ed., *Russian Foreign Policy Since 1990* (Boulder, Colo.: Westview Press, 1995): 37. For a detailed account of Russian military involvement in these conflicts, see Baev.

60. Deborah Yarsike Ball and Celeste Wallander, "Interests, Institutions, and Involuntary Defection: The Effects of Russian Civil-Military Relations on International Security Cooperation," Program on New Approaches to Russian Security, Conference Working Paper (Cambridge, Mass.: Davis Center for Russian Studies, Harvard University, 1998).

61. For proponents of this view see S. Meyer, "The Devolution of Russian Military Power," *Current History* (1995): 322–328; and Deborah Yarsike Ball and Theodore P. Gerber, "The Political Views of Russian Field Grade Officers," *Post-Soviet Affairs*, vol. 12, no. 2 (1996): 155–180.

62. "The Armed Forces Transit to a State of Emergency," *Defense and Security* (November 16, 1998).

63. William Zartman, ed., *Collapsed States: The Disintegration and Restoration of Legitimate Authority* (Colorado: Lynne Rienner Publishers, 1995).

64. Lee, 394.

65. See Lieven.

66. The Nunn-Lugar program allocates U.S. funds to help Russia transport, store, safeguard, and destroy its weapons of mass destruction. For a detailed description and assessment of Nunn-Lugar initiatives, see Graham Allison, et al., *Avoiding Nuclear Anarchy: Containing the Threat of Loose Russian Nuclear Weapons and Fissile Material* (Cambridge, Mass.: MIT Press, 1996).

67. Presidential Decree No. 725 of July 16, 1997, "On Priority Measures to Reform the Armed Forces of the Russian Federation and Improve their Structure." See "The Reform of the Russian Armed Forces Gets Under Way," *Military News Bulletin* 8 (1997).

68. This would leave more or less intact the Northern Military District (the previous Leningrad District), the Moscow Military District, the Far East Military District, and the North Caucasus Military District.

69. Major-General (Reserve) Aleksandr I. Vladimirov, "Russia: Systems for Control of Military Viewed," *Nezavisimoe Voennoe Obozrenie* 49 (December 28, 1998 to January 14, 1999): 4; trans. in *FBIS Daily Report* (December 1, 1999) and Mark Galeotti, "Decline and Fall—The Right Climate For Reform?" *Jane's Intelligence Review* 11 (January 1, 1999): 1. Retrieved from Lexis-Nexis.

70. See Christopher Bluth, "Turmoil Looms for the Russian Military," *Jane's Intelligence Review,* vol. 8, no. 10 (1996). Retrieved from Lexis-Nexis.

71. Mikhail Shevtsov, "Russia: Russian Budget Allocations to Meet Army's Minimum Needs," Moscow ITAR-TASS in English 11H02 GMT (November 12, 1998); trans. in FBIS-UMA-98-316.

72. For a recent assessment of these initiatives see Kimberly Zisk, "Contact Lenses: The Realist Neglect of Transparency and US-Russian Military Ties," Program on New Approaches to Russian Security Conference Working Paper (Cambridge, Mass.: Davis Center for Russian Studies, Harvard University, May 1998).

6

Is the Center Too Weak or Too Strong in the Russian Federation?

STEVEN L. SOLNICK

The Soviet Union, Yugoslavia, and Czechoslovakia were all multinational Communist federations that disintegrated during the transition to non-Communist rule. The largest remnant of the former Soviet Union, the Russian Federation, was also a multinational federation, and during 1992 to 1994, it seemed as if the Russian Federation might also be headed for disintegration. Several of Russia's constituent ethnic "republics" declared themselves to be "sovereign," and in 1994 Russia waged a civil war in the North Caucasian Republic of Chechnya to maintain the territorial integrity of Russia. The conflict in Chechnya left Russia deeply divided, Chechnya economically ruined, and countless thousands dead.

The state-building challenge that Russia faced in the post-Soviet period is not unique. A fundamental problem in the evolution of state institutions during any change of political regimes is to create a central government that is strong enough to keep the country whole, yet limited enough to prevent a return to tyranny. This fundamental problem led the authors of the *Federalist Papers* to advocate a system of government for the newly created United States of America that would divide responsibility horizontally through the separation of powers and vertically through federalism. More recently, political scientists have been grappling with ways states can create a balance between governmental capacity and governmental restraint. To some, the federal solution represents the best of both worlds, because it provides for *carefully delimited* areas of jurisdiction in which one level of government has ultimate authority.[1] From this theoretical perspective, the central government's authority can be held within certain clear and agreed-upon boundaries only by ensuring that any attempt to overstep these boundaries will provoke a unified response from the constituent units of the federation.[2] In other words, if constituents (e.g., states within a federation) can agree to jointly oppose a transgression against the rights of any one of them, the central government can be effectively constrained. The problem lies in guaranteeing that a challenge to the rights of one will always be perceived as an affront to the rights of all.

A related but distinct literature has applied similar tools to problems of exploitation by rulers that produces either nondemocratic outcomes or pathological and exploitative democracies.[3] Authors contributing to this literature have long recognized that if some citizens or citizen groups possess greater bargaining power than others, questions of coordination among them become vastly more difficult to resolve. Governmental actors can collude with privileged citizens or citizen groups to exploit less powerful social actors. This chapter extends this insight to the dynamics between national and subnational governments in transitional federations.

In particular, this chapter considers the problems of creating strong but limited central government in Russia. It begins by looking at how subjects of a federation (i.e., constituent regions) can coordinate their responses to attempted exploitation by the central government. It then looks at institutions and bargaining dynamics within Russia during the post-Soviet period. It concludes with some brief considerations of the normative implications of strong or weak central governments in a federal system.

Cooperation, Co-optation, and Collective Goods: Theoretical Perspectives

One way to look at the problem of limiting central government power is to discuss it as a "transgression game" between a ruler and a pair of citizens, A and B; such a model has been proposed by Barry Weingast.[4] For the purposes of this discussion, I will treat the central government (or, more simply, the national president) as the sovereign, and constituent states (or their chief executives) as citizens. In Weingast's model, a sovereign needs the support of at least one citizen in order to retain power. In the federal context, this may be analogous to a nascent federation (such as one that has just gained independence) in which the federal government can act autonomously but lacks the capacity to unilaterally collect revenue, impose rules, and retain power without at least some support from subnational governments.[5]

In Weingast's model, citizens coordinate to oppose (and defeat) transgressions committed by the central government because they fear that later predation could be directed against them. The fundamental problem, for Weingast, is devising effective mechanisms of coordination, in which all constituent units can agree on what constitutes a transgression by the center and can enforce unified opposition by all remaining subjects.

To usefully extend Weingast's model to the Russian case, we must consider the problems that arise when constituent units are unequal.[6] In the Russian federation, a handful of regions control a majority of the country's economic resources: Sakha controls most of its diamonds; Yamalo-Nenets is home to much of its natural gas; Moscow is home to 70 percent of its financial capital. In such a federation, if one region can unilaterally oppose transgression by the sovereign, the capacity of other regions to enforce cooperation will be eroded. The result will be an asymmetric equilibrium in which the center exploits weaker regions and shares the confiscated surplus with the strong region. A similar logic applies if a *subset* of regions succeeds in forming a *coalition* capable of defeating transgression by the sovereign. This coalition can deter transgression by the sovereign directed against it, and it has no need to come to the aid of weaker regions that may find themselves the target of predation.

In other words, any solution to the problem of coordination among regions that allows a strong coalition to form will lead to an asymmetrical outcome rather than the universalist "rule of law" that proponents of democratic federalism aspire to. If the mechanism that triggers coordinated regional resistance to the center is selective enough to allow members of a coalition to recognize when transgressions are not directed at them, then they may only act when coalition interests are threatened. In that case, the emergence of a universal coordination mechanism (i.e., one that united *all* regions) would actually deprive the coalition partners of the surplus that they enjoy in the asymmetric equilibrium. Thus, when both the democratic and exploitative outcomes rely upon interregional coordination mechanisms, the crucial question is *whose* actions are being coordinated.

To understand the final point, it is enough to recognize why regions that succeed in developing a limited coalition will have little incentive to replace it with a universal one. Once the bargaining unit is strong enough to be able to resist the sovereign on its own, its constituents will seek to limit the number of players with a claim on the confiscated surplus.[7]

The capacity of regions to act in a coordinated manner depends critically on institutions that might foster limited or universal collective action. As I will show in this chapter, however, the center, or central government, is not powerless to influence the bargaining environment. In particular, the center might seek to encourage or disrupt certain coalitions of regions, perhaps by constructing vertical institutions or restricting the flow of information needed for coordination to function effec-

FIGURE 6.1   Actors' Preferences Over Collective Bargaining

	Central Actor	*Regional Actor*
Most preferred	Bilateral bargaining (no coordination among regions)	Selective Collective Action (minimal strong coalition of which it is a member)
to	Selective Collective Action	Universal Coordination
least preferred	Universal Coordination	Bilateral Bargaining

tively. One might expect the center to try to prevent any player or coalition from growing powerful enough to be able to unilaterally depose her. Upon closer examination of the strategic incentives, however, it should be clear that a predatory center should prefer the asymmetric outcome, because in the symmetric democratic equilibrium the center's powers are effectively constrained.

In other words, if it must deal with regions bargaining collectively, a predatory center will prefer the collective bargaining unit to be no larger than necessary. A central government that fears that regions might solve the society-wide coordination problem and enforce limits on the center's behavior might therefore prefer co-opting a single strong region or coalition of regions whose support makes exploitation of weaker regions possible.

This preference ordering is captured in Figure 6.1.

The next section considers how certain institutions of the Russian state may foster or hinder coordination among regions, either universal or selective. In essence, federal dynamics in Russia from 1990 to 1998 can be recast as a struggle between federal and regional actors to create institutions that maximize their bargaining leverage.

Federal Institutions and Maintenance
of Federal Control in Russia

The Russian Federation was "born" asymmetrical. When the Soviet Union collapsed in 1991, Russia inherited a multitiered patchwork of different types of subnational units. In the Federation Treaties signed in March and April 1992, this asymmetrical structure became the formal basis of the new state. The twenty-one "autonomous republics," defined in the Soviet era as "homelands" for non-Russian ethnic groups, were deemed to be "sovereign" units and received the right to have their own citizenship and constitutions and greater control over natural resources on their territory. Predominantly Russian *oblasts* (regions) and *krais* (territories), and the two "federal cities," Moscow and St. Petersburg, objected to this formulation and were offered their own version of a treaty to sign, though without the recognition of "sovereignty." A third group of territories—sparsely populated *okrugs* created by Soviet governments as the homelands of smaller ethnic groups—received their own texts to sign.

The 1993 Yeltsin Constitution only muddied the waters. The distinction between republics, *oblasts/krais*, and *okrugs* was retained, though any references to "sovereignty" were dropped and all eighty-nine federal subjects were declared to be "equal." Through 1994, the republics (excepting Chechnya) were widely considered to enjoy an elevated status, both constitutionally and fiscally.[8] In part, the explicit recognition of a subset of regions as autonomous republics may have provided a sufficient coordination mechanism for them to preserve these benefits at least for the first years of the federation. Any threat to the privileges of one republic was viewed as a threat to the very constitutional status of all republics and evoked a coordinated response.[9]

As noted above, institutions can greatly affect the capacity of regions to coordinate their responses to central government encroachment. Both the federal government and regional governments can attempt to utilize a variety of institutional structures to foster collective action of a universal or more selective scale. The remainder of this chapter examines how such institutions have functioned in Russia since the early 1990s.

"Pure" Bilateralism: Institutions That Disrupt Collective Action

Treaties

Beginning with Tatarstan in February 1994, the federal government began negotiating and signing a series of bilateral "power-sharing treaties" with territories to resolve disputes over both jurisdictional and distributional issues. The treaties were initially promoted as a means of settling standoffs with Tatarstan and Chechnya, both of which had refused to sign the 1992 Federation Treaties and had boycotted the 1993 constitutional referendum. Once the Tatarstan Treaty was signed, creating a new class of "privileged" republic, federal authorities came under intense pressure to extend similar privileges to other republics.[10] In time, *oblasts* and *krais* began demanding similar treatment. By the end of 1996, 24 treaties had been signed with a total of 26 federal units. By 1998, more than half of Russia's 89 constituent units had signed bilateral treaties with the center.

Each treaty consists of an umbrella "political" document and a series of specific "intergovernmental agreements." These ancillary agreements constitute the real shifts of power negotiated between the two sides. They concern both jurisdictional questions, such as which side names officials in the judiciary or sets environmental policy, and distributional questions, such as which federal properties are transferred to regional ownership, or what percentage of the Value Added Tax is to be retained by the regional budget. While the umbrella "treaty" is a permanent quasi-constitutional document, these intergovernmental agreements generally require renegotiation every four or five years. In some cases these agreements concern very specific issues relevant only to the signatory region; the agreements are clear examples of "isolated" benefits, unlikely to provoke similar claims from other regions.[11]

In other cases, more fundamental issues are at stake. Three republics—Sakha, Tatarstan, and Bashkortostan—received "special tax regimes" in which they assumed financing of certain federal obligations on their territory in return for a much greater control over the collection and division with Moscow of tax revenues. More recently, "inter-budgetary" agreements accompanying the treaties have been used to short-circuit the flow of tax revenues to Moscow, to be discussed in the next section.

Though the establishment of such treaties became a routine matter after 1994, subtle differences remained among the individual packages, suggesting that each deal is tailored to local demands and constraints. For instance, some agreements include a provision for the agreement to automatically renew unless one side serves six months' notice; others simply expire and require renegotiation.[12]

An examination of the treatment of military affairs in some treaty packages provides another illustration of the latitude for fine tuning.[13] The Tatarstan Treaty of February 1994 was accompanied by a bilateral agreement (*soglashenie*) "on military affairs" signed on March 5, a few weeks after the main treaty. Article Eight of that agreement provides that Tatarstan citizens drafted into the army are to serve beyond Tatarstan's borders "only on a voluntary basis." Article Six of the same agreement provides that the top draft official (*voenkom*) for Tatarstan is to be appointed only with the agreement of the Tatar government (the same is true for the heads of the military schools). The treaty with Bashkortostan, signed in August 1994, apparently lacks an accompanying agreement on "military affairs." A minor concession on the draft is contained in Article Three of the treaty, which grants the republic the right to establish alternative civilian service on the territory of Bashkortostan, but only for individuals entitled to a deferral of military service *under federal legislation*. Other treaties also lack "military affairs" agreements, and provisions within the main treaties differ considerably. The North Ossetia Treaty, for instance, seems silent on the question of military service, whereas the

Sverdlovsk Treaty includes a clause on alternative civilian service similar to that in the Bashkortostan document.

Though these treaties apportion tangible benefits to regions that have signed them, they are far from an infallible guide to the relative regional distribution of benefits. In some cases, not all clauses of all agreements have apparently been implemented, and in other cases, the agreements themselves are highly ambiguous.[14] Nevertheless, the treaties represent a clear mechanism through which the federal government can exercise broad discretion to grant specifically tailored privileges to regions. Several of these privileges—like the clause in Bashkortostan's treaty exempting it from provisions of the federal constitution on land privatization—place some regions beyond the constraints of the Constitution they seemed to accept in 1993. Given the difficulty such selective benefits mechanisms create for the establishment of any broader-based interregional coordination, we should expect to see potential coalitions of regions who are seeking to constrain this federal prerogative of signing bilateral treaties.

One prominent opponent of the bilateral treaty mechanism has been Yegor Stroev, the Speaker of the Federation Council (the upper house of Russia's Parliament). Since the Federation Council is composed of the heads of each region's legislative and executive branch, it should be a natural institutional locus for a more universal coordination mechanism to police the central government (i.e., the president). In September 1997, Stroev attacked the bilateral treaties, arguing that regions "should not gain at each other's expense."[15] In January 1998, he complained that the treaties contributed to the "arbitrary" nature of federal relations and left weaker regions almost completely dependent on the Kremlin.[16] In both statements, Stroev seemed to recognize that the treaties granted the central government sufficient discretionary power to sustain an asymmetrical, exploitative equilibrium and frustrated more widespread interregional coordination.

While Stroev might personally gain from heading a more powerful Federation Council, its more privileged members (and those still seeking particularistic benefits for their own regions) have much to lose. In April 1997, the Duma passed a law that would severely restrict the president's discretion over treaty drafting and signing by requiring all bilateral treaties to have enabling legislation passed at the federal level. In effect, this would subject the treaties to legislative ratification. The law was to apply to all treaties, including those already in effect.[17] The law was promptly killed in the Federation Council. A much weaker law, providing only for "consultation" with the Federation Council and regional assemblies, was finally approved in June 1999. The new law did not directly overturn existing bilateral treaties.

Subsidies

The most tangible distributional benefits preferentially offered to specific regions are budgetary resources. The federal government can allow regions to retain a higher share of "split" taxes (like the Value Added Tax, roughly 75 percent of which is supposed to go to the federal budget), or it can offer direct block grants. Since these transfers are determined by formulas based upon public data, any preferential treatment shown by federal authorities has become difficult to camouflage.[18] In practice, fiscal benefits flow through a large number of channels, across and within budgets, making comprehensive accounting particularly problematic.

Especially difficult to track is federal largesse that fails to register as an explicit transfer from federal to regional budgets. Regional distribution of federal expenditures *within* the federal budget remains largely undocumented, as does the critical issue of the *timing* of the payment of federal obligations.[19] In 1996, for instance, while 57 trillion rubles were distributed through inter-budgetary transfers, an additional 74 trillion went to expenditures at the regional level wholly *within* the federal budget.[20]

In addition, some of the most valuable concessions won by regional leaders from the federal government are precisely the rights to retain valuable resources at the regional level. An example is the Sakha region's concession that allowed it to market a share of its diamond output independently. Such concessions fail to register as inter-budgetary transfers. Furthermore, since mutual indebtedness continues to run rampant in the Russian economy, simply getting the federal government to meet its obligations to a regional enterprise, or to forgive that enterprise's obligations to the federal treasury, can represent a significant show of favoritism.

One particularly egregious example of this kind of federal discretion over such privileges occurred in June 1997. Yeltsin phoned the mayor of Chelyabinsk to congratulate him on his fiftieth birthday. During the call, Yeltsin announced a two-year deferral on tax payments for the Chelyabinsk Tractor Factory, worth as much as 400 billion rubles (approximately $80 million).[21] One can surmise that for each isolated incident reported in the national press, dozens more go unreported.

The analysis presented in the previous section suggests that such budgetary favoritism is difficult to track, not merely because the budget is technically complex, but because federal and regional officials *want* such information to remain hidden. Since data on explicit transfers between the federal and regional budgets are readily available to regional politicians, any attempt to favor a selected group of regions through such an inter-budgetary mechanism would be easy to track. Once known, this show of preferential treatment would likely trigger a coordinated response from the remaining regions, whose taxpayers are ultimately paying the price. On the other hand, "invisible" privileges are far less likely to serve to unite either those regions "profiting" from preferential transfers or those regions shouldering the burden of subsidizing their neighbors.[22]

The *mechanisms* for distributing the budget can also be manipulated to the advantage or disadvantage of regional authorities in ways that are difficult to quantify. The federal treasury (*kaznacheistvo*) system, established in 1995, provides an institutional network for budgetary administration independent of the national banking system. The treasury network has also created a means for certain regions to control the flow of taxes collected on their territory that are earmarked for federal programs in that region. By agreement with the federal government, they are allowed to retain these revenues in the region, up to the limit of all taxes collected within that region, rather than send them to Moscow and wait for their redistribution through centralized ministerial channels.[23] Tax revenues flow into the regional *kaznacheistvo* and are used to directly finance federal obligations in the region.

Under this new system, officials at the regional level can reward favored constituencies directly, without having to lobby an array of federal officials to force prompt payment of federal obligations. Control over the fiscal flow also creates extensive opportunities for corruption or favoritism at the regional level, particularly if regional officials are ultimately allowed to keep some of these funds in accounts of "authorized banks."[24] Finally, the scheme creates a structure for Moscow to engage in annual negotiations with selected regions over the target for net federal expenditures within the region, a practice unsustainable on a national scale, given the federal government's gross inability to fulfill all of its fiscal obligations.

Institutions of Universal Collective Action

The most obvious institution constructed for facilitating regional coordination on a federation-wide scale is the Russian Parliament, and specifically its upper house, the Federation Council. Since December 1995, the Federation Council has been composed, *ex officio*, of the executive and legislative heads in each region.[25]

Though Remington argues that the very composition of the Federation Council after 1995 represented a significant concession to the collective interests of regional leaders, the capacity of that body to organize regions for collective action on specific issues has proven extremely limited.[26] Debates within the Council, even on fundamental questions such as the respective jurisdictions of the federal and regional governments, reveal deep cleavages among the members.[27] Republics and *oblasts/krais* regularly divide on the subject of asymmetrical treatment for federation subjects. In addition, regions having concluded bilateral treaties with Moscow, and those without them, regularly square off over the desirability of continuing the entire treaty process.[28] In a recent example of the sort of divisions that limit the effectiveness of the Federation Council as a collective body, Aman Tuleev, the powerful governor of Kemerovo *oblast*, complained: "At a Federation Council session in Moscow we see 21 flags of the Federation members, and not a single flag or pennant of a region. Why such discrimination?"[29]

Clearly, the pervasiveness of the federal government's web of bilateral deals with the regions—epitomized by the bilateral treaties—amounts to a selective provision of money and privilege to specific regions that undermines incentives for interregional collective action. Property transfers and subsidies sent directly to regions are not shared by any neighboring regions, and as a result they may easily be more valuable to regional leaders than "public goods" that, by their nature, must be shared, like a common economic or legal space, or protection of property rights. While a collective institution like the Federation Council should, in principle, encourage coordination to achieve the longer-term goals of limited government and economic growth, the body's part-time work schedule means that governors spend far more time as free agents negotiating independently with the center than as senators acting collectively. There have been few issues on which regional leaders have preferred universal collective action through the parliamentary chamber over more limited collective action or aggressive bilateralism.

Russian institutional designers have also hoped to see the party system emerge as a locus for interregional collective action on a national scale.[30] Half the seats in the Russian Duma are elected through party-list voting, and parties in 1993 and 1995 concentrated most of their efforts on Moscow-based national campaigns with few real roots at the regional level. In December 1995, among the four parties to cross the national threshold of 5 percent in the PR ballot, only the Communists were able to elect more than a third of their total deputies from the district-level vote. Other than the Communists, whose grass-roots network has its origins in the days of the Soviet party-state, no political party has managed to consistently gain representation in the executive and legislative branches at the regional level.[31] Just as parties have failed to effectively link the executive and legislative branches, so too have they failed to organize regions into more powerful and united blocs.

Institutions of Selective Collective Action:
Regional/Sectional Coordination

Selective groupings of regions stand a better chance of acting collectively, if they define themselves essentially as "clubs" whose benefits are shared only by members.[32] Within the Russian federation, several examples of regional associations based on geographic proximity operate like clubs. Some have been more successful than others.

The most prominent illustration of regional clubs is probably the assortment of "interregional economic associations" in existence since the Soviet period.[33] These organizations took on greater prominence during the 1992–1993 confrontation between the Parliament and the president, as some sought to elevate their status into macro-regional "super-states."

These "interregional associations" have functioned essentially as economic cooperation blocs, with little political impact overall. Even the most prominent, the seventeen-region "Siberian Accord," has been focused on fostering intra-regional trade. It has also promoted the development of Siberian regional securities and financial markets. This limited focus, when it yields results as it has in Siberia, may lay the groundwork for the achievement of more political goals as a by-product. Although member regions may support the association in order to receive preferential economic relations with neighboring regions, their support puts an alliance in place that may position the association to pursue more elusive objectives, such as restrictions on the unchecked discretion of the federal government.

For example, in May 1997, Deputy Prime Minister Chubais visited the Siberian center of Krasnoyarsk for a meeting of the Siberian Accord, which was devoted to a discussion of the draft Tax Code. Chubais was lectured by Krasnoyarsk's governor, Valerii Zubov, against offering extensive privileges to a limited number of republics. Zubov claimed that continued special treatment of Sakha—and especially its right to market a share of diamonds outside Russian federal channels—would provoke the wrath of all the remaining governors of Siberia, who felt they were subsidizing their eastern neighbor's sweetheart deal.[34] Chubais then traveled on to Sakha, where he called for the republic to make a greater contribution to the federal budget.[35] Two months later, a presidential decree terminated the 20 percent set-aside of diamonds that Sakha had been permitted to market independently.[36] In this case, the interregional association proved a more effective institution for lobbying federal authorities over regional policy than the Federation Council.

More ambitious plans for interregional associations to elevate their political profile have met with less success. The fate of the short-lived "Urals Republic" provides a particularly striking example.[37]

In 1990, five *oblasts* in the Urals region (Kurgan, Orenburg, Perm, Chel–iabinsk, and Sverdlovsk) formed a "Greater Urals" interregional association to promote intra-Urals development.[38] In 1993, these five *oblasts* criticized the ongoing constitution-drafting process for preserving the distinction between *oblasts* and republics.[39] The first proposals began to circulate for converting the Grand Urals association into a "Urals Republic."

At roughly the same time, federal authorities began seeking to disrupt the unity of the "Urals Five." Prime Minister Chernomyrdin visited Orenburg *oblast*, bearing a draft decree, "On the Socioeconomic Status of Orenburg Province." Such decrees were then the standard format in which the center delivered economic rewards (in the form of tax breaks, subsidies, investments, free enterprise zone status, etc.) to individual regions. Not long afterward, the governor of Orenburg was heaping scorn on the Grand Urals scheme, claiming that "as soon as the first signs of glorious Yekaterinburg's [Sverdlovsk's] bid for leadership were apparent, the other members of the association lost interest in their offspring."[40]

Undeterred by the defections of its neighbors, on July 1, 1993, Sverdlovsk *oblast* declared "that it is upgrading the status of Sverdlovsk *oblast* to a republic within the Russian Federation (the Urals Republic)."[41] The move was described as a direct response to dissatisfaction with the "existing asymmetrical federal model"; no secessionist claims were advanced.

The Sverdlovsk declaration invited other Urals *oblasts* to join the republic, but their immediate reactions were mixed.[42] The governor of Perm complained about the ethnic republics' "unjustified advantages and privileges" and declared, "ideally our aim is . . . exactly the same status the republics have." The Speaker of the Chelyabinsk Soviet agreed that "the important thing is for us to get rid of discrimination."[43] Neither region moved to join, however. The governor of Orenburg, not surprisingly, was more openly skeptical, declaring, "The formation of individual republics will lead to nowhere."[44]

The response of the ethnic republics to the Urals Republic was predictably hostile. Murtaza Rakhimov, soon to become president of the republic of Bashkortostan, saw the hand of Moscow behind the declaration from Sverdlovsk: "Who gave them the right to call themselves a Urals Republic? The Bashkirs, Tatars, Chuvash, Maris, Mordvins, and Udmurts lived in the Urals long before the coming of the Russians."[45] Perhaps reflecting his confidence in the ability of republics to reject this challenge, Rakhimov concluded by shrugging off the entire episode: "Many stupid things are being done today."

By September, as the political showdown in Moscow between Boris Yeltsin and the Russian Parliament was coming to a head, the Urals Five again pledged to consider political integration.[46] According to Aleksei Vorobiev, an adviser to Eduard Rossel, who was the governor of Sverdlovsk *oblast*, neighboring regions supported political integration, but "as soon as it came down to signing memoranda of intentions people would get up from the negotiating table. . . . You would have had to have been there to understand just how awkward it felt sometimes."[47] Undeterred, the Sverdlovsk Soviet drafted a "Constitution" for the new Republic.

According to Vorobiev, Sergei Shakhrai warned the Sverdlovsk leaders that Yeltsin would not approve any Urals Republic scheme unless it included several regions. After the subsequent disbanding of the Russian Parliament that month, however, "all the rest [of the Urals regions] felt extremely intimidated, and our agreements collapsed." On October 27, the Sverdlovsk Soviet, acting alone, approved a "Constitution" for the Urals Republic that went into force on October 31.[48] On November 9, 1993, Yeltsin dissolved the Urals Republic as well as the Sverdlovsk Parliament, citing gross violations of the Constitution. On the following day, he fired Sverdlovsk's Governor Rossel.[49]

The Urals Republic episode suggests the limits of interregional collective action, especially when the "natural" association of geographically clustered territories ends up yoking together regions with highly divergent economic and political objectives. Institutions whose membership is more voluntarily than geographically determined may stand a better chance of collaborating over the long term.

Institutions of Selective Collective Action:
Cross-"Sectional" Alliances

In geographically defined, or sectional, associations, benefits from collective action are generally available to all states physically located in the macro-region. "Pro-Urals" policies implemented by the federal government will presumably benefit all provinces in the Urals, and not just those with membership in the interregional association. Some regions can therefore free-ride (i.e., enjoy the benefits of collective action without bearing its costs), forcing other regions to shoulder a disproportionate share of the burden.

The quest to promote more effective collective action among selective groups of regions therefore led naturally to the creation of interregional groups not defined solely in terms of physical location. Most prominently, in Russia, a Council of Heads of Republics defended the interests of the ethnic republics during the 1992–1993 constitutional negotiations and subsequent constitutional crisis. The group was an effective interlocutor with the federal government, in large part because its members could point to specific benefits of status, autonomy, and economic privilege that flowed from their profile as republics and that also defined their membership in the group.[50] Not surprisingly, a corresponding Council of Governors (i.e., of the heads of the Russian *oblasts* and *krais*) was formed to agitate against the constitutional and economic asymmetries.[51]

There have also been efforts to create a lobby within the Federation Council of the regions that are net "donors" to the federal budget, as well as associations like the Union of Northern Peoples, that seek to link subregional groups. Federal officials have recently attempted to offset the power of governors and heads of republics by fostering the establishment of nonfederally defined associations. Most significant has been the Congress of Municipalities, linking mayors across the Russian federation. The new organization offers mayors an opportunity to deal directly with federal officials, bypassing regional leaders, and offers the Kremlin a competing channel for the distribution of money and favors. One Moscow analyst called the new organization "a fifth column in every region as a balance against the governors."[52]

Conclusion:
When Is the Center *Too* Weak or *Too* Strong?

This chapter began by casting federalism as a delicate balance between governmental capacity and constraint. Federal institutions were devised specifically to permit a strong central government to set and implement policies over a well-defined and limited set of questions. Keeping this objective in mind, how might we recognize a central government that has grown *too* weak or *too* strong? And has Russia crossed over either line?

A central government that has grown too strong denies to regional governments the autonomy necessary to derive the benefits of federalization most often cited by its proponents. In particular, for federalism to *make government more representative and responsive to local demands*, subnational politicians must be able to respond to constituents' demands with policy proposals and be able to be held accountable for the implementation of that policy. Excessive centralization makes that accountability problematic, as it provides local officials with a real or imagined scapegoat for local policy failures. Similarly, to *deliver "ethnic peace,"* a federalist arrangement must grant minority groups autonomy over cultural and some political activities in the groups' "homelands." Without that guarantee, the territorially defined interests that represent the building blocks of a federation could easily become the seedbeds of secession. And, finally, for federalism to *stimulate economic growth*, regional governments must have sufficient latitude to set economic policy at the regional level and stimulate competition among jurisdictions to attract scarce investment and improve the regional tax base. This competition among jurisdictions is the engine that produces innovation and efficiency gains in governmental policy and regulation.

This chapter argues that, in the Russian case, the central government's power comes not from its capacity to impose its will and usurp decision-making authority. Rather, the center's strength derives from the disunity and heterogeneity of regional administrations. Rather than question whether regions preserve areas of competence over which their say is final, we might well ask whether the federal government has policy areas where *it* has the unambiguous last word. Since the debacle in Chechnya, the federal government's capacity to impose its will by force has seemed unrealistic at best, and after Yeltsin's inability to replace Governor Nazdratenko of Primorskii *krai* in summer 1997, the center increasingly resembled a paper tiger.

Since the central government in Russia has suffered more openly from *weakness* than from a surfeit of control, we might therefore ask if the center might, or has, become *too* weak. Here, it is important to recall the functions played by the central government in most developed economies. In addition to providing public goods, like a stable currency and national defense, governments also ensure the survival of a single economic space. Without this guarantee of contract enforcement and the free movement of labor and capital, the virtues of competition among subnational governments would be lost (i.e., the *incentive* for regions to . compete with each other through policy innovation is the *fear* that capital and skilled labor will move to more hospitable regions, taking their tax revenues with them). A strong central government also limits the corrosive effects of corruption at lower levels, either by mounting an effective fight against corruption or, at second best, by coordinating that corruption so that it does not produce market failure.[53]

From this perspective, the Russian government has begun to look disturbingly weak. Even before 1998, the regional strategy pursued by federal authorities was distressingly ad hoc. The financial crash of 1998 left the government hard pressed to deliver the few discretionary benefits that it had managed to produce to that point. Without these ad hoc privileges, the center's leverage over regions—and especially its ability to exploit interregional rivalries for scarce resources—was sharply curtailed. Although the steady erosion of power from the center may seem to be a step in the direction of grass-roots democracy, the survival of any federal state requires a federal government that can at least exploit its strategic position to enforce the rules of interregional competition. Without a central government strong enough to play this role, the increasing flow of authority out of Moscow might produce not robust grass-roots democracy, but rather a beggar-thy-neighbor "race to the bottom," and a threat to the very territorial integrity of Russia.

Notes

1. William H. Riker, "Federalism," in *Handbook of Political Science*, Fred Greenstein and Nelson Polsby, eds. (New York: Harcourt Brace, 1975); Barry R. Weingast, "Constitutions as Governance Structures: The Political Foundations of Secure Markets," *Journal of Institutional and Theoretical Economics*, vol. 149, no. 1 (1993): 286–320.

2. Barry R. Weingast, "The Political Foundations of Democracy and the Rule of Law," *American Political Science Review*, vol. 91, no. 2 (1997).

3. Robert H. Bates, *Markets and States in Tropical Africa* (Berkeley, Calif.: University of California, 1981); Margaret Levi, *Of Rule and Revenue* (Berkeley, Calif.: University of California, 1988); Douglass North, *Structure and Change in Economic History* (New York, N.Y.: Norton, 1981).

4. This approach is adapted from Barry R. Weingast, "The Economic Role of Political Institutions: Market-Preserving Federalism and Economic Development," *Journal of Law, Economics and Organization*, vol. 11, no. 1 (1995): 1–31; Weingast, "The Political Foundations of Democracy and the Rule of Law"; and Weingast, "Constitutions as Governance Structures."

5. To elaborate more fully, I consider this developmental stage of a federation to be one in which two primary constitutional issues and one fundamental distributive question remain to be solved: Which policy questions are decided by which level of government, how are jurisdictional disputes resolved, and how are the public goods created by the federation distributed? I do not consider the question of how many or which states join the federation, but treat that as a separate and prior question. Issues of democratic polities—in particular the degree to which the sovereign (center) should be portrayed as a *representative* of citizens (states) rather than as an autonomous actor—is deferred for later analysis (as it is set aside as well by Weingast).

6. For such an extension developed in detail, see Steven Solnick, "Hanging Separately: Cooperation, Co-optation, and Cheating in Developing Federations," a paper presented at the Annual Meeting of the American Political Science Association, Boston, Mass. (September 3–6, 1998); and Steven Solnick, "Territorial Coalitions in Transitional States: Russia in Comparative Perspective," a paper presented at the Annual Meeting of the Midwest Political Science Association, Palmer House, Chicago, Ill. (April 1998). The discussion here draws on these analyses.

7. This focus on institutions of coordination suggests that cooperative game models may proved useful analytic tools, and the observation that strong players seek to limit the size of the partnership is simply a restatement of the well-known "size principle" from coalition theory. See William H. Riker, *The Theory of Political Coalitions* (New Haven, Conn.: Yale University Press, 1962). For a useful comparison of cooperative and noncooperative approaches to modeling political bargaining, see the special issue of *Journal of Theoretical Politics*, vol. 7, no. 3 (July 1995).

8. Oksana Dmitrieva, "Political Games Around the Budget," *Moskovskie novosti*, no. 28 (July 11, 1993): 8–9; Leonid Smirniagin, "Political Federalism Versus Economic Federalism," *Segodniia* (June 25, 1993): 2; Daniel Treisman, "The Politics of Intergovernmental Transfers in Post-Soviet Russia," *British Journal of Political Science* (July 1996).

9. Steven L. Solnick, "The Political Economy of Russian Federalism: A Framework for Analysis," *Problems of Post-Communism*, vol. 43, no. 6 (1996).

10. In essence, the Tatarstan Treaty moved the federation toward a greater degree of asymmetry, by revealing that the federal bargaining position was weaker than other regions had suspected.

11. One example of an "isolated" benefit is Buryatia's Agreement, signed together with its treaty, for financing of programs to support the Lake Baikal ecological region.

12. One important agreement with an automatic rollover clause is Tatarstan's unusual and highly valued agreement establishing a State Bank of Tatarstan. While the right to a "national" bank is an important promise in the top-level treaty, the implementation of this promise required an enabling document in the form of a simultaneous ministerial-level agreement. Presumably, however, while the Kremlin could renege on the agreement, the treaty-level clause would be difficult to disavow. All the Tatar documents, including some preliminary drafts, are available on the republic government's Web site at <http://www.kcn.ru/tat–ru/politics/pan–for/tombk.htm>.

13. Reference texts for the treaties are taken from the State Duma's published compendium of these documents though 1996, *Sbornik dogovorov i soglashenii mezhdu organami gosudarstvennoi vlasti rossiiskoi federatsii i organami gosudarsvennoi vlasti sub"ektov Rossiiskoi Federatsii o razgranichenii predmetov vedenii i polnomichii* (1997).

14. The treaty with Tver, for instance, granted it the right to a "special tax regime," subject to subsequent authorization by the administration and Duma. Although regional officials saw this as approval of a sweeping devolution of taxing powers, the Duma ultimately authorized a much more modest package of regional taxes and federal tax breaks.

15. *Rossiiskaia gazeta* (September 18, 1997). Stroev himself is governor of Orel *oblast*, which has no bilateral treaty with Moscow.

16. *Kommersant Daily* (January 20, 1998).

17. *Kommersant Daily* (April 29, 1997).

18. To be more precise, the "inter-budgetary transfers" captured by these data were primarily within the "Federal Fund for Regional Assistance," which provides subsidies for regions whose per capita tax collections fall below 95 percent of the norm for the region's economic zone (the formula for calculating these transfers is set by federal law, but the Ministry of Finance exercises some discretion over the timing of the actual transfers). According to Aleksei M. Lavrov, "Mify i rify Rossiiskogo biudzhetnogo federalizma" (manuscript, Moscow: December 1996), 70 percent of "inter-budgetary transfers" flowed through this mechanism in 1996. The remainder included special categories of block grants and mutual settlements, which were far more prevalent up to 1994.

19. Lavrov, "Mify i rify."

20. Aleksei M. Lavrov, "Donors and Dependents," in *Rossiiskie vesti* (August 6, 1997).

21. *Kommersant Daily* (June 11, 1997).

22. In particular, various efforts to unite the "donor" regions (net contributors to the federal budget) into a more powerful unified lobby have fallen flat in recent years. See, for instance, the accounts in the *Russian Regional Report* OMRI (November 20, 1996); and the *RFE/RL Newsline* (October 29, 1997). In fact, estimates on the number of "donor" regions vary widely, from as low as 10 to as many as 32, depending on which revenues and expenditures are counted. See Lavrov, "Donors and Dependents." Furthermore, membership in the club of "donors" is at least as dependent on federal tax policy as on the structural characteristics of regions, making it a tenuous coalition at best for the purposes of lobbying the federal center.

23. These arrangements were initially established through agreements on inter-budgetary relations attached to some but not all bilateral treaties since 1995. The Finance Ministry moved to universalize the system by signing special agreements on inter-budgetary relations with all regions in 1998.

24. It is highly profitable for banks to handle federal and regional budget accounts. Bank officials would presumably be more than willing to share some of their windfall profits with the officials who decided which banks are to receive government accounts.

25. In 1993, the first Federation Council was constituted by regional elections, but in 1995 Yeltsin seized on language in the Constitution (Article 96) stipulating that the Federation Council was to be "formed" whereas the Duma was to be "elected." Since gubernatorial elections in most regions did not take place until 1996 to 1997, Yeltsin's innovation placed many of his hand-picked appointees into the upper house. The new arrangement also had the inevitable effect of transforming the Federation Council into a part-time body, as all the deputies had full-time jobs in their home regions.

26. Thomas F. Remington, "Political Conflict and Institutional Design: Paths of Party Development in Russia," *Journal of Communist Studies and Transition Politics*, vol. 14, no. 1/2 (1998): 201–223.

27. These are evident, for instance, in the roundtable chaired by Yegor Stroev, speaker of the Federation Council, in the "Stenogram of 'Roundtable' on Problems of Development of Russian Federalism," Moscow: Federal Assembly of the Russian Federation (June 4, 1996).

28. For a sampling of different leaders' opinions on the treaties, see A. N. Arinin, "Problems of Development of the Russian State at the End of the Twentieth Century," in *Federalizm vlasti i vlast' federalizma*, M. N. Guboglo, ed. (Moscow: Inteltekh, 1997): 6–107.

29. Aman Tuleev, "Russia's National-Territorial Structure: A Cause for Anxiety," in *Trud* (August 19, 1998).

30. Peter C. Ordeshook and Olga Shvetsova, "Whither Russian Federalism?" (manuscript, November 1996); Peter C. Ordeshook, "Russia's Party System: Is Russian Federalism Viable?" *Post-Soviet Affairs*, vol. 12, no. 3 (1996): 195–217; William H. Riker, *Federalism: Origin, Operation, Significance* (Boston, Mass.: Little, Brown and Co., 1964); and Riker, "Federalism."

31. On executive elections, see Steven L. Solnick, "Gubernatorial Elections in Russia, 1996–97," *Post-Soviet Affairs*, vol. 14, no. 1 (1998). On legislative elections, see Darrell Slider, "Elections to Russia's Regional Assemblies," *Post-Soviet Affairs*, vol. 12, no. 3 (1996): 243–264; and Aleksei Titkov, "Regional Elections: November-December 1997," *Politicheskii landshaft Rossii*, no. 4–5 (Nov.-Dec. 1997): 16–21.

32. On clubs and club goods, see Todd Sandler, *Collective Action: Theory and Applications* (Ann Arbor, Mich.: University of Michigan Press, 1992); and more specifically Alessandra Casella and Bruno Frey, "Federalism and Clubs: Towards an Economic Theory of Overlapping Political Jurisdictions," *European Economic Review*, vol. 36, no. 2/3 (1992): 639–646.

33. On the general phenomenon see Natal'ia Zubarevich, "Interregional Associations in 1997," *Politicheskii landshaft Rossii*, no. 4–5 (Nov.-Dec. 1997): 28–31. For a discussion of the early development of the most prominent example, the Siberian Accord, see James Hughes, "Regionalism in Russia: The Rise and Fall of the Siberian Agreement," *Europe-Asia Studies*, vol. 46, no. 7 (1994): 1133–1161.

34. *Kommersant Daily* (May 14, 1997).

35. *Kommersant Daily* (May 15, 1997).

36. *Kommersant Daily* (July 22, 1997).

37. This Urals Republic account is adapted from Steven L. Solnick, "Will Russia Survive? Center and Periphery in the Russian Federation," in *Post-Soviet Political Order*, ed. Barnett Rubin and Jack Snyder (London: Routledge, 1998). For an alternative account, see Gerald Easter, "Redefining Centre-Regional Relations in the Russian Federation: Sverdlovsk Oblast,'" *Europe-Asia Studies*, vol. 49, no. 4 (1997).

38. Sergei Ryabov, "The Urals Community: Five Plus Three," *Pravda* (January 3, 1992): 3.

39. *Rossiiskaia gazeta* (May 19, 1993).

40. Bulat Kalmantaiev, "Who Needs a Ural Republic and Why?" *Rossiiskie vesti* (May 20, 1993): 2. In January 1996, Orenburg was further rewarded with its own bilateral treaty with the center. The treaty was announced by Chernomyrdin in December 1995, on the eve of the Duma elections and of Orenburg's gubernatorial elections.

41. *Rossiiskie vesti* (July 3, 1993).

42. *Rossiiskaia gazeta* (July 6, 1993).

43. *Rossiiskie vesti* (July 6, 1993).

44. ITAR-TASS (July 6, 1993).

45. *Nezavisimaia gazeta* (July 7, 1993).

46. *Izvestiia* (September 17, 1993).

47. Vorobiev was quoted in the Yekaterinburg paper *Oblastnaia gazeta* (March 14, 1996). Translated in FBIS-SOV-96-093-S, 57–63.

48. The Constitution was published in *Vash Vybor*, no. 5 (1993).

49. Rossel was reelected to the governorship two years later and moved quickly to sign a bilateral treaty between Sverdlovsk *Oblast'* and the federal government. He quietly dropped the campaign for a Urals Republic.

50. In part, republics received higher levels of federal subsidies, paid a smaller share of taxes collected to the center, had greater influence over personnel appointments, exerted greater control over natural resource exploitation, had greater control over regional elections, etc.

51. Arinin, "Problems of Development of the Russian State."

52. Nikolai Petrov, quoted in the *Saint Petersburg Times* (June 23, 1998). The founding congress of the new association is also described in *Russkii Telegraf* (June 20, 1998).

53. On corruption and competing jurisdictions, see Andrei Shleifer and Robert W. Vishny, "Corruption," *Quarterly Journal of Economics*, vol. 108, no. 3 (1993): 599–617.

7

Liberal Transformation:
Labor and the Russian State*

STEPHEN CROWLEY

In Russia during the spring of 1998, as coal miners were blockading the Trans-Siberian Railway and other main rail arteries for days on end, demanding the resignation of President Yeltsin and the payment of their wages, which many had not seen in months, and some for over two years, the newspaper *Nezavisimaya Gazeta* ran a headline that asked ominously, "On the Threshold of Revolution?" About the same time, Oleg Chernovets, a forty-year-old scientific researcher, who had not been paid in six months, stated, "Russians are the world's most patient people. We put up with things that cause revolutions in other countries. But history tells you that even Russians have their breaking point. If things get much worse, there will be a revolution here too."[1]

There is a paradox concerning labor in Russia. One constantly hears phrases like "social explosion" and "revolution" uttered in Russia. And yet despite conditions that are nearly catastrophic, no social explosion has occurred, and despite dramatic exceptions like coal miners' protests, there has been little sign that it might soon appear.

From the perspective of workers in particular, the conditions in Russia at present are distressing indeed. Between 1991, when Russia embarked on a move from central planning to a market system, and 1999, the Russian economy has experienced a downturn worse than that of the Great Depression. According to official statistics, the gross domestic product has been reduced roughly in half since the start of "reforms" in 1991; in

*The author is grateful for the comments of Steve Hanson, Regina Smyth, and Valerie Sperling.

other words, factories and other economic units are producing about half of the goods and services they did prior to the collapse of communism.[2] Some seven years after the start of Russia's movement away from central planning, the economy is still in decline. According to the government's accounting, some 40 percent of the population lives below the poverty line, and most of these people are "working poor."[3] There has been a chronic problem with wage arrears—many workers simply are not getting paid for months at a time.[4] While some recent improvement has been made in wage arrears since the collapse of the ruble in August 1998, the value of those wages that do get paid has dropped in real terms. In fact, Russia's average hourly labor costs, including benefits, as of March 1999, is 56 cents an hour—less than half the labor costs in Guatemala.[5]

Most would expect that under such conditions of rapid decline, workers, who make up Russia's largest social group, would protest. Yet, relative to this grim social and economic picture, very few strikes have taken place. The FNPR, Russia's main trade union federation and the successor to the Communist-era trade union, has proven to be largely impotent against wage delays and other crucial working-class concerns. Nor does it have any significant rivals that could better defend Russia's workers. Indeed, aside from some strike activity in limited sectors of the Russian economy, as in the case of the coal miners mentioned above, workers in Russia have remained remarkably quiescent.

This chapter will attempt to examine this paradox of Russian labor through the prism of the Russian state and the role it has set for itself in labor relations. The Russian state, as we shall see, is central to explaining labor's position in the ongoing political and economic transformations.

Politically, as a number of the classics of political sociology and comparative politics point out, labor has formed the backbone of civil society in democratic countries. Labor is often the critical variable in determining such political outcomes as social democracy or dictatorship.[6] As in any country, workers are crucial to the Russian economy. Indeed, Russia might be postcommunist, but it is not "postindustrial." In other words, Russia might have too much industrial capacity, of the wrong kind, and more industrial workers than it needs. But besides having natural resources, such as oil, Russia's "comparative advantage" in the global economy is that of low-wage, even if well-educated, producers. This places labor at the center of Russia's economic success or failure. In short, the state's incorporation of labor as political and economic actor is pivotal to the overall relationship between state and society. Russia is not facing this issue for the first time, but it is witnessing a fundamental transformation of relations between workers, the firms in which they work, and the state.

The rest of this chapter will proceed as follows: We will briefly place Russia's changing labor relations in comparative perspective, and then see how labor's quiescence was anticipated neither by social theorists nor political actors. The bulk of the chapter will examine four distinct areas where the Russian state attempted either to disentangle itself from labor or to exert some control over it: privatization; labor legislation; the state's relationship with unions; and finally the issue of unemployment, wage arrears, and general enterprise restructuring. Finally, we will return to the relationship between labor, the Russian state, and the feared social explosion to examine how workers might further impact Russia's economic and political transformation.

The Challenge of Liberal Transformation

What role does the state claim for itself in Russian labor relations? What possible models might it rely on as it makes its transition from communism? For one, Russia could look to the corporatist model of Western Europe, where unions, employers, and the state negotiated wage increases and full employment policies in exchange for pledges not to strike.[7] Alternatively, Russia might look to a labor repression model, pursued with some success in the newly industrialized countries of East Asia, like South Korea. In this approach, the state sought to subordinate labor and exclude it from the political process as a means of improving the country's comparative advantage in labor costs.[8] Or Russia could attempt some combination of subordinating labor and mobilizing its support, as was successful in Latin America.[9]

Each of these models is aimed at coming to grips with a strong (or at least potentially strong) labor movement, albeit from different levels of development and positions in the global economy. One clear difference between these models and the Russian situation is in the relationship of labor movement to the state. In Russia, no strong labor movement presents a challenge to the state. The second major difference between Russia and these other cases is that the Russian state is not simply seeking to accommodate and/or subordinate labor; it is trying to bring about a liberal transformation—that is, a diminished role for the state in the economy.

The Russian state faces a paradox—it is both trying to transform society and withdraw from it at the same time. Nowhere is this withdrawal more clear than in the sphere of labor relations. The state is attempting to extract itself from a tradition of paternalistic labor relations inherited from the Communist past. This extraction of the state from direct responsibility for workers' well-being has been largely successful. The outcome thus far has been a system of labor relations that is largely decentralized, even anarchic. Yet the specter of potential "social unrest" still haunts the state and pervades a wide variety of government actions.

It was not initially clear that labor would be a weak social actor in Russia. In fact, at the beginning of these transformations a wide range of sources believed the situation to be otherwise. The experience of developing countries suggested that actions, such as the lifting of food subsidies, which occurred in Russia in 1992, frequently lead to riots.[10] Those studying the political economy of structural adjustment—the sorts of market reforms typically demanded by the International Monetary Fund—argued that for reform to be successful, labor had to be either defeated or marginalized.[11]

Analysts of the Soviet Union also believed that Soviet society had a potentially strong labor movement. Some scholars argued that the Soviet state maintained the political status quo through a "social contract," whereby workers received full employment and price subsidies in exchange for social peace.[12] Since the postcommunist liberalization would entail quite a bit more hardship than merely raising the prices of basic commodities, the specter of a "social explosion" was raised repeatedly by political analysts, labor experts, and politicians in Russia and elsewhere in the post-Soviet region. Several years into the transition, the fear of social unrest among workers is still invoked to explain the state's failure to pay its foreign debts and to impose such steps as factory closures in Russia.[13]

The economic decline since the fall of communism has been much greater than anyone anticipated. And yet it has occurred with few visible signs of resistance from workers. There are a number of potential explanations for this lack of protest among Russian workers. Still, it is worth emphasizing that the weakness of Russian labor seems inevitable only in hindsight. The Russian state, from the outset of these changes, had strong reasons to disentangle itself from labor relations and to try to weaken labor's hold on enterprises, while at same time preventing the proverbial "social explosion" from breaking out.

Privatization and the State's Economic Role

One initial and crucial step the Russian state took in its liberalizing efforts, which had a direct impact on labor, was the abandonment of central planning and the privatization of state enterprises. Under the old regime, where the invisible hand of the market had little influence, the very visible hand of state planners acted as a lightning rod for labor conflict, quickly politicizing it. For example, when coal miners in the Siberian Kuzbass region first struck in July 1989, initially in a single mine over local issues, the strike soon spread to the entire industry. Miners in the Ukrainian Donbass region struck after the strike in the Kuzbass region ended, just to make sure, despite promises from top state officials, that the strike agreement covered them, too.[14] The question of why other workers did not join the miners' strikes, then and subsequently, has been examined elsewhere, but in this first strike miners were united by the coal industry, or more precisely the Coal Ministry, which was handing out the concessions.[15] That is, the strike followed channels set up by the state.

With the advent of market reform, the role of the state has changed significantly—it is no longer the central employer. The importance of this is evident if we compare the protest actions that took place in Indonesia and Russia, both of which, in 1997 and 1998 respectively, suffered a severe economic crisis.[16] The conventional explanation for the lack of protest in Russia has been the purported stoicism of the Russian people. As *The New York Times* glibly put it, the ability to withstand suffering is in Russians' "genetic code."[17] But Indonesians also had a reputation for subservience before authority. And yet in Indonesia, student protests and riots brought down the Suharto regime in 1997. In Russia, by contrast, a "Day of Protest" called by the main trade union federation and opposition parties in October 1998—just months after the August collapse—was even weaker than the ineffective attempts at such protest in the past.[18]

The difference, or at least one major one, between these two countries is the role of the state in the economy. In Indonesia, the state maintains direct control over much of the economy, not unlike the case in the Soviet Union. Control of the state and the economy were both popularly perceived by Indonesians as focused in one individual and his family, who then served as a target for economic protests. By contrast, in Russia, control over the economy was perceived as dispersed and diffused and no longer under the direct control of the state.[19]

The state's success in withdrawing from direct responsibility for the economy in general and labor in particular is even more evident if we look at strike activity. In Russia from 1992 to 1996, a total of 24,185 strikes were reported, for an average of 4,837 per year.[20] When we break down these figures by sector, however, a different picture emerges. The large majority of these strikes were led by teachers. More precisely, fully 87 percent of all strikes in Russia from 1992 to 1996 took place in the education sector, and these figures have since remained largely consistent. Manufacturing and mining combined account for less than 5 percent of the official strike figures; almost certainly most of these strikes took place in the strike-prone mining industry. This means that, since the start of the painful "transition," very few strikes have occurred in any industry other than in coal mining.

Rather, the bulk of strikes occur in the "budget sector"—that is, the branches of the economy such as education and health care, where employees are paid (or more often not paid) directly from the state budget. The coal mining industry also remains predominantly state-owned as well. However, two caveats are in order. First, if one looks at the intensity of strikes—not only the number of strikes but the number of strikers and the strikes' duration—the disparity between strikes in the budget sector and those in mining/manufacturing are not quite so lopsided. Even with this correction, however, one finds very few industrial strikes outside mining. Second, the fact that few industrial workers, aside from coal miners, engage in strikes predates privatization, suggesting there are more factors at work than the state/private sector distinction. Nevertheless, the strike figures strongly suggest that the government has succeeded in no longer being perceived as directly responsible for the state of affairs in most workplaces; or perhaps workers in newly privatized firms simply are not sure whom to strike against.

Labor Legislation

If the state is no longer directly responsible for conditions in the workplace, it is certainly responsible for establishing a legal framework for labor relations. There are a number of laws on the books, such as the Labor Code, the Law on Collective Bargaining Agreements, the Law on Trade Unions, and the Law on Collective Labor Disputes.[21] With the state no longer directly responsible for the state of affairs at individual enterprises, these laws take on increased importance. In the legal realm, the trend is the reverse of liberalization. Here, the state has not withdrawn from its previous commitments; in fact, partially out of inertia and partially out of resistance by trade unions and others, just the opposite has occurred. And yet the results have had a perverse effect on labor. The state legally stipulates so much in the sphere of labor relations, including unions' rights and privileges, that trade unions are effectively tied to the state.

In the Soviet period, workers had some of the strongest legal protections anywhere in the world—on paper. Surprisingly, despite tremendous changes elsewhere in the economy, little of this legal framework has changed. Despite a large number of amendments and presidential decrees, the Russian Labor Code remains largely the same as the Brezhnev-era Labor Code of 1972. Among the legal protections in the Labor Code is the trade unions' traditional right to prevent layoffs without union approval.[22] There have been a number of attempts to rewrite the Labor Code, and as of this writing, a draft law has been submitted to parliament. The changes would, among other things, make it easier for firms to fire workers.[23] Not surprisingly, trade unions have opposed the changes, and the current parliament has given consideration of the Labor Code a very low priority.

One area of labor law that is not simply left over from the Soviet era is the law on strikes (or more specifically, the Law on Collective Labor Disputes). Before the first miners' strike in 1989, there was not even a strike law on the books, since strikes were simply not supposed to occur in the Soviet Union. The law on strikes is therefore newer, first written in 1991, and extensively revised in 1995.

The law itself is arcane and lays out extremely bureaucratic procedures for calling a strike.[24] For example, half the workforce must first vote for a strike, and then employers and employees must create a conciliation commission, which has five days to resolve the dispute. If that fails, the conflict goes to mediation and/or arbitration. Workers can at this point call a one-day warning strike, provided they have given three days' written notice to the employers. Ten days' written notice, along with the above steps, is required before calling for a full strike; the notice must include the points of contention, the time the strike is to begin, the expected number of participants, and so on. Only then can a strike be considered "legal." Moreover, the walkout can only be considered a strike, with legal protections, if the demands concern a "collective labor dispute," that is, questions about the implementation of the labor contract. If not, workers can simply be dismissed for absenteeism.

The upshot of this bureaucratic procedure is that spontaneous strikes are almost always illegal, as are political strikes, or strikes about any issues that do not appear in the labor contract. This is a significant problem, because most overt conflicts have been small-scale, localized, and spontaneous.[25] This means that a lot of conflict can easily overflow these official, legal channels.[26]

The basic function of the state is to enforce its laws. While discussing strike laws, we might ask how the state enforces such laws. Put differently, what might the Russian state's response be if the oft-mentioned social explosion ever actually occurred? The example of the coal miners' "rail wars" of the spring of 1998 provides some evidence in this regard. When confronted with miners blockading the main rail arteries of the country, state officials responded with threats and invoked laws stating that strikes at power stations were subject to criminal prosecution. They called out the infamous OMON police units to move miners off the tracks. Yet they did so rather gingerly, forbidding the OMON units to use "riot gear or weapons."[27]

Despite the serious economic costs of the rail blockades, and the deliberate flouting of laws through this civil disobedience, state officials were clearly concerned about the political fallout of any labor repression. As the newspaper *Kommersant* put it, in talking about regional governors, "we can say with certainty that no elected governor who cares about his future career will give the order to use rubber truncheons or water cannons against striking voters."[28] One survey found considerable support for the miners and showed about 80 percent of respondents considering it "impermissible under any circumstances to use force against participants in railroad blockades."[29] This example suggests the state's resources are limited in repressing strikes or labor unrest.

The law on strikes aside, with Soviet laws still largely in place in the other realms of labor law, workers still have extensive legal protections. Yet, it is hardly news that the law in Russia is often flouted with impunity. Moreover, in the labor sphere, the juxtaposition of these sweeping laws protecting labor rights alongside systematic violation of the same makes the notion of the rule of law for most workers a cruel joke. Rules on layoffs are routinely ignored, and union activists are harassed with impunity, to give but two examples.[30] Most obviously, it is against the law, in Russia as elsewhere, to withhold salaries from workers, a practice that has become widespread in recent years. These problems are not simply the result of some flaw in Russian culture. Foreign firms also routinely violate labor laws. According to an American Chamber of Commerce survey, 32 percent of U.S. companies operating in Russia admitted to deferring the payment of wages.[31]

Unions do seek legal redress for their grievances, and this strategy seems sensible, especially given the fact that Russian unions have not been very successful in leading strikes or other collective actions. With backing from the AFL-CIO, the new alternative unions that sprang up with the collapse of communism have pursued the legal path vigorously. In 1997, 6 percent of the total Russian workforce sought redress for the nonpayment of wages through the courts.[32]

But this legal strategy requires a tremendous amount of time and resources, which further detracts from unions' ability to engage in organization-building and collective action. The process typically involves getting tied down in the courts.[33] Even when the court decides in the union's favor, there is still the problem of enforcement. Some factory directors claim to have piles of these court orders sitting on their desk.[34]

There is a reason why these labor laws are so hollow, beyond the general lack of rule of law in Russia. These legal protections were not brought about, as in Western Europe for example, through union pressure from below. Rather, Russian labor protections are either legacies of the Soviet period, or they were handed down from the state. The only way these legal protections can have any bite is if they are backed up by strong trade unions that can make violators pay.[35]

Trade Unions and the Russian State

If laws are not sufficient to protect workers, what about unions themselves? Here we will look in particular at the unions' relationship with the state. The main trade union federation (FNPR) is predominant, not only in terms of numbers—which, while declining, are still quite high—but also in terms of state recognition and legal standing. The changes that have occurred in labor laws and state policy have privileged the once official union—the FNPR—as opposed to new alternative trade unions.[36] For example, the rules determining who can represent the workforce in collective bargaining privilege the dominant trade union in the enterprise, almost always an FNPR member union. Moreover, in the tripartite bodies (which bring together representatives of unions, employers, and the state, as discussed below) the Russian government has sanctioned the FNPR as virtually the sole national representative of labor.[37] In these and other ways, the Russian state has signaled its desire to make the FNPR the single intermediary between workers and the state. In other words, in some ways the FNPR remains the official trade union.

In most sectors of the economy, the FNPR is the only union that matters. Polls show that the demands trade unions raise are popular: People's greatest concerns are often unemployment and delayed wage payments.[38] Yet poll after poll shows that the FNPR, and unions generally, are among the least respected public institutions in Russia.[39] Put differently, unions—the organizations that in theory should be the most capable of achieving the goals of most people—are among the least trusted institutions in society and have proven themselves largely incapable of mobilizing their members in support of those goals.[40]

Why have Russian unions been so ineffective? Unions remain doubly dependent, on both management and the state. At the factory level, managers in many cases are still trade union members, as they were in the Communist era. In 1993, 95 percent of union leaders saw themselves as part of management's team.[41] A more recent survey found that two-thirds of trade union presidents and the same number of enterprise directors think it is normal for workers and managers to be members of the same trade union since "this helps to avoid conflict."[42] Given the lack of other institutions, unions are still called upon to fulfill state functions at the workplace. For instance, health and safety inspections are supposed to be conducted by an independent government agency, but given the lack of state funding such inspections are done by unions, if at all.[43] More important is the provision of social services and in-kind benefits, which in the Communist era was the main function of trade unions. Such benefits were once funded by the state. Now, if they exist at all, they are provided by management, although, as before, they are most often distributed through the unions. A 1995 survey found that more than twice as many people turn to the union with questions about social benefits as with questions about pay, even when many workers were not getting paid for months at a time.[44]

Russian unions face a paradox: Given the unions' long and continued legacy of being an arm of management that exists to provide social services, workers do not look to them to defend their rights. But given the dire economic and social conditions at most workplaces, workers more than ever need whatever goods and services unions can provide. However, because managers provide the resources for such services, union leaders are effectively prevented from taking a tough stance against management. Union leaders can easily be cut off from these resources and thus further lose their standing with their members.[45] In these conditions, it is not surprising that unions are not viewed by workers as real defenders of their interests.

At the national level, the FNPR remains dependent on the state. As with health and safety and social welfare provisions within the factory, although social insurance funds were supposed to be administered by a government agency, by default a large portion of these funds are still administered by the FNPR. The FNPR inherited an enormous amount of property from the Communist period, including revenue generating concerns like vacation resorts and other real estate. The continued control over these and other resources helps explain the continued, even if declining, high rates of membership, especially in comparison to the new trade unions that do not have access to such resources. Yet, as the newspaper *Izvestiya* put it, "Being one of the greatest landlords in Russia, the FNPR is not interested in confrontation with the state. The government may decide to privatize its property at any moment."[46] The Russian government has used this dependence successfully to keep the FNPR in line. The removal of such resources from union control was explicitly threatened after the union sided with the defenders of the Russian "White House" in October 1993.

This explains the impotence of the main union federation in pressing demands against the state. A telling example was the March 27, 1997, national "day of protest" called for by the FNPR. Despite the fact that a large portion of its members had not been paid in months, the union leadership refused to put forth any political demands at all, merely calling for "a change in the course of reforms."[47] After the August 1998 collapse of the ruble, FNPR did strengthen its rhetoric for its October 1998 day of protest to include demands for Yeltsin's resignation.[48] With the president's popularity rating in the single digits, however, Russia's main trade union was not exactly climbing out on a limb.

In short, the state has managed to keep the FNPR dependent on the goodwill of the Russian government. This state dependence and lack of popular trust are all the more troubling when we recall that the FNPR is probably the biggest single example of civil society in Russia.

Despite, or perhaps because of, the dependence and impotence of Russia's unions, the state has sought to integrate labor, as well as employers, in a tripartite arrangement of "social partnership," modeled roughly on the corporatist arrangements of Western Europe.[49] Walter Connor has written a monograph on this topic, calling the attempts at tripartism a "sideshow" among other things, and there seems to be little reason to substantially revise this conclusion.[50]

One obvious problem with setting up an arrangement whereby the state mediates labor conflict between unions and employers is the continued problem of differentiating interests in a society still experiencing radical economic transformation. We have already mentioned that at the plant level, unions and managers often see themselves as working on the same side. This phenomenon is also evident at the national level. In tripartite negotiations, unions and industrialists do not look to the state as a neutral body to help them settle their conflicts; instead, they unite along sectoral lines to lobby the state for more resources. Further, it is not always clear who the state represents. This is especially obvious in branch tariff agreements, which cover a given industry. Since there is typically no employers' organizations for a given branch, branch unions fill this role, as do industrial ministries. In other words, unions and branch ministries, in the absence of an employers' organization, work out and sign an agreement aimed at extracting more resources from the rest of the state.[51]

As an example of how unions differentiate between "their" ministry and other parts of the state, consider the September 1998 meeting of the central committee of the health care workers trade union. Union leaders at the meeting stated sharply: "We demand the president step down," hardly a surprising demand given that many members had not received their meager salaries from the government in the last six months. Yet according to a correspondent for *Nezavisimaya Gazeta*, "Interestingly enough, after blasting the president, union activists uttered hardly a single word of reproach for the Public Health Ministry officials attending the plenum."[52]

Besides seeing ministry officials as their potential allies, unions remain committed to tripartite bargaining in large part because they are so weak in the workplace. Tripartite negotiations give the unions an additional reason for existing beyond the provision of goods and services. However, these negotiations are nearly meaningless. One clear example is that the General Agreement is normally signed long after the federal budget for the relevant year has been set.[53] Most striking is the level of the minimum wage. The most basic function of corporatist negotiations is generally to establish an effective minimum wage—for a given industry and for society as a whole. And yet the minimum wage in Russia, as of December 1998, was 87 rubles a month, or about four dollars. This is a tiny fraction of the state-defined physiological subsistence minimum.[54] Clearly, Russia's "tripartite" or corporatist arrangement is not protecting workers as it was intended to.

Why has corporatism failed so badly in Russia? We have raised one explanation: the difficulty of separating privatized employers from the state, and separating the interests of workers from those of managers, practices that are considered "normal" for most capitalist societies. Yet it is not clear that the hardening of private property rights will make corporatism more effective in Russia. If this were so, we would expect stronger corporatist institutions to develop once privatization became more meaningful, and the state, having ceased to be the owner, could no longer be appealed to by both workers and employers. And yet, in Hungary for example, where privatization is much more deeply established than in Russia, corporatism is not demonstrably stronger than it is in Russia.[55] The state/private differentiation argument also fails to account for the exact opposite tendency empirically: The more "private" the enterprise, the less likely it is to be unionized at all.[56]

The main reason why the corporate model does not work in Russia—and in other postcommunist countries—is that unions bring next to nothing to the negotiating table. They are unable, for example, to mobilize a credible strike threat. As with strong labor legislation, these tripartite institutions, created artificially from above, will not have the same impact as they do in societies where they arose historically, through labor pressure, from below. From the perspective of the state, the most these tripartite institutions can do, and what the state hopes unions generally will continue to do, is to act as a stabilizing factor, expressing discontent in ways that are, in effect, quite harmless.

The Labor Market, Unemployment, and Wage Arrears

Let us now turn to questions concerning the labor market. As stated above, by most indicators, Russia's decline has been worse than that of the Great Depression. And yet, in all major countries during the Great Depression, real wages remained stable, while unemployment rose between 20 to 25 percent, and somewhat higher in Germany. In Russia, the opposite has happened. Unemployment levels have remained low relative to the fall in output, but real wages have been cut by about half.[57] Put differently, in the Great Depression, workers bore the brunt of the crisis through unemployment; in the postcommunist depression, workers took the hit through wages. To the Russian situation must also be added the phenomenon of workers officially kept on the payrolls, even though there is no work, and even though they are not getting paid. Returning to the notion of corporatism for a moment, it is worth pointing out a standard definition of corporatism—wage restraint in exchange for full employment.[58] From this perspective, Russia seems to be a case of corporatism gone mad!

How has state policy influenced this phenomenon of exchanging unpaid wages for what amounts to outright unemployment? In the wage arrears crisis, we find another example of the state's withdrawal from responsibility for labor relations. When the state assumes responsibility, it is only for unpaid wages in the "budget sector"—those paid directly from the state budget. Even here, the federal government often argues that regional governments are to blame, not Moscow. Of course, government employees are the state's immediate obligation, and regional leaders have no doubt been squandering funds assigned for this purpose. And yet who is ultimately responsible for ensuring that basic social and economic obligations, such as paying workers their wages, are met? What kind of state is there in Russia if it is unable to meet its most basic obligations to those who work?[59]

Arguably the phenomenon of avoiding massive layoffs despite the economic depression has evolved as a defensive mechanism within Russian enterprises. Yet the Russian government is at least implicitly part of this arrangement. Not only has it acquiesced, but it has taken steps to encourage it. The state's policy of issuing soft credits and subsidies to factories, which soon followed the attempts at "shock therapy" begun in 1992, was rather clearly an attempt at, among other things, avoiding mass unemployment and potential unrest. The stricter fiscal and monetary policy after 1994 led directly to the rise in delayed wage payments.[60] In effect, one could say without too much exaggeration that the state balanced its books on the backs of workers and their wages.

That the result was delayed wage payments, rather than open unemployment, was in no small part a result of the state's failure to create other social institutions to deal with the dilemma of labor surplus. Some seven years into the transformations, the Russian state has failed to create a functioning unemployment service. The existing unemployment service has proven ineffective in placing laid-off workers in new jobs, and thus it plays very little role in making the labor market more flexible.[61] There is still a wide disparity between the number officially registered as unemployed and those actually looking for work. Not only are benefits abysmally low—they have averaged about 10 percent of the subsistence minimum—but even unemployment benefits are in arrears. Some laid-off workers might find jobs in the informal economy and thus not be captured in official figures. Yet it is clear that the number registered as unemployed is so low because there is little incentive to register with an unemployment service unable to provide meaningful benefits.

The Soviet welfare state was administered through the workplace. The typical Soviet factory not only provided employment, but also housing, day care, vacations, and often a wide range of consumer goods to workers and their families. The state, in the course of market reforms, has officially transferred social assets from enterprises to local governments, but without providing the funds to pay for them. To the extent these social services exist at all, they are still paid for and administered through the workplace. Managers, typically the new owners of privatized firms, continue to provide some benefits to employees because, like the state, they also fear a social explosion, which might signal their vulnerability to outside takeover, or perhaps the renationalization of their firms by regional governments. While the level and quality of the benefits provided at the workplace have declined significantly, they take on more importance given people's struggle to escape poverty.[62] The continued dependence of workers and their families on these workplaces makes the bankruptcy and closure of unprofitable firms extremely problematic.

The Russian government has taken a number of very large steps along the road of structural reform. It has liberalized prices, dismantled central planning, opened up to the world market, and privatized enterprises. Yet it could not get past the step, so crucial for a capitalist economy, of removing workers from unprofitable enterprises and shutting them down. In short, there appears to have been an implicit deal between the state and industrial enterprises—enterprises might not pay their workers, pay their bills to creditors, or pay their taxes to the government, but they should continue to take care of the "collective." The state thereby loses revenue, but it prevents social unrest. There are additional factors to help explain Russia's nonpayment crisis and its relatively low level of unemployment, but this is clearly a crucial one.

As of March 1999, unemployment in Russia was at 12.4 percent.[63] This is "low" only relative to the deep economic contraction Russia has experienced. The relationship between the state and workplaces in Russia is something like a war of attrition. Enterprises are starved of cash and credit. Managers are implicitly permitted to use whatever means they can, legal and otherwise, to induce workers to quit without massive layoffs.[64] The government hopes these factories will not explode, but instead will wither away, as workers eventually leave of their own volition.

Conclusion

We began this chapter by saying that Russia's liberal transformation involved the state extracting itself from labor relations. As we have seen, it has not extracted itself from labor law, but has done so in effect by not enforcing those laws that exist. In its relations with unions, especially the FNPR, the state has co-opted and controlled unions more than it has withdrawn from them. But in the areas of privatization and the labor market, especially the twin problems of unemployment and wage arrears, the Russian state has succeeded significantly in extracting itself from labor relations. The state is no longer seen as directly responsible for the plight of most workers, and it is no longer a lightning rod for social unrest. Labor conflict and protest remain, but they have been dispersed, fragmented, and localized.

There is still much talk in Russia of the threat of a "social explosion," but the threshold for that explosion has been raised dramatically. In Soviet times it was argued that simple price rises were enough to set it off.[65] Now the question has become, What, if anything, could bring about this social explosion? It would seem the Russian government, and many others, believe that threshold would be crossed by massive bankruptcies, factory closures, and widespread and open, as opposed to hidden, unemployment.

The Russian state has clearly failed to protect labor in the most basic sense of raising the minimum wage to the physiological subsistence level and enforcing laws on the timely payment of wages. The resulting outcome has been keeping virtually "cost-free" workers on the books and giving them access to the only part of the welfare state that exists—the workplace. The Russian state has succeeded with labor to this extent—its weakness becomes a strength, in that it has both willingly and of necessity shed much of its responsibility for workers' well-being.[66]

If the state has had some success in extracting itself from labor relations, it clearly has failed to put other institutions in its place. Leaving workers' welfare at the mercy of enterprises and their managers has so far prevented massive unemployment and perhaps ensuing social unrest. On other hand, it is here that "economic reform" comes to a halt—just short of closing down unprofitable firms and forcing workers to find employment elsewhere.

Perhaps most troubling for the future is the state's failure to create institutions that might effectively channel the grievances of workers and others in a time of wrenching social change. As Simon Clarke has argued, this "underlies the dual fear that the bulk of the population will, in its passive moment, vote for the authoritarian leader who can make the most radical promises and, in its active moment, take to the streets in outbursts of mass civil unrest."[67]

The repeated raising of the specter of "social explosion" is curious in that outside of coal mining, education, and a few other sectors, there has been no sign of it. And yet when it has emerged in these militant sectors, it has shown every sign of being spontaneous and unchanneled, as was seen in the miners' "rail wars," in episodes of managers taken hostage, in hunger strikes, and even the self-immolation of those who despaired over unpaid wages.[68] This is what is so frightening, to the state and others, about a potential "social explosion": No effective institutions are available to channel it, not state institutions, not political parties, and not trade unions. Russian workers are clearly angry, and they have good reason to be. But without representative institutions to express workers' grievances, and without an effective state to respond to their demands, the probability of a social explosion in Russia, however remote, and whatever the political direction it might take, looks to those in power quite frightening indeed.

Notes

1. *Nezavisimaya Gazeta* (May 19, 1998); Fred Weir, as posted in Johnson's Russia List, no. 2143 (April 9, 1998).

2. While official figures may fail to capture informal economic activity, other measures put the decline at only slightly lower levels. See Branko Milanovic, *Income, Inequality, and Poverty During the Transition from Planned to Market Economy* (Washington, D.C.: The World Bank, 1998).

3. See Milanovic.

4. In June 1998, wage arrears were equivalent to over 25 percent of Russia's gross domestic product. *Financial Times* (August 14, 1998).

5. *The New York Times* (March 18, 1999).

6. For the classic perspective, see Reinhard Bendix, *Nation-Building and Citizenship* (New York, N.Y.: John Wiley and Sons, 1964); T. H. Marshall, *Citizenship and Social Class* (Cambridge, U.K.: Cambridge University Press, 1950); Guenther Roth, *The Social Democrats in Imperial Germany* (New York, N.Y.: Putnam, 1959). More recent interpretations along these lines include Dietrich Rueschemeyer, Evelyne Huber Stephens, and John D. Stephens, *Capitalist Development and Democracy* (Chicago, Ill.: University of Chicago Press, 1992); Gregory Luebbert, "Social Foundations of Political Order in Interwar Europe," *World Politics*, vol. 39, no. 4 (July 1987).

7. For a thorough review of corporatism as a model for Western Europe, see Kathleen Thelen, "Beyond Corporatism: Toward a New Framework for the Study of Labor in Advanced Capitalism," *Comparative Politics*, vol. 27, no. 1 (October 1994): 107–124.

8. Frederic C. Deyo, *Beneath the Miracle: Labor Subordination in the New Asian Industrialism* (Berkeley, Calif.: University of California Press, 1989).

9. Ruth Berins Collier and David Collier, *Shaping the Political Arena: Critical Junctures, the Labor Movement, and Regime Dynamics in Latin America* (Princeton, N.J.: Princeton University Press, 1991).

10. John Walton and D. Seddon, *Free Markets and Food Riots: The Politics of Global Adjustment* (Cambridge, Mass.: Blackwell, 1994).

11. Stephen Haggard and Robert Kaufman, *The Political Economy of Democratic Transitions* (Princeton, N.J.: Princeton University Press, 1995); Adam Przeworksi,

Democracy and the Market: Political and Economic Reforms in Latin America and Eastern Europe (New York, N.Y.: Cambridge University Press, 1991).

12. Linda J. Cook, *The Soviet Social Contract and Why It Failed* (Cambridge, Mass.: Harvard University Press, 1993); Peter Hauslohner, "Gorbachev's Social Contract," *Soviet Economy* 3 (1987).·

13. One of Russia's new tycoons, Vladimir Potanin, soon after the August 1998 devaluation of the ruble, "flustered financial markets when he warned that Russia would sooner default on its [foreign] debt than risk disrupting 'social peace.'" The *New York Times*, section 3 (September 27, 1998): 1. Yeltsin warned then Internal Affairs Minister Sergei Stepashin about the same time that "the situation in the country could explode." *Izvestiya* (September 23, 1998).

14. Stephen Crowley, *Hot Coal, Cold Steel: Russian and Ukrainian Workers from the End of the Soviet Union to the Postcommunist Transformations* (Ann Arbor, Mich.: University of Michigan Press, 1997); Theodore Friedgut and Lewis Siegelbaum, "Perestroika from Below: The Soviet Miners' Strike and Its Aftermath," *New Left Review* (Summer 1990); Simon Clarke and Peter Fairbrother, "The Origins of the Independent Workers Movement and the 1989 Strike," in Simon Clarke, et al., *What About the Workers? Workers and the Transition to Capitalism in Russia* (London, U.K.: Verso, 1993).

15. Crowley, *Hot Coal, Cold Steel*; Crowley, "Barriers to Collective Action: Steelworkers and Mutual Dependence in the Former Soviet Union," *World Politics*, vol. 46, no. 4 (July 1994).

16. Between June 1997 and December 1998, the value of the Indonesian stock market decline by 80 percent and the Russian stock market by 86 percent. More painfully for average citizens, both local currencies were sharply devalued. The *New York Times* (February 17, 1999).

17. The *New York Times* (September 6, 1998).

18. *Nezavisimaya Gazeta* (October 8, 1998); *Segodnya* (October 9, 1998).

19. Paul T. Christensen, "Why Russia Lacks a Labor Movement," *Transitions* (December 1997). While many blamed the handful of economically powerful Russians, the so-called oligarchs, it was unclear how to target them, and their offshore bank accounts, for protest.

20. *Yearbook of Labour Statistics: 1997* (International Labour Office: Geneva).

21. For an in-depth discussion of recent changes in Russian labor law, and one I rely on considerably in the following analysis, see Simon Clarke, "The Development of Industrial Relations in Russia: Report for the ILO Task Force on Industrial Relations." See also Linda J. Cook, *Labor and Liberalization: Trade Unions in the New Russia* (New York, N.Y.: The Twentieth Century Fund, 1997).

22. Clarke, "Development of Industrial Relations."

23. *Russia and Commonwealth Business Law Report* (August 12, 1998).

24. Clarke, "Development of Industrial Relations."

25. Since many of these conflicts do not fit the legal definition of a strike, they are not officially counted as such, another caveat to strike statistics cited above.

26. See also Clarke, "Development of Industrial Relations."

27. *Izvestiya* (July 30, 1998, and August 13, 1998).

28. *Kommersant-Daily* (August 5, 1998).

29. *Nezavisimaya Gazeta* (July 18, 1998).

30. Christensen, "Why Russia Lacks a Labor Movement."

31. The *Moscow Times* (September 28, 1998). Another source found that "many employers, both Russian and foreign, have resorted to firing employees without notice, severance pay or unemployment compensation," in direct violation of the Labor Code. *Russia and Commonwealth Business Law Report* (November 18, 1998).

32. *Izvestiya* (January 6, 1999); Christensen, "Why Russia Lacks a Labor Movement."

33. Paul Christensen cites a cartoon in a St. Petersburg labor newspaper that depicts a judge addressing a skeleton in a suit covered with cobwebs, announcing, "Congratulations, the court has reinstated you at work!" He also notes that managers "on many occasions" have taken union organizers to court as a means of delaying union recognition and obstructing their activity. "Why Russia Lacks a Labor.Movement," 47.

34. *Russia and Commonwealth Business Law Report* (November 18, 1998).

35. Clarke, "Development of Industrial Relations."

36. This is ironic because some of the new alternative unions, especially the Independent Union of Miners, helped propel Yeltsin to power back in 1991. See Crowley, *Hot Coal*.

37. Connor, *Tattered Banners*, 109; Clarke, "Development of Industrial Relations."

38. For example, a September 1998 poll by the Institute of the Sociology of Parliamentarianism found that when asked what problems in their personal life anger them the most, 60 percent of the respondents answered wage arrears and 55 percent answered low wages. *Izvestiya* (September 23, 1998).

39. One survey found the new independent unions were less trusted than even the former Communist-led trade unions, with respondents placing them second from the bottom of trusted social institutions, just percentage points above "[W]esterners advising the Russian government." Richard Rose, Stephen White, and Ian McAllister, *How Russia Votes* (Chatham, N.J.: Chatam House Publishers, 1997).

40. A survey conducted by the All-Russian Center for the Study of Public Opinion in February and March 1998 found that respondents placed trade unions at the very bottom of institutions that "have influence" (with only 4 percent of those surveyed saying unions had influence), but when asked "who ought to have influence," unions came in second place (below the intelligentsia) with 64 percent of respondents saying unions ought to have influence. *Obshchaya Gazeta*, no. 29 (July 23–29, 1998), as translated in *The Current Digest of the Post-Soviet Press*, vol. 50, no. 29 (1998).

41. Clarke, "Development of Industrial Relations."

42. Clarke, "Development of Industrial Relations."

43. Clarke, "Development of Industrial Relations."

44. T. Chetvernina, P. Smirnov, and N. Dunaeva, "Mesto profsoyuza na predpriyatii," *Voprosi Ekonomiki* 6 (1995); Clarke, "Development of Industrial Relations."

45. Chetvernina, et al.

46. *Izvestiya* (April 9, 1998).

47. The trade unions were especially criticized by the Communist opposition for the lack of stronger demands. *Pravda* 5 (March 29, 1997); *Kommersant-Daily* (March 29, 1997); *Moscow News*, no. 13 (March 30 to April 6, 1997).

48. *Nezavisimaya Gazeta* (October 8, 1998).

49. Triparitism refers to centralized and formal negotiations between representatives of labor, employers, and the state.

50. Walter Connor, *Tattered Banners: Labor, Conflict and Corporatism in Post-Communist Russia* (Boulder, Colo.: Westview Press, 1996): 170.

51. Clarke, "Development of Industrial Relations."

52. *Nezavisimaya Gazeta* (September 18, 1998).

53. Clarke, "Development of Industrial Relations."

54. *Segodnya* (June 19, 1998); Guy Standing, "Reviving Dead Souls," in Simon Clarke, ed., *Structural Adjustment Without Mass Unemployment* (Cheltenham, U.K.: Edward Elgar, 1998): 151; Tatyana Chetvernina, "Minimum Wages in Russia: Fantasy Chasing Fact," in Guy Standing and Daniel Vaughn-Whitehead, eds., *Minimum Wages in Central and Eastern Europe* (Budapest: Central European University Press, 1995). As this last volume makes clear, this situation is similar in most postcommunist societies.

55. Marc Ellingstad, "The Maquiladora Syndrome: Central European Prospects," *Europe-Asia Studies*, vol. 49, no. 1 (1997).

56. This complements the previous argument about how privatization has dispersed labor conflict.

57. Milanovic, *Income, Inequality, and Poverty*, 28–29.

58. Thelen, "Beyond Corporatism," 110.

59. It should be noted that the problem of wage arrears has appeared in other postcommunist societies, in cases as diverse as Croatia and the Czech Republic.

60. Thus, the amount of delayed wage payments by the end of 1993 in industry, construction, and agriculture was 17 percent of the total monthly wage bill, but by the beginning of 1996 the amount had risen to 83 percent of the total wage bill. Bertram Silverman and Murray Yanowitch, *New Rich, New Poor, New Russia* (Armonk, N.Y.: M.E. Sharpe, 1997): 98–99.

61. Simon Clarke, "Structural Adjustment Without Mass Unemployment, in Clarke, ed., *Structural Adjustment*, 47.

62. See Guy Standing, "Reviving Dead Souls."

63. The figures were calculated according to International Labor Organization methods. The number of officially registered unemployed remained much lower, at 2.7 percent of the economically active population. Itar-Tass News Agency (March 18, 1999).

64. Clarke, "Development of Industrial Relations."

65. While such open protests were rare, so were price rises, the most dramatic confluence of the two phenomena being the violent repression of protesting workers in Novocherkassk in 1962. Regardless of the empirical validity of the claim that price rises in the Soviet Union would lead to protest, this perception was widespread, inside and outside of the Soviet Union.

66. Viewed differently, workers and others have little incentive for collective action if the state has so few resources to distribute and few protections that it can provide.

67. Clarke, "Development of Industrial Relations."

68. These extreme forms of protest by miners and others are examined in Stephen Crowley, "Between a Rock and Hard Place: Russia's Troubled Coal Industry," a paper presented to the Olin Seminar on Business and the State in Russia, Davis Center for Russian Studies, Harvard University, February 1998.

8

The Executive Deception: Superpresidentialism and the Degradation of Russian Politics

M. STEVEN FISH

Anyone who has conducted field research on political questions in the postcommunist area or in developing countries in other regions is likely to have encountered enthusiasm for the idea that "strong executive power" provides a key to progress and security. Particularly in the post-Soviet states, including in Russia, as well as in Latin America, East Asia, and Africa, ordinary citizens, scholars, politicians, and authors of constitutions have touted the concentration of power in the executive, and particularly in a mighty president, as a "guarantee" of all good things, including stability, reform, national sovereignty, and development. In scholarly debates in the West among specialists on constitutions in new democracies, the lion's share of energy is expended on controversies over where to concentrate power—in parliament or in the presidency. Relatively few scholars have been greatly concerned with separating and dividing powers. The success of the American and French models, which separate power at the national level and distribute it between the president and the legislature, are usually overlooked or dismissed as eccentric cases. Some scholars argue that these countries maintain high-quality democracy in spite of, rather than due to, their constitutional systems. During the "third wave" of democratization that began in Spain and Portugal in the mid-1970s and that continues today in parts of the postcommunist world, East Asia, and Africa, the ideas of Montesquieu and James Madison, the great foundational apologists for the institutional separation and dispersion of state power, are largely overlooked in debates on constitution-making.

Not since scholars and politicians in the West blindly declared an "end of ideology" at the beginning of the 1960s—at precisely the moment when a new wave of intensely ideological conflict was gathering steam, soon to rend the fabric of societies from San Francisco to Paris and from Beijing to Jakarta—has the gap between perceptions and reality on a question of fundamental political importance yawned so widely. Super-executivism, meaning concentrated executive power that is not checked by assemblies or state agencies outside the executive, and especially superpresidentialism, the form of superexecutivism currently found in Russia as well as in many other countries, including Peru, Venezuela, and the Philippines, has delivered on none of its promises and has created a host of maladies. It has relegated one polity after another to chronic underdevelopment. Chief executives themselves, of course, have a great deal of interest in bolstering popular and elite perceptions regarding the indispensability of a national father-figure, invested with great power and authority. Their success in promoting such an idea, even in polities in which the president himself is personally unpopular, represents one of the greatest global political frauds of the last quarter of the twentieth century. In few places is the fraudulence of superpresidentialism's promise clearer than in post-Soviet Russia.

What Is Superpresidentialism?

Superpresidentialism is a form of democratic, or partially democratic, regime. Regular, reasonably open elections are held for holders of high office. Superpresidentialism therefore may be distinguished from autocracy. In the postcommunist world, as of the beginning of the 2000s, Azerbaijan, Belarus, Kazakhstan, Serbia, Tajikistan, Turkmenistan, and Uzbekistan stand as the postcommunist region's autocracies. While their rulers take the title "president," nothing resembling open political competition and free elections occurs in these polities, which are best classified as authoritarian or autocratic, and their rulers as dictators. Super-presidentialism also differs from moderate presidentialism, such as is found in the United States, and semipresidentialism, the leading exemplar of which is France. In the postcommunist region, Georgia, Lithuania, Moldova, Mongolia, Poland, and Romania have moderate presidential or semipresidential regimes. Parliamentary regimes, under which the national legislature holds considerably more power than does the president, are found in Bulgaria, the Czech Republic, Estonia, Hungary, Latvia, Macedonia, Slovakia, and Slovenia. In contrast with moderate presidential, semipresidential, and parliamentary systems, superpresidentialism is characterized by the following attributes: a huge apparatus of executive power that overshadows other state agencies and the national legislature in terms of its size and the resources it uses; a president who controls most or all of the levers of public expenditure; a president who enjoys the power to make laws by decree; rules that make impeaching the president exceedingly difficult or impossible; a legislature that enjoys little real oversight authority over the executive branch; and a judiciary that is appointed and controlled largely by the president and that cannot in practice check presidential prerogatives or even abuse of power.

In the postcommunist region at the onset of the 2000s, Russia, Kyrgyz-stan, and Armenia represent clear cases of superpresidentialism. Ukraine may also be included in this group, though along some dimensions it is closer to moderate presidentialism than to superpresidentialism. Several countries adopted constitutions that were semipresidential or parliamentary in form but also had presidents who exploited constitutional ambiguities and national crises to set up essentially superpresidential regimes. Croatia under Franjo Tudjman and Albania under Sali Berisha are the examples of this phenomenon in the postcommunist region.

Why Superpresidentialism in Russia?

The emergence of a superpresidential regime in Russia resulted from a confluence of several circumstances.[1] The system's origins may be traced to the drive by the democratic movement in the late Soviet period to undermine the power of the Communist Party by asserting the "sovereignty" of the Russian Republic within the USSR—a move that was designed to break up the USSR—and to the simultaneous effort by prodemocratic forces to create a powerful post for the leader of the anticommunist movement. The spring 1991 referendum in the Russian portion of the USSR, in which a majority opted to found a directly elected presidency of the republic, amounted to a vote against the Communist Party system of domination, since practically all voters then knew that Boris Yeltsin, the leader of the anticommunist movement, enjoyed unparalleled popularity and authority in Russia and would win the new office. The office was in a sense therefore created for Yeltsin himself. The forces that forged the institutions that would soon grow to become the superpresidency, therefore, paradoxically acted out of a fervent desire to bring down the authoritarian regime and usher in a more open polity.

The superpresidency's advent was made still more likely by the institutional breakdown that characterized Russian politics during the late Soviet era. Personalization sometimes accompanies de-institutionalization, and superpresidentialism reflected and codified the personalization of power. As previously strong institutions, including and especially the Communist Party and its many auxiliary organizations, crumbled at the turn of the decade, persons, rather than organizations and abstract ideas, were left as the only entities with which large portions of the citizenry could readily identify and on which political groups could focus their causes. Yeltsin's intrepid and politically ingenious behavior during the last-ditch effort by the forces of nostalgia to shore up the old order in August 1991, following on four years of courageous leadership of the anti-communist movement, established him as a genuine hero and national father figure with whom a substantial majority of the population identified closely. The likelihood of the advent of superpresidentialism was enhanced by the presence of such a figure, who many felt could fill the new office and who himself also enjoyed the self-confidence that he could do so. Analogous figures were also found in Armenia (in Levon Ter Petrossian), Kyrgyzstan (in Askar Akaev), Croatia (in Franjo Tudjman), Albania (in Sali Berisha), and, arguably, in Ukraine (in Leonid Kravchuk). Many polities that did not adopt superpresidentialism, including Romania, Latvia, Mongolia, Estonia, and Bulgaria, lacked such dominating figures at the time of regime change. The presence of a national hero-figure was not a sufficient condition for the establishment of a superpresidential regime, as shown by the Polish and Czechoslovak experiences, where such figures (in the persons of Lech Walesa and Vaclav Havel, respectively) were present but superpresidentialism was not established. A national hero may have been necessary for the nascence of such a regime, however; there is no country in the region that adopted superpresidentialism (again, this category excludes dictatorships) that lacked such a personage.

Support for an overweening presidency was also bolstered by mass popular perceptions that Russia needed a "decisive" executive to guard the country's great power status and to match wits with the leaders of other great powers, especially the United States. Russian elites and ordinary citizens, who tend vastly to overestimate the political freedom of movement of the U.S. president and to underestimate the weight of congressional constraints, often regard America's great power status as arising in part from the presence of strong, decisive executive power. In conversations in Russia during field research at the end of the Soviet era and the beginning of the post-Soviet period, this author often encountered the expression of sentiment that Russia needed a mighty president to handle its foreign policy, "just like you have in America."

Conditions in Russian domestic politics that favored the establishment of a superpresidential regime were reinforced, or at least not countered, by external influences. Few of the many Western advisers who descended on Russia during the late-Soviet and early post-Soviet periods were concerned with distributing power among branches and averting the concentration of power in a single branch. To the extent that they were concerned with dispersing power at all, the vast majority of foreign advisers, who were made up largely of lawyers, constitutional specialists, and economists from the United States and northern Europe, focused on decentralization. Preoccupied with the specter of ethnic conflict and deeply convinced of the virtues and applicability of American and German models, these advisers concentrated on creating a new Russian "federalism," whereby power would be shared between the central government and Russia's many regional subdivisions. The distribution of power *within* the central government was given far less attention. The near-obsession with rapid decentralization was inspired in part by a laudable concern for protecting the rights of ethnic minorities and promoting human rights more generally, but, as a result, the problem of how to distribute power among state agencies at the center was often relegated to the margins of consultation and debate. For their own part, the foreign consultants who advised the Russian government on economics were, as is normally the case among neoclassical economists, convinced of the virtues of concentrating, rather than dispersing, power. Many felt that the concentration of power would fortify the forces most committed to rapid economic change, minimize the dangers of "gridlock," and marginalize the bothersome interference of "politics" in restructuring a moribund economy.

The Fatal Attractions of Superpresidential Power

The appeal of superpresidentialism, however, has rested on a set of theoretical and practical arguments that cut more deeply than the proximate causes that helped bring superpresidentialism into existence in the first place. The first two arguments for superpresidentialism are made more generally in and about polities in the postcommunist and other developing regions and are not specific to Russia itself. The first of these is that the concentration of executive power creates a firmer basis for a "strong state" than does the separation of power. Indeed, if there is an area in which superexecutive authority would intuitively *seem* most clearly and unequivocally to provide advantages, it is in the realm of state strength.

In practice, however, superpresidentialism has actually undermined state capacity. Measuring state capacity is complicated, but establishing the weakness and the decline of the state in Russia under superpresidentialism is not difficult. The Russian national state, as of the beginning of the 2000s, is very low on extractive capacity. Despite one campaign after another to try to get enterprises to pay their taxes, tax collection capacity fell in the second half of the 1990s. The agencies of coercion in charge of maintaining public order virtually disintegrated, relegating some realms of society and regions of the country to the control of criminal and semi-criminal forces. The armed forces almost fell apart during and following the disastrous campaign in Chechnya. Central power deteriorated relative to regional power, and in a manner that promoted the formation of region baronies and that deepened corruption rather than bringing government closer to the people. The weakening of central power did not result from orderly decentralization. In practice, the center simply hemorrhaged power and capacity and the regions picked up whatever they could. This process had nothing in common with, nor did it yield structural arrangements that in any way resemble, the federalism found in the United States, Germany, or Brazil or the semifederal system in place in Spain. Rather, Russia underwent a poorly orchestrated, largely anarchic decentralization-by-default, which seriously impaired the coherence and capacity of the Russian state.[2]

Superpresidentialism's debilitating effect on state capacity stems largely from the way that it promotes personalism and discourages institutionalization. By investing so much power in one person, it offers that individual enormous discretion as well as incentives to thwart or distort the formation of institutions. Leaders who seek to control everything themselves—that is to say, most leaders—prefer direct control to ruling through impersonal, established rules and agencies. Leaders in systems in which power is divided often must build institutions in order to compete effectively with other leaders, so competitive politics in polities in which power is separated often takes on the character of competitive institution-building. But if a single agency holds most of the power, its custodian will often feel himself or herself capable of unmediated control of all of political life, and will regard institutions more as nuisances and obstacles than as necessities and potential allies. Yeltsin provides a study in how superpresidentialism encourages the president to regard all power as his own patrimony, and how he in turn regards any attempts to regularize the exercise of power in the form of institutions as a threat to his prerogatives.[3] The phenomenon is not, of course, unique to Russia. It is also found in some other countries in the post-Soviet states as well as in Latin America, East Asia, and Africa.

In sum, the argument that superexecutive authority promotes the development of a "strong" state is entirely unfounded. On the contrary, in practice it undermines state capacity.

The second virtue sometimes attributed to superpresidentialism is that it provides a superior basis for carrying out economic reform. A powerful executive, unencumbered by constant interference from the legislature and the courts, is seen as a particularly effective and important agent for pushing through difficult reforms.[4] As mentioned above, this view was held by many foreign economists who advised the Russian government in the early post-Soviet period. It was and is still shared by many economists and politicians in Russia and other postcommunist countries, as well as by their counterparts in other regions. According to the logic of this argument, mighty and unconstrained executive power may be most felicitous during the early stages of regime change, when a crucial, temporary "window of opportunity" for implementing painful reforms may be open. Superpresidential systems therefore might suit countries that face the imperative of a major overhaul of economic policy particularly well.

Despite widespread belief in such a notion, there is little empirical evidence to support it. In the postcommunist region, the half-dozen countries in which economic reform was most extensive in the first half of the 1990s all had semipresidential or parliamentary systems. Russia did indeed undertake a great deal of privatization in the early years following the demise of the Soviet system. But quantitative indicators showing extensive privatization in Russia necessarily fail to account for the *quality* of privatization there, and in particular for the inequality-exacerbating, criminalized, and crime-inducing manner in which privatization was carried out. While Russia's privatization program did produce a rapid change in property relations and some benefits for the economy, and while Yeltsin's ability to push the program through without a great deal of parliamentary interference probably did hasten its implementation, the second half of the 1990s showed the profoundly pathological consequences of the privatization program for political and social as well as economic life in Russia. What is more, Russia's performance in the realms of liberalization and enterprise restructuring, two other crucial aspects of economic reform, was lackluster at best during the entire 1990s.[5]

The other two arguments made in support of superpresidentialism are more specific to Russia. One is that this form of regime suits Russian political culture. This argument comes in two related versions, both of which inform a great deal of thinking on postcommunist politics. The first posits that Russia has always been led by a figure of overwhelming authority, be he or she a tsar or a Communist Party first secretary. Thus, from among all possible forms of democratic regimes, one that has at its center an overwhelmingly powerful and authoritative individual provides, in broad historical perspective, the best fit and the least disruptive discontinuity.[6] A variation on this argument asserts that contemporary Russia, after centuries of harsh despotism, has been left with an underdeveloped, even infantile, political culture. Given their historically conditioned orientation toward politics and authority, Russians crave a strong hand. Under such conditions, superpresidentialism, a system in which the masses can have their father figure and vote for him too but need not participate extensively in political life between elections, represents the most appropriate brand of democracy for Russia. Adherents of such a view do not necessarily celebrate the superpresidential constitution; they may even criticize it. But they do regard it as consistent with Russia's political-cultural norms.[7]

Whether or not such generalizations provide an accurate portrait of Russian political culture must be left to question here. Certainly those who hold such an image may find evidence to support it, including recent public opinion surveys showing that Brezhnev and Andropov would come in first and second and Stalin would finish in the top five in a hypothetical presidential election in which the dead were able to run.[8]

Even supposing that such a portrayal of Russian political culture is on target, however, one may question whether a constitutional system that revolves around a powerful executive provides the most appropriate institution. The main theoretical question to be pondered is whether an institution that reinforces extant political-cultural tendencies is most auspicious. If Russians are relatively unaccustomed to and incapable of sophisticated political participation, and if they are used to laboring under a "strong hand," is it really best to choose an institution that reproduces these conditions ad infinitum, or might arrangements that countervail such tendencies be more appropriate? As of the end of World War II, Japan had a long historical legacy of autocratic rule, conditioned by a hierarchical social structure and the near-absence of traditions of individualism and free political participation. Would reestablishment of the monarchy on prewar terms or the creation of a democracy based on the rule of a single, elected individual therefore have provided a more favorable basis for postwar political development than did the parliamentary system that Japan (with a great deal of guidance from the occupying power) adopted in fact? Would postwar Germany, given what many regarded as that society's highly authoritarian political culture, also have been better off in the postwar period with superpresidentialism than with the vigorous, competitive parliamentarism that it adopted?

Analogous questions may be asked of countries within the postcommunist world. Most countries in the region, like Russia, actually enjoy precious little in the way of democratic tradition. Political culture in most countries in the region, notwithstanding a great deal of local mythmaking, has been shaped no more strongly by democratic thought and pluralist practice than has Russia's political culture. Many leaders who sought superpresidencies for themselves, in fact, asserted that cultural and historical circumstances necessitated such institutions. Poland's first postcommunist president, Lech Walesa, made such an argument. So too did Nursultan Nazarbaev, independent Kazakhstan's first and still-sitting president. Walesa did not get what he sought. Poland adopted a semipresidential system with a strong parliament. Despite some arbitrary antics on the part of Poland's first postcommunist president,

Poland enters the 2000s as a vibrant democracy with Europe's fastest-growing economy. Nazarbaev, by contrast, got what he wanted. Following the adoption of a superpresidential constitution in the early 1990s, the country slid toward presidential dictatorship, with genuine electoral politics reduced to parades of dubious referenda on extending the president's term in office in perpetuity, as well as presidential "elections" in which Nazarbaev disqualifies any serious opponents on the basis of bogus technicalities shortly before balloting. The Kazakh economy remains in a tailspin, with economic conditions so dire that the country lost some 15 percent of its population to emigration—an extraordinary figure for a country not at war—between the end of the Soviet period and the end of the 1990s. Perhaps superpresidentialism, as Nazarbaev and his cronies regularly reiterate, is entirely consistent with Kazakhstan's "political culture and traditions." On the other hand, perhaps a constitution that is less "consistent" with preexisting cultural conditions would have provided a firmer basis for avoiding a slide into the soft dictatorship, crony capitalism, and national disintegration that now afflict Kazakhstan.[9] In sum, even if superpresidentialism indeed appears to "fit" a given "political culture" better than does a form of regime that disperses power, it is by no means clear that achieving a close "fit" is a worthy goal. Institutions that countervail some aspects of existing political culture may actually provide a superior basis for political progress.

The final basis for defense of superpresidentialism in Russia rests on counterfactual thinking about what *would have* happened in Russian politics in the first post-Soviet decade had the national legislature been invested with more power and the president with less. Given the dominance of the parliament's lower and more powerful house, the Duma, by communist, nationalist, and various other manifestly antiliberal forces, one could plausibly maintain that a stronger legislature and a weaker president would have harmed democratization even more than the superpresidential regime did. Indeed, one may argue that semipresidentialism was even "tried" in Russia in 1991–1993, and that this regime produced only deadlock and rancorous interbranch conflict, culminating in the violent confrontation between supporters of Yeltsin and the largely (but not exclusively) communist and nationalist backers of parliament in October 1993.[10]

Such an argument, while prima facie compelling and widely held among liberals in both Russia and the West, suffers from several empirical and logical shortcomings. First, the constitution that Russia lived under between August 1991 and October 1993 did not embody genuine semipresidentialism, or for that matter moderate presidentialism, parliamentarism, or any other normal form of democratic regime. The constitution in force at the time was a motley document inherited from the Soviet era, filled with legal fictions and liberalizing amendments attached during the Gorbachev period. On paper, the then-parliament, the Supreme Soviet, held supreme power; in fact, as president, Yeltsin enjoyed a host of decree powers that he secured at the onset of the post-Soviet period. The holdover constitution's contestedness and utter lack of clarity were far more formidable barriers to the establishment of normal, nonviolent interbranch conflict and cooperation than was the circumstance that power was, at least ostensibly, shared between the president and the parliament.[11]

The contention that a stronger parliament would have invested democracy's antagonists with more power than they have in fact enjoyed is not implausible. There is no denying that Yeltsin, despite his enormous shortcomings as an administrator and as a democrat, maintained antiauthoritarian positions more clearly and consistently than did his major communist and nationalist enemies in parliament. But the argument that a more balanced system would have yielded more antidemocratic outcomes holds only if one assumes that both the legislature and the electorate would have behaved in exactly the manner that they did from late 1993 until the present day even under a different constitution. This counterfactual assumption cannot be tested, but there are good reasons to doubt that everything would have been the same, except that the communists and nationalists would have held more sway, had the Duma enjoyed more authority. First, one must consider the possibility that the Russian electorate would have voted differently, had it been voting for a body that had real power and whose decisions could not be annulled or circumvented by a highhanded president. If they were really voting for a body that held a great deal of power, would the same electorate that handed Yeltsin an overwhelming victory over his communist opponent, Gennadii Ziuganov, in mid-1996, have voted for a parliament with a communist-nationalist majority at the end of 1995? It is not farfetched to think that if the electorate believed that the outcome of the parliamentary elections would deeply and rapidly mark public policy, rather than merely send a disgruntled message of protest to those who really held power, its voting behavior in parliamentary elections might have been different.[12]

Even had voters behaved as they did in fact under a different system, may one reflexively assume that parliament would have behaved no differently? The many parliamentary deputies who have acted as if they regarded the body they constitute as little more than a debating club, or a soapbox from which to advance personal ambitions to become president or secure a job in the executive branch, have in fact acted in accordance with institutional reality. The surest way to encourage irresponsibility in an individual or an organization is to withhold real responsibility from that same individual or organization. It is possible, of course, that even a more puissant parliament still would have become a forum for racist tirades, fistfights, and rampant absenteeism. But one may also conjecture that a legislature endowed with greater authority would have been taken more seriously by its own members. It certainly would have been afforded more media attention. More thorough press coverage would have exposed members to greater public scrutiny. Such conditions would have offered politicians better opportunities to build political careers by virtue of their work in the legislature alone, much the way many members of the U.S. Congress or the Polish parliament who harbor no presidential pretensions make their names and careers by sustained, dedicated work in the national legislature. As with any counterfactual exercise, one cannot establish definitively what "would have been." But it merits note that the usual assumption that greater parliamentary power would have spelled more influence for antidemocratic extremists is not necessarily sound. One must consider also how different institutional arrangements would have changed voters' and parliamentarians' calculations and behavior.

In sum, the main justifications for superpresidential power in Russia are either demonstrably false or, in the best case, impossible to sustain logically or empirically. Yet not only has superpresidentialism not delivered benefits; it has also engendered a host of pathologies in multiple realms of political life. Three major areas in particular merit discussion.

The Damaging Effects of Superpresidentialism

The first way in which superpresidentialism in Russia has actively degraded political development is by reducing the legitmacy of the democratic regime itself. "Legitimacy," of course, is a complex and elusive concept, and is hard to measure and observe. But whether one relies on public opinion surveys, investigation of the behavior of political groups, or evidence of citizens' compliance with the law, it is clear that the political regime in Russia at the outset of the 2000s suffers from a dire crisis of legitimacy. Public trust in public institutions is low even by postcommunist standards. Problems of public order and respect for the law, while common in societies in transformation, are especially acute in Russia. By the middle of the 1990s, anti-system political parties, meaning parties that seek to bring about a change of regime, rather than mere political change within the regime, were the largest and strongest parties in Russia. The Communist Party of the Russian Federation (CPRF), the rump successor to the CPSU, and the misnamed Liberal Democratic Party of Russia (LDPR), an ultranationalist party led by a bizarre demagogue, finished first and second, respectively, in the December 1995 parliamentary elections. Other substantial organizations, such as the ultra-militant Communists-Working Russia party, as well as several openly fascist organizations, also enjoy considerable popular backing. The mere existence of such parties does not necessarily signify weak regime legitimacy. But the popularity of such organizations, combined with extremely low trust in public institutions and widespread contempt for the law, do spell a legitimacy crisis.[13]

Superpresidentialism exacerbates legitimacy problems by identifying the regime itself with a single, fallible individual. Such a state of affairs is especially dangerous under conditions of rapid transformation that necessarily induce popular hardship. From the standpoint of maintaining the legitimacy of the new regime and of democracy in particular, it was crucial that Yeltsin, as the de facto leader of the democratic movement at the time of the anti-Soviet revolution, create institutional arrangements that would have enabled him to share the blame for the trials of transformation with the legislature and with politicians of diverse political orientations. Yeltsin's thirst for absolute power and his personal hubris blinded him to the possibility that sharing blame might become necessary to preserve the legitimacy of the regime—and his own rule. He foolishly saw no danger of failing and so sought to invest all power in the office that he himself held.[14] Under a system that concentrated so much power in a single pair of hands, the post-Soviet regime itself came to be identified in the popular imagination with the government's policies, and the government's policies with Yeltsin alone. Superpresidentialism converted an inevitable crisis of Yeltsin's popularity into an avoidable crisis of regime legitimacy.[15]

Superpresidentialism also promotes unaccountable, irresponsible behavior on the part of officeholders in the executive branch. This problem may reinforce the one just discussed, since irresponsible behavior by state officials, if adequately severe and persistent, may contribute to the erosion of regime legitimacy. Official accountability is difficult to measure, but it may be assessed in several realms. The extent to which officials' manner of governing reflects respect for and fear of the electorate and the extent to which important government decisions express or at least do not contravene the popular will represent two indicators of official accountability.

Russian officials' habits of governing during the first post-Soviet decade showed little respect for and fear of the electorate. Despite the presence of regular, open elections for the president, the legislature, and many local and provincial-level offices, officialdom's approach to the governed was marked by arrogance and aloofness. Russia shows the insufficiency of elections alone to secure democracy with accountability. It demonstrates that the episodic intervention of the citizenry in politics in the form of voting, while an absolutely necessary condition for accountable rule, is not sufficient.

The clearest sign of unaccountable government is massive official corruption, since citizens always oppose the appropriation by officials of resources that otherwise could be invested in public services. High corruption always reveals low official accountability, though a handful of authoritarian polities exist, most notably Singapore, where both corruption and accountability are low. Anyone who has lived in Russia for an extended period has seen that corruption is the essence of political life there. Cross-national surveys provide more systematic comparative evidence. In the most recent study conducted by Transparency International, Russia ranked 76th out of the 85 countries evaluated, meaning that in only nine countries was corruption more severe. Russia received the worst rating of the 12 postcommunist countries included in the study, which included Bulgaria, Belarus, Serbia, Ukraine, and Romania. Corruption was also found to be worse in Russia than in 14 of the 17 African countries included in the study.[16]

The link between corruption and superpresidentialism is found in the executive's control over public expenditure and in the absence of meaningful external checks on executive-branch officials. Since the regime invests most of the powers of the purse at the national level in the executive branch, the latter controls the disposal of the lion's share of the state's resources. To the extent that parliamentary cooperation is needed, the president's enormous discretionary powers enable him easily to buy the support of parliamentarians with patronage. Thus, Yeltsin was able to secure backing for his budgets from a parliament whose majority was openly hostile to him. Corruption within the executive branch also rages unchecked due to the absence of agencies and mechanisms for interbranch oversight. Since neither the courts nor parliament possesses the means to investigate and monitor the executive, those who control the state's resources at the national level ultimately are accountable only to the president himself. Were he deeply committed to and capable of controlling his subordinates, perhaps the president could limit the use of office for private gain. But Yeltsin's inability or unwillingness to exercise such control enabled many of his closest subordinates to route large portions of the national wealth into their own pockets.

The accountability shortage engendered by superpresidentialism is evident in several major governmental missteps that probably never would have happened had the constitution provided the legislature and the courts with more power to rein in the executive. The most flagrant and disastrous of these blunders was the war in Chechnya, which was plotted by Yeltsin and a handful of officials in charge of the agencies of coercion, without consultation with the legislature or public debate. From its outset the war was wildly unpopular. Opponents of the war included not only Yeltsin's traditional communist opponents but virtually all major liberal politicians and organizations as well. If the parliament had enjoyed more authority, the war might never have been launched. If the Duma and public opinion had been able to assert themselves and restrain Yeltsin after the war had been initiated, forces very likely would have been withdrawn quickly from Chechnya, saving Russia a futile campaign that claimed 40,000 civilian lives and what remained of the army's fighting capacity, prestige, and morale.

In addition to damaging the legitimacy of the regime and undermining the accountability of the rulers to the ruled, superpresidentialism checks the growth and development of political-societal organizations. One of the most salient aspects of post-Soviet Russian politics has been the lethargy of political society. Membership in political parties in Russia remains among the lowest in per capita terms in the postcommunist region. Nor did trade unions, professional associations, business associations, or social movement organizations develop robustly during the 1990s. Indeed, even by postcommunist standards, Russian political society has developed particularly slowly.[17]

A number of factors, including Soviet legacies of repression of all non-state forms of association, play a substantial role in retarding the development of political society.[18] But superpresidentialism exacerbates the problem. It reduces the incentives for political and economic actors to invest in autonomous societal organizations. The strength of the stimulus to build parties depends in large part on the status of the legislature. Parliaments and parliamentary elections are where parties attract attention and resources, build their reputations, and find their voices. Parties normally control the nomination of candidates in elections for the legislature and organize competition within the legislature between elections. Parties do fulfill such functions in the Duma, but the weakness of this body compared to the executive branch provides ambitious politicians and societal actors with scant reason to seek their fortunes and advance their interests by constructing and contributing to political parties. Targeting—and perhaps buying off—the relevant official or officials in the executive branch agency who control policy over the area of one's concern provides a much more efficient way of pursuing one's goals than does lobbying or aiding this or that political party or launching organizations that pressure the legislature. A superpresidential system therefore encourages the formation of small, closed, compact societal organizations that are adept at currying favor with individuals in ministries and other executive-branch agencies. Such groups, in the form of highly personalistic, well-endowed cliques representing business and financial interests, constituted the growth area in the political-societal realm in Russia during the 1990s. They, much more than political parties, interest groups (in the traditional meaning of this term), professional associations, trade unions, or social movement organizations, have defined the character and complexion of post-Soviet Russian political society. Other factors, including the type of privatization carried out in Russia, also contributed to the emergence of the peculiar type of political society found in Russia at the outset of the 2000s. But this form of political society bears an affinity with superpresidentialism, and it is particularly likely to emerge under such a regime.

In sum, superpresidentialism's promises—a stronger state, more economic reform, a regime consonant with existing political culture, weaker extremists and stronger liberals—all turn out upon inspection to find little or no support in real-world experience. On the other hand, superpresidentialism's pernicious effects—on regime legitimacy, on the accountability of officialdom, and on the development of political society—are found in spades in actual practice. While many economists and other social scientists, politicians, and ordinary citizens will undoubtedly continue to tout the indispensability of "strong," highly concentrated executive power, their arguments should now be seen for what they are—baseless apologies for a regime whose only effect can be perpetuation of political underdevelopment and decline.

Notes

1. The generalizations offered in this section are based largely on personal observation and conversations with relevant actors carried out during field research in Russia between 1990 and 1993.

2. Stephen Holmes, "What Russia Teaches Us Now," *American Prospect* 33 (July-August 1997): 30–39; M. Steven Fish, "The Roots of and Remedies for Russia's Racket Economy," in Stephen S. Cohen, Andrew Schwartz, and John Zysman, eds., *The Tunnel at the End of the Light: Privatization, Business Networks, and Economic Transformation in Russia* (Berkeley: University of California International and Area Studies, 1998): 86–137; Kathryn Stoner-Weiss, "The Russian Central State in Crisis: Center and Periphery in the Post-Soviet Era" (unpublished ms., 1999); Anatol Lieven, *Chechnya: Tombstone of Russian Power* (New Haven: Yale University Press, 1998).

3. On Yeltsin's consistently destructive posture on institution-building, see George W. Breslauer, "Evaluating Yeltsin as Leader" (unpublished ms., 1999).

4. A sophisticated, qualified version of this argument is found in Stephan Haggard and Robert R. Kaufman, *The Political Economy of Democratic Transitions* (Princeton: Princeton University Press, 1995): 163–165, 336–338, 348–355.

5. M. Steven Fish, "The Determinants of Economic Reform in the Post-Communist World," *East European Politics and Societies*, vol. 12, no. 1 (Winter 1998): 31–78; Fish, "The Roots of and Remedies for Russia's Racket Economy."

6. See, for example, Dmitry Mikheyev, *Russia Transformed* (Indianapolis: Hudson Institute, 1996): 182–221.

7. Remarks of Victor Zaslavsky at the Carnegie Conference on Russia on the Eve of the 21st Century, May 14, 1999, University of California, Berkeley; Vladimir Brovkin, "The Emperor's New Clothes: Continuity of Soviet Political Culture in Contemporary Russia," *Problems of Post-Communism*, vol. 43, no. 2 (March-April 1996): 21–28.

8. "Primakov Beaten Out by Brezhnev, Andropov," *Radio Free Europe/Radio Liberty Daily Report* (September 13, 1999).

9. See Andrew A. Michta, "Democratic Consolidation in Poland after 1989," in Karen Dawisha and Bruce Parrott, eds., *The Consolidation of Democracy in East-Central Europe* (Cambridge: Cambridge University Press, 1997): 66–108; Martha Brill Olcott, "Kazakstan: Nursultan Nazarbaev as Strong President," in Ray Taras, ed., *Postcommunist Presidents* (Cambridge: Cambridge University Press, 1997): 106–129.

10. Such an argument is offered in, for example, Mikheyev, *Russia Transformed*, 76–111.

11. See Yitzhak M. Brudny, "Ruslan Khasbulatov, Aleksandr Rutskoi, and Intraelite Conflict in Postcommunist Russia, 1991–1994," in Timothy J. Colton and Robert C. Tucker, eds., *Patterns in Post-Soviet Leadership* (Boulder, Colo.: Westview, 1995): 84–87.

12. For prescient ruminations on this point, see Timothy J. Colton, "From the Parliamentary to the Presidential Election: Russians Get Real About Politics," *Demokratizatsiya*, vol. 4, no. 3 (Summer 1996): 371–379.

13. Richard Rose, "Postcommunism and the Problem of Trust," in Larry Diamond and Marc F. Plattner, eds., *The Global Resurgence of Democracy*, 2nd ed. (Baltimore: Johns Hopkins University Press): 251–263; Fish, "The Roots of and Remedies for Russia's Racket Economy"; Veljko Vujacic, "Gennadiy Zyuganov and the 'Third Road,'" *Post-Soviet Affairs*, vol. 12, no. 2 (1996): 118–154; Gennadii Ziuganov, *Za gorizontom* (Orel: Veshnie vody, 1995).

14. See Boris Yeltsin, *The Struggle for Russia* (New York: Times Books, 1995): 126.

15. For an acute analysis of this problem that includes a remarkably accurate prediction, see Edward W. Walker, "Politics of Blame and Presidential Powers in Russia's New Constitution," *East European Constitutional Review* 2/3, 4/1 (Fall 1993/Winter 1994): 118–119.

16. "The Transparency International 1998 Corruption Perceptions Index" at <http://www.transparency.de/documents/cpi/index.html>.

17. Marc Morjé Howard, "Demobilized Societies: Understanding the Weakness of Civil Society in Post-Communist Europe" (Ph.D. dissertation, University of California, Berkeley, 1999).

18. M. Steven Fish, *Democracy from Scratch: Opposition and Regime in the New Russian Revolution* (Princeton: Princeton University Press, 1995).

9

Russian Courts:
Enforcing the Rule of Law?

PAMELA JORDAN

In the Soviet period, instead of establishing a set of laws as the legal foundation of society, leaders continually remade the rules in response to their changing interests. Many average citizens saw law as something to be circumvented. They were more attuned to appealing to certain key personalities of the moment—local administrators or Party officials, for example—instead of to the courts. By rejecting this mind-set, legal reformers in post-Soviet Russia demonstrated that they have envisioned a rule of law based on judicial independence, procedural regularity and fairness, and universal adherence. But, years after the USSR's fall, are Russia's courts adequately fulfilling their reform mandates, from reinforcing a separation of powers system to strengthening civil rights and liberties?

Reform in Russia, as in any country, is a developmental—and not always linear—process. Since the late Gorbachev period, Russian judicial reformers have confronted a series of problems that have obstructed the implementation of both structural and substantive reforms. These include a number of Soviet legacies, prevailing antireform attitudes among state officials and the population, the state's lack of legitimacy and material resources, and center-periphery conflicts. This chapter will outline how there has been progress in some quarters of judicial reform and back-pedaling in others. In the long run, what will determine the success of reform measures will not be the precise wording of laws or increased assistance from the West, so much as the extent to which a legal culture evolves once the older generations with their conservative attitudes exit the stage.

Overview of the Judicial System and Reforms:
The Soviet Versus Post-Soviet Eras

In the Soviet period, no court possessed powers of judicial review, which would have enabled the courts to rule acts and laws of the other two branches of power and lower levels of government as unconstitutional. Instead, judges acted as civil servants who applied various kinds of laws and governmental and Communist Party enactments in their daily proceedings. Judges lacked their own autonomous organizations, were underpaid, and were often not well educated; many received their credentials from correspondence law schools. The courts were not a separate branch of power; they were supervised and administered by the Ministry of Justice (*Miniust*) and its regional offices. Courts and judges were dependent on local officials for various resources, including facilities and housing. In some instances, labeled telephone law, members of local Party organs advised judges on how to rule on politically sensitive cases.

The structure of the Soviet court system was unitary. The USSR Supreme Court was situated at the top of the hierarchy of "courts of general jurisdiction," or ordinary courts, as the highest appeals court, and it also issued instructions to the lower courts. Next were the republican-level Supreme Courts. Below these stood the regional (*oblast*) and territorial (*krai*) courts, which heard a mixture of appeals and first-instance cases. The regional courts impaneled one judge and two court assessors, or two judges. At the district level, the so-called people's courts sat at the bottom and heard only first-instance cases, with one judge and two assessors presiding. People's court judges were popularly elected in single-candidate elections for five-year terms, while the judges on the higher courts were appointed by the legislature (*sovet*) on their same level. In addition, for minor infractions, comrades' courts operated in workplaces and housing units; and arbitration tribunals settled disputes between suppliers in the command economy.

Soviet criminal procedure was strongly inquisitorial; the judge acted as a partner with the procurator's office and generally did not rule in favor of the defendant.[1] The USSR Constitution of 1977 made several provisions for civil liberties, but those it guaranteed in name were seldom observed in reality. Civil law existed to resolve private and organizational disputes, as well as to teach Soviet citizens lessons about socialist legality and to protect the social and state system from unintended influences. Many civil and arbitration disputes, however, were settled outside the courts, in local administrative offices, ministries, procurators' offices, and state enterprises.

The Russian Federation (RF) Constitution, adopted in December 1993, is deemed as the highest source of law, followed by legislative law, and then administrative law created by executive agencies. The Constitution set general guidelines on individual rights, the basic structure of the political system, and center-periphery relations. In theory, new constitutional stipulations about rights set post-Soviet legal thinking significantly apart from Soviet thinking. But the fact that Russia has a constitution does not resolve the conflicts inherent in its complex legal system. The legal system continues to be congested by various types of contradicting laws and other types of legal pronouncements, including court rulings; this congestion has detracted from the legitimacy of legal institutions and their capacity to support procedural regularity and fairness. Reformers have confronted a weak—some argue, collapsing—state that lacks the capacity, money, and legitimacy to enforce its laws. For example, the breakaway republic of Chechnya adopted Islamic *Shari'a* law as the supreme law, and summary executions have been carried out in public squares; these practices violate federal constitutional provisions.

The Constitutional Court and
Its Role in the Separation of Powers

The Russian judiciary is conceptualized in the Constitution as a separate branch of power. Most interestingly, judicial practice is beginning to be acknowledged as a source of law in itself, as courts fill gaps in regulation.[2] These developments include the new ability of courts to hear individual appeals concerning the actions and decisions of state agencies and officials and judicial review.

But many judges are still not being paid regularly, the conditions of most courts remain substandard, judges rely on local officials for some of their benefits, and jurisdictional questions still lie unresolved; judges themselves admit that their independence is tentative. Moreover, the court system is divided into three hierarchies: first, the courts of general jurisdiction with the RF Supreme Court on top, which include supreme courts of the republics, territory and regional courts, courts of the cities of Moscow and St. Petersburg, courts of the autonomous regions and autonomous national areas, district courts, and military tribunals and other specialized courts; second, the RF Constitutional Court; and finally the arbitration court system.[3] While not dissimilar to the German model, this system may jeopardize the political authority of the judiciary because of its complexity and its overlapping jurisdictions.[4] This chapter will concentrate on the first two hierarchies.

The fifteen-member Constitutional Court, theoretically the court with the most leverage, was created in 1991 by the Russian government, then still part of the USSR, to ensure that the laws and decrees of the other two branches observe constitutional principles.[5] The Constitutional Court initially held exclusive power of judicial review. In fact, the Court declared acts of both the legislative and executive branches unconstitutional in seven of its first nine cases.[6] But the Court, under the chairmanship of Valerii Zorkin, became politicized; a majority of its members turned against Yeltsin and openly sided with Parliament. Yeltsin dissolved the Court in October 1993, after it ruled his decree to disband the Russian parliament unconstitutional. It would not be reconstituted until February 1995; this delay—caused by the drafting of a new law on the Court and controversies over the appointments of six new justices—jeopardized the Court's legitimacy.

The 1993 Constitution and the 1994 RF "Law on the Constitutional Court," largely drafted by the justices themselves, changed certain parameters of the original Court. For example, the Constitutional Court's size was increased to nineteen justices, to be nominated by the president and appointed by the Federation Council, the upper house of the new parliament. A term in office was limited to twelve years or until a justice turns seventy years of age. Most importantly, the framers of the Constitution and the 1994 law sought to prevent the Court from again becoming politicized. The Constitution eliminated the Court's earlier ability to initiate cases on its own and issue advisory opinions. Only through the petitions of the appropriate official bodies can the Court review various types of legislative acts, including federal laws, acts of the president, the republican constitutions, special treaties signed by the national government and federal subjects, and international treaties.[7] It also restricted the access of elected officials to the Court; for a petition from the Duma to be accepted, at least one-fifth of the Duma membership must sign on.

The 1994 law denied the Court the power to make determinations related to the impeachment of high officials, weakened the chairman's powers, and narrowed the scope of the Court's jurisdiction. The Constitutional Court no longer may initiate a review of the constitutionality of the government's actions in implementing laws and treaties; this power was transferred to the courts of general jurisdiction. It now accepts individuals' appeals only on the basis of an inquiry on the constitutionality of legislation pertinent to a particular case from an ordinary or an arbitration court. In addition, individuals and ordinary courts no longer may petition the Constitutional Court to perform abstract review (i.e., not arising from concrete litigation) of the legality of presidential and governmental acts.[8] On the other hand, the Court's authority was enhanced in some ways. For example, the 1994 law granted the Constitutional Court the exclusive right of abstract review over acts of the RF president and government, as initiated by specific parties, including one-fifth of the members of either house of the Federal Assembly, the RF Supreme and High Arbitration Courts, and the bodies of legislative and executive power of the eighty-nine subjects. Moreover, the Court's decisions cannot be appealed and, in theory, any act that is found unconstitutional must lose force immediately.

Whereas, in its initial form, the Constitutional Court was more activist in its interpretation of laws, in its present form, the Court has adopted a more civil-law reliance on statutes (e.g., strict constructionism). As a consequence, it has sometimes been criticized by legal reformers, as well as members of the Federal Assembly, for sympathizing with executive authorities. Critics point to the way that the Court ruled largely in favor of Yeltsin and the RF government in the 1995 Chechnya case. In this case, both the State Duma and the Federation Council challenged the constitutionality of several presidential and governmental enactments that initiated Russia's civil war in Chechnya in 1994. Yet it appears that the Court was attempting to maintain its strict constructionist approach—in basing its decision on a constitutional stipulation that the president must uphold the country's territorial integrity—rather than to serve Yeltsin himself. Western scholars have criticized the Court for ignoring certain laws that could have been used as a basis for finding more decrees illegal and for not championing human rights.[9] But the Court does not rule in favor of human rights without a solid statutory basis. For example, in July 1998, it rejected a journalist's petition concerning how she was kept under surveillance and detained without explanation by local Ministry of Internal Affairs (MVD) officials in Volgograd and requesting that the Court rescind portions of the law on undercover investigative work.[10]

In certain areas of the law, including freedom of movement, Constitutional Court justices have typically ruled against executive agencies, particularly local organs. The Court, for example, has consistently found unconstitutional acts issued by Moscow authorities and local officials elsewhere that had strengthened the residence permit (*propiska*) regime to the detriment of the constitutional freedom of movement and right to housing.[11] Soviet citizens were required to obtain residence permits before moving to a new city or even neighborhood. After 1991, residence permits have been used in cities such as Moscow to prevent non-Russian ethnics, particularly migrants from the Caucasus, from relocating there. The Constitutional Court ruled in a case brought by a citizen in Astrakhan in 1995 that the absence of a *propiska* in itself cannot serve as a basis for refusing someone housing. Unfortunately, the capacity of the Constitutional Court to enforce rulings in this area has been low. The Court, unlike the ordinary courts, lacks organs of enforcement and thus must rely on the other branches—namely the RF president—for implementing its decisions. Yeltsin, however, did not intervene to enforce the *propiska* rulings.

In sum, the Constitutional Court has acted in significant ways to check the power of the two other federal branches; it has also found unconstitutional laws and enactments of Russia's regional governments. But, due to a number of factors—its losing a good deal of its legitimacy after being disbanded in 1993, its reputation for siding with Yeltsin, and the curbing of some of its original powers—the Court has lacked the authority to enforce many of its rulings.

The RF Supreme Court and the Question of Diffusion

One added obstacle to establishing procedural regularity in the legal system has been the rivalry between the RF Constitutional Court and RF Supreme Court. As defined in the Constitution, the Supreme Court is the highest tribunal for civil, criminal, administrative, or other cases heard in the courts of general jurisdiction. Divided into *collegia* for civil cases, criminal cases, and military cases, it supervises the activities of the lower courts. The Court's powerful Presidium may review by way of supervision any lower court's rulings. In addition, the Supreme Court justices provide clarification, or explanations and interpretations of the written law, on issues of judicial procedure, and in a sense they act as a source of law and a tool for maintaining uniformity in court decisionmaking.[12] The Court sometimes hears first-instance cases; these include challenges to laws or to acts of state bodies, as well as disputes between two regional governments.

Supreme Court justices have influenced the development of a post-Soviet diffused model of constitutional control of legislation, with the aim of decentralizing control over judicial decisionmaking.[13] In October 1995, the Supreme Court issued an explanation directing the lower courts to consider, in relevant cases, the constitutionality of laws and various other legal enactments. In so doing, it narrowed the Constitutional Court's exclusive jurisdiction in that area. However, in practice typically this meant that ordinary courts did not annul a law outright, but just refused to apply it.[14] For instance, some lower courts chose not to observe the existing regulations on compulsory military conscription by ruling in favor of conscientious objectors who asserted their constitutional right of alternative service. In addition, the Supreme Court ruled that essentially all courts could exercise the same authority in reviewing the constitutionality of subjects' legal enactments.

There are both potential benefits of and problems with this diffused system of judicial review. Potential benefits include making the adjudication process speedier and accessible, having a system of enforcement already in place in the lower courts, and finding more pre-1993 legislation obsolete. The problems with diffusion center on redundancy of function between the ordinary courts and the Constitutional Court.[15] What has typically resulted is confusion and an opportunity for the Supreme Court to assert its jurisdiction vis-à-vis the Constitutional Court. For example, the Supreme Court examined decisions from lower courts concerning subnational electoral laws, despite the fact that the Constitutional Court had already ruled that regional legislation could establish schedules for subnational elections.

In a June 16, 1998, ruling, the Constitutional Court prohibited all courts except itself from deciding on the constitutionality of federal laws or laws issued by any of Russia's eighty-nine territorial subjects. The Court also prohibited all other courts from reviewing complaints about enactments issued by the president, the RF government and any subnational organs of power that conflict with federal laws. Now, in instances when laws and enactments contradict the Constitution, lower courts are obligated both to apply the Constitution and request that the Constitutional Court review the case. Critics are concerned that the decision prohibits courts from scrutinizing certain types of laws and administrative regulations of subnational governments and will deter citizens from filing complaints concerning the constitutionality of legal norms on such divisive issues as residence permits, immigration, and freedom of religion.[16] But it is still too early to conclude whether this ruling will work as intended, to centralize the court system and strengthen the authority of the Constitutional Court to check the other two branches of power.

The Courts of General Jurisdiction and Judicial Independence

Structural Reform

In the late 1980s, Gorbachev's regime aimed for courts to become more independent from local governmental and Communist Party bodies. In 1989, the USSR Supreme Soviet adopted the "Law on the Status of Judges," which expanded a judge's tenure from five to ten years. It also stipulated that the legislative body at the next higher territorial level select trial judges. This procedure was initiated to prevent judges from becoming dependent on the same local officials for appointment and benefits. The 1989 law created judicial qualifications panels staffed and chosen by judges themselves, although there is some evidence that local Party officials may have influenced their composition.[17]

While the Gorbachev reforms may have improved the status of lower court judges somewhat, they did not eliminate their dependence on justice officials or their direct superiors in the courts.[18] It is also important to point out that, unlike what occurred in other former Soviet-bloc countries, such as the Czech Republic and East Germany, in Russia there was

no retributive purging of Soviet-era officials, including judges and procurators. Many of the same law-enforcement officials and judges who
worked under "socialist legality" now serve the new laws that are an-
chored in democratic and capitalistic principles. This policy may be in-
hibiting the courts from acting as stronger protectors of human rights
and due process.

To present Russian legal reformers, what is meant by an independent
judiciary is that few de facto external constraints should remain on individual decisionmaking. In tangible terms, this means that courts themselves should have administrative control, judges should devise their
own qualifications and disciplinary policies, and all judges should be
awarded higher salaries and more benefits. The first two legal documents
that outlined the new judiciary were the 1992 "Law on the Status of
Judges" and the 1993 RF Constitution. The June 1992 RF law on judges
and its subsequent amendments were meant to fulfill these goals of judicial independence and professionalization. The 1992 law establishes a
fair salary scale, a generous benefits package, and lifetime tenure after
serving a five-year probationary period; and it asserts that judges are
subordinate only to the law. In addition, it grants judges the power to
find people in contempt of court and, to underscore their impartiality,
prohibits judges from joining political parties.[19] The Constitution stresses
that judges are now required to have higher legal education, cannot be
removed for political reasons, and are immune from prosecution. It also
requires courts to be financed exclusively by the federal budget.

The "Law on the Court System of the Russian Federation," signed by
Yeltsin on December 31, 1996, was meant to fill in the various gaps remaining in the Constitution, as well as the 1992 law. In fact, it did not resolve all jurisdictional or organizational issues. The law asserts that all
sitting judges are a part of a unified federal court system, thus asserting
federal supremacy.[20] In promoting judicial independence, the law removed from *Miniust* the right to administer the courts of general jurisdiction and transferred it to new court-operated judicial departments.

These laws have granted judges the right to form autonomous organizations, the Council of Judges of Russia, the All-Russian Congress of
Judges, and the judicial qualification commissions. The Council of Judges
is now permitted to participate in budgetary proceedings. Judicial qualification commissions, composed of senior judges, administer entrance
exams to candidates, help nominate judges to the bench, and discipline
and remove judges. Reformers hope that judicial qualification commissions will offset executive and legislative power in the appointment
process. There is some evidence, though, that the judicial qualification
commissions have harbored more conservative elements. In August 1998,
a young, pro-reform judge on the Moscow City Court, Sergei Pashin, was

removed by the judicial qualification commission in Moscow, as well as the national judicial qualification commission, on the grounds that he had violated procedural etiquette by postponing the proceedings of a criminal case in order to attend a conference. Pashin filed a complaint with the Supreme Court, claiming that the grounds for his dismissal were unsubstantiated; in September 1998, the Court overturned the two decisions, arguing that Pashin's actions did not shame the honor and dignity of the bench.[21] Therefore, judges who fall prey to powerful conservative forces at least can be protected by grievance regulations.

Two other innovations in the 1996 law are the creation of the justice of the peace courts and constitutional and charter courts. Modeled on a tsarist-era version, justice of the peace courts are expected to relieve district courts of almost 60 percent of their caseload, which consists of hearing over 90 percent of all criminal and civil cases. They will handle lower-level cases, including misdemeanors, administrative transgressions, and civil cases mainly related to family law. The 12,000 justices of the peace will be elected on the local level for five-year terms and will not be required to be jurists. The 1996 law on the court system also permits the eighty-nine federal subjects to establish and fully finance their own constitutional courts for the twenty-one republics, or charter courts for the remaining territories. These courts have exclusive powers to review the consistency of local legal norms with the fundamental law of a particular subject. For the time being, most judges on these courts are treating the federal Constitution as the supreme law and respecting the hierarchy of the federal courts system.

In civil law cases, judges have been granted the right to issue orders compelling losing parties to comply with court decisions; in certain instances, judges now can rule in camera, in the absence of one or both parties.[22] But the boldest court innovation has been the reintroduction of jury trials for criminal cases in 1993. They are often referred to by more conservative jurists as an experiment, even though jury trials are stipulated for in the Constitution. In courts with jury trials, twelve jurors are impaneled to decide questions of fact.[23] Initially, jury trials were introduced in five *oblast* courts: Moscow, Riazan', Ivanovo, Saratov, and Stavropol'.[24] As of 1998, jury trials had expanded only to nine regions and covered no more than 23 percent of the country's population.

The prerevolutionary Russian jury trial system has acted as more of a model for the post-Soviet jury trial system than Western jury trial systems have. Changes and amendments to the RSFSR Criminal Procedure Code (UPK) pursuant to jury trials have strengthened the meaning of the adversarial principle, the presumption of innocence, the privilege against self-incrimination, and the exclusion of evidence under circumstances of procedural violations.[25] Jurors are compensated a fair amount, which has pleased them but overtaxed courts. The RSFSR UPK mandates that the judge's role is to reflect a neutral stance; in the Soviet period, judges sometimes gathered incriminating evidence to bolster investigative reports and acted as inquisitors at trial. In 1998, the average acquittal rate in jury trials was approximately 25 percent, while that in regular criminal trials averaged between 0.5 and 0.7 percent.[26]

Despite such encouraging trends, no consensus on jury trials has been reached. Complaining of lack of funding, the Procuracy and law enforcement officials have called for their curtailment, while a recent Constitutional Court ruling strengthened the justification for jury trials. On February 2, 1999, the Court ruled that a death sentence could not be carried out unless the prisoner had been convicted by a jury. The main problem, however, is that eighty regions have not yet instituted juries; moreover, in order to maintain membership in the Council of Europe, Russia must abolish the death penalty.

Reformers are concerned that the new laws will not remedy certain problems. For one, shortages of judges plague many courts. In 1997, there were 15,564 sitting judges in the courts of general jurisdiction, although approximately 8 percent of positions were vacant.[27] In some areas, courts have closed.[28] Shortages are partly due to the fact that judges and courts themselves have been underfunded or do not receive any federal funds—despite the fact that, in 1997, the government made courts a protected category in the federal budget.[29] In some parts of Russia, judges have struck over lack of financial support. Most courts remain without adequate staffing and technical support. Lacking funds to afford their own housing, judges have remained dependent on regional and federal officials for such non-salaried perks. Several subnational governments—and even private businesses—have funded the courts just to keep them operating. The implications are serious: Average Russians will view private funding as organized crime's way of holding the courts captive and local government funding as a way for subnational officials to bribe judges. On occasion, judges have reported that they have received calls from local Duma deputies who urged them to rule a certain way.[30] Meanwhile, inside courts, court chairmen have exerted a great deal of control over rank-and-file judges and are responsible for providing their benefits. The Soviet-era practice of basing a judge's performance evaluation on how many of his or her rulings have been overturned is still in use; this method discourages judges from exercising their own professional judgment, for fear of placing their careers in jeopardy. But perhaps the most disturbing aspects of working on the bench today are the occasional murders of judges and bomb threats in courthouses. Judges may now carry firearms. It is not surprising, then, that the position is still not a highly desirable one.

Another major concern about the judicial system that legal reformers have raised is compliance problems in civil cases. The judicial enforcers, an office that in the Soviet period was supervised by the courts of general jurisdiction, were unarmed, without material resources, and overworked. They collected on civil judgments and carried out evictions. In the mid-1990s, only around 50 percent of court decisions related to property suits were being enforced.[31] In 1997, a federal law on bailiff-guards and bailiff-enforcers was adopted. While the bailiffs largely service the courts, the bailiff-enforcers are involved in executing civil, arbitration, and administrative decisions chiefly at the district level and are supervised by *Miniust*. For now, more regulations governing the bailiff institution still need to be written.

Last, in the long run, the judicial selection process may most inhibit the strengthening of judicial independence. Besides the screening process completed by the judicial qualification commissions, further vetting is carried out by the president, as well as regional legislatures and the Supreme Court and High Arbitration Courts. The president appoints all lower federal judges and nominates justices to the RF Constitutional Court, the RF Supreme Court, and the RF High Arbitration Court. The Federation Council then confirms the president's nominations. For the selection of lower court judges, the legislative body of the region or republic in which a candidate's post is located gives its consent after the candidate receives the approval of the judicial qualification commission and before his or her application is submitted to the president. Legal reformers fear that judges seeking promotion will undergo unfair legislative scrutiny. Indeed, officials in some subjects have ignored the law by filling vacancies for regional, city, and district courts themselves.[32]

Substantive Reform

Courts of general jurisdiction have heard many of the same types of cases in the post-Soviet period as in the Soviet period: civil cases involving private disputes over housing and personal property; inheritance disputes and other family law matters; pension law matters; and criminal cases involving typical misdemeanors and felonies. However, the post-Soviet milieu has introduced new categories. In criminal courtrooms, in light of Russia's high crime rates in the 1990s, judges now hear cases involving organized crime groups and contract murders. In civil courtrooms, judges are expected to run objective trials; they are no longer supposed to play an inquisitorial role, although in practice old behaviors have often prevailed and judges have often sided with powerful political and economic interests. For example, in the hundreds of lawsuits brought by federal and local governments or individual officials against journalists for allegedly damaging their honor and reputation, courts usually rule in favor of the state's interests and slap journalists with large fines and sometimes even jail sentences.[33]

On the other hand, judges are deliberating on cases in such new areas as consumer and environmental protection law and citizens' complaints against the malfeasance of officials and state organs. In such cases, judges seem more disposed to rule in favor of the plaintiffs, particularly in citizens' complaints. A law was approved in 1989 and introduced in 1990 that permitted citizens to file complaints against both individual officials and state organs. In 1993, the Supreme Soviet passed an RF version, under which the courts have jurisdiction over appeals concerning all state and local governmental organs, institutions and enterprises, societal associations, and officials themselves. Complaints often concerned such matters as the issuing of hunting licenses, residence permits, and internal passports; the awarding of pensions; and the leasing of land. It appears from initial statistics that many judges have taken the law seriously. In 1991, citizens brought 3,941 complaints to court; in 1995, they brought 34,000 complaints; and in 1997, they brought 80,600. Claimants were winning 70 percent of the time.[34] On the other hand, most complaints are still being brought to the Procuracy and to administrative agencies outside the court system, which are cheaper and more familiar options.

In no other sphere of legislation do the issues of procedural regularity and fairness in the judicial system come into play more than in criminal procedure. By the late Gorbachev era, when significant reforms in criminal procedure began to be adopted, some judges started to accept a stronger adversarial component in their courts, and acquittal rates increased slightly. However, both Gorbachev-era and subsequent reforms have been inadequate and under-implemented.

The Constitution grants the courts supervisory functions over preliminary investigations and other pretrial activities. But judges will not have exclusive jurisdiction over deciding matters of pretrial detention, search and seizure, or surveillance until a new UPK is adopted. Suspects and the accused are incarcerated on average for up to ten months in pretrial detention centers (SIZOs). In the late 1990s, 168 SIZOs that were built to detain only 81,000 people were actually holding 295,000.[35] Many procurators continue to issue sanctions to arrest suspects without fully reviewing whether grounds were sufficient for detaining them. Many detainees have been tortured by investigators, in order to obtain confessions.

In 1992, legal reformers succeeded in adding Articles 220.1 and 220.2—equivalent to the right of habeas corpus—to the RSFSR UPK Criminal Procedure Code that was still in force. The articles grant courts the power to review the legality of arrests authorized by procurators' offices and the extension of the time a suspect or the accused remains under custody. For the time being, much of this supervision is done by procurators.[36] In the mid-1990s, the courts were satisfying under one-fifth of habeas corpus complaints.[37] On a number of occasions, law-enforcement officials and procurators across Russia sabotaged courts' decisions by rearresting detainees. Yet a few courts have asserted their independence. In February 1998, for example, a court in Saransk for the first time in Russia's history convicted police officers of torturing to death a murder suspect.[38]

The most damaging measure taken to limit the use of habeas corpus was Presidential Decree Number 1226, which was in force from June 1994 to June 1997. The decree gave law-enforcement officials wide discretion in fighting organized crime but contradicted stipulations in the UPK. It ensured that suspects could be held for up to thirty days without being charged. The RSFSR UPK calls for a seventy-two hour maximum period of detention without being charged, and the Constitution allows only for a 48-hour window. Yeltsin's rescission of the decree at least indicates that he was swayed by journalists' and human rights activists' criticism. Now, under a 1997 law, law-enforcement agencies are allowed to detain suspects without charge only for up to ten days. But law-enforcement officials can still extend a suspect's stay for up to thirty days by charging him with an administrative infraction.[39]

Another threat to court authority is the Federal Security Service (FSB), a descendant of the Soviet KGB. This agency has been viewed by foreign and Russian observers alike as non-reformed, both in structure and attitude. For three years, the FSB has been central to keeping alive the treason case against former Soviet naval officer Aleksandr Nikitin, who was accused of publishing classified information about the Russian Navy's polluting of waters off the Kola Peninsula in a newsletter of a Norwegian environmental group. Although sufficient evidence was never unearthed, neither the St. Petersburg court hearing the case in October 1998 nor even the RF Supreme Court, in a February 1999 ruling, dismissed it. Instead, they ordered a supplementary investigation, which is a Soviet-era practice that contradicts the constitutional presumption of innocence.

Local officials are also impairing due process, especially in human rights cases. In 1996 and 1997, local authorities arrested and charged at least four human rights activists with libel, contempt of court, making death threats, and statutory rape. The real reason for their arrests likely was to silence their criticism of local authorities. The procurator's offices chose to release some of the activists, only after being pressured by human rights groups.[40] Trials are often delayed, sometimes for months, and as mentioned earlier, judges still sometimes return the case to supplementary investigation, particularly when the procurator has political support or the case involves a political controversy.[41] In the 1998 trial of Krasnodar human rights activist Vasilii Chaikin, the judge rejected a plea for medical assistance and consistently sided with the procurator's office on other matters.[42] However, now individuals who have exhausted all appeals in Russian courts have the right to appeal to the European Court of Human Rights. On February 20, 1998, the Duma ratified the European Convention on Human Rights, which provides for this mechanism. By the late summer, more than 800 complaints had been filed by Russian citizens—an indication that a number of Russians perceive that domestic courts are falling short of protecting human rights.

Conclusion

Many of the new laws on Russia's courts hold some promise that the country is moving toward a system of rules that promote procedural regularity and fairness, long-term stability, and democratic governance. These include, first, the creation of a Constitutional Court and arbitration court system; second, the adoption of measures to strengthen judicial independence, inject more elements of adversarial play without eliminating the inquisitorial approach altogether, and promote compliance with court rulings; and third, some allowance for experimentation on the local levels, such as the formation of constitutional and charter courts. The jurisdiction of Russian courts has expanded greatly in the post-Soviet era. Judges now are deciding cases involving pretrial detention, the misuse of official power, the constitutionality of laws and certain regulations, and commercial disputes. In a 1997 survey of judges, 72.1 percent of respondents considered themselves to be independent, and 51 percent saw themselves as more independent in the post-Soviet period than they had been previously.[43]

Compelling evidence shows that some segments of the population, particularly the young and well educated, may be gaining a stronger respect for the law. Using survey data collected in 1990–1992 and 1995, a group of American social scientists found that those Russian respondents committed to legal procedures tended to be younger, urban, and ethnically non-Russian citizens who desire market reforms.[44] In a survey of legal opinions conducted in 1995 by the Center for Rights Protection in Perm, respondents were divided into eight social groups and were first asked about what kinds of actors had most violated their civil rights.[45] All but one group answered that bureaucrats were the foremost offenders, trailed by salespeople, the police, politicians, tax inspectors, and physicians. In a second question about who most defended their rights, the largest number answered nongovernmental organizations, including consumers and human rights groups; their employers; and private law offices. Even judges fared well on this question. City councils and local administrative offices, as well as trade unions and political parties, fell lowest on the list.

In a 1996 survey conducted by *Itogi* magazine, 1,600 Russians were asked what they thought "order" meant. The results (see Table 9.1) indicate that a majority of Russians prefer not to live under a dictatorship. Most promising for a future rule-of-law society are the responses from those surveyed who found that a strong observation of laws (32 percent) and the opportunity for all citizens to realize their own rights (11 percent) are the factors that determine an orderly country.

While these data offer hope for long-term progress, there are still indications of back-pedaling: Structural and substantive reforms have not been sufficient in cultivating a legal culture in which average citizens respect law and find that it responds to their interests—and in which state officials are subordinate to the law. Many laws that were adopted reflect compromises on the reformers' part and favor the conservative interests of the Procuracy and MVD. Meanwhile, a new criminal procedure code and a statute governing the bar have yet to be adopted. Some evidence points to how average Russians still rely on the old methods of resolving conflicts: the use of *blat* (influence-peddling) and petitioning executive officials for redress. The poor, moreover, feel that they lack access to sound legal advice. What continues to be most reprehensible is the persistence of anti-Semitism and anti-immigrant sentiment throughout Russia, attitudes that hinder the protection of civil rights and thus prevent equality before the law. Legal reform in Russia will be a long developmental process, which in some ways will be distinctly Russian and in other ways will not be unlike the struggles for equality before the law that countries of Western and Eastern Europe were and still are facing.

The judicial branch, arguably the weakest of the three branches of power, has lacked the daily authority and budgets that executive agencies have been awarded. Specific external factors that have negatively influenced court reform include the state's inability to fund courts adequately; the government's failure to nurture democratic and market-supporting institutions; conflicts between the executive and legislative branches; center-periphery problems; the power of crony capitalism in undermining economic and political reform; and organized crime elements, which have exerted a disquieting influence over local officials and economies. Internally, courts are suffering from a dearth of judges and funds; they are burdened by high numbers of ordinary criminal and civil cases, and yet they are underused in some areas, such as that of commercial law. The compliance problem for civil rulings may subside once bailiffs are fully operational, but lack of compliance with federal laws and Constitutional Court rulings on the subject and local levels is

TABLE 9.1   What Does "Order" Mean? (in percentages)

40	Political and economic stability of the country
32	Strong observation of laws
26	Stoppage of power struggles and collapse of the country
23	Stoppage of looting of the country
18	Social defense of the less affluent
15	Strong discipline
11	Opportunity for everyone to realize his or her own rights
6	Use of the army to combat crime
.8	Other
.5	Limitation of democratic rights and freedoms
.3	Dictatorship

SOURCE: "Russkii poriadok," *Itogi* (February 25, 1997): 7.

more insidious. Moreover, the rivalry between the Constitutional Court and the Supreme Court has underscored the problem of redundancy, and the Supreme Court's control over the decisionmaking of lower court judges has hurt judicial independence.

International factors have typically played only a minor role in judicial reform in Russia. Those who have drafted Russian legislation have been most influenced by civil-law approaches. In many countries of the former Soviet bloc, including Russia, laws on the legal system have tended to follow the German approach; some specific laws, like on stock exchange regulations, are based on a French format.[46] In some instances, as was the case with American legal experts who were ignorant of Russian legal practices and advised Russian legislators to adopt American approaches to legislation on trusts, American influences have been ill advised.[47] Moreover, only a minority of legal professionals in Russia have participated in these legal reform seminars, so their impact on legal practice has been minimal.

On the other hand, some programs sponsored by the American Bar Association's Central and East European Law Initiative (CEELI), University of Maryland's IRIS, the British Council, and the EU's TACIS, as well as exchanges between German and Russian Constitutional Court justices, have introduced hundreds of lawyers to new training methods and legislative options. World Bank moneys have funded the operations of the Russian Fund for Legal Reform, which, among its more useful projects, sponsored judicial training programs and supported annual congresses of judges. A sister-state legal reform program, the Vermont-Karelia Rule of Law Project, has offered Russian jurists in Petrozavodsk jointly developed training programs, assistance in operating a legal aid clinic, new communications technologies, joint research projects, and faculty exchanges. It is now acting as an umbrella organization for other American-Russian sister-state and sister-city law programs, including a pairing of Maryland and the Leningrad *oblast*. These programs are geared toward meeting the reform goals of lawyers in particular regions of Russia, allowing for experimentation and autonomy from Moscow bureaucrats. While it is difficult to evaluate the overall effectiveness of this and other joint programs, Russian participants by and large have found their involvement in them to be beneficial.[48]

In sum, Russians are not doomed to repeat the authoritarian patterns of behavior that plagued the Soviet political system. A new incentive structure favoring rule of law may emerge from generational change. Moreover, already Russians are becoming more aware of their rights and how to protect them. Ultimately, then, it is the domestic forces—the courts, politicians and business leaders whose interests are protected by law, and pockets of civil society—not imported forces, that are most likely to free Russia from centuries of arbitrary rule.

Notes

1. The legal system of the former Soviet Union, and of Russia today, is based on the civil, or continental, law tradition. Under it, laws tend to be strictly codified, and the judiciary is responsible for applying them. In addition, criminal procedure is based on an inquisitorial approach, whereby court actors tend to work together in seeking out the truth, beginning in the crucial preliminary investigation. Conversely, under a common-law system, a more adversarial approach is taken in criminal cases, whereby an "objective" court resolves conflicts between two opposing sides.

2. R. Z. Livshits, "Judicial Practice as a Source of Law in Russia," *Sudebnik* 2 (1997): 628–638.

3. The new arbitration courts resolve disputes between legal entities, both state and private. For more on these courts, see Kathryn Hendley, "The Role of Law in the Russian Economic Transition: Coping with the Unexpected in Contractual Relations," *Wisconsin International Law Journal*, vol. 14, no. 3 (1996): 624–650; also Hendley, "Temporal and Regional Patterns of Commercial Litigation in Post-Soviet Russia," *Post-Soviet Geography and Economy*, vol. 39, no. 7 (September 1998): 379–398; and Katharina Pistor, "Supply and Demand for Contract Enforcement in Russia: Courts, Arbitration, and Private Enforcement," *Review of Central and East European Law*, vol. 22, no. 1 (1996): 55–87.

4. Eugene Huskey, "Russian Judicial Reform After Communism," in Peter H. Solomon, Jr., ed., *Reforming Justice in Russia, 1864–1996: Power, Culture, and the Limits of Legal Order* (Armonk, N.Y.: M. E. Sharpe, 1997): 330.

5. The Constitutional Court did have a distant Soviet parallel, the USSR Committee of Constitutional Oversight. A Gorbachev-era creation, the Committee was a twenty-seven-judge panel that acted only as an advisory body on the constitutionality of legislative and executive acts. The Committee lacked the authority of

a high court, although it could declare a law unconstitutional if it violated human rights.

6. Robert Sharlet, "Russian Constitutional Crisis: Law and Politics under Yeltsin," *Post-Soviet Affairs,* vol. 9 (1993): 323.

7. The Russian Federation has eighty-nine territorial units, which are called subjects of the federation.

8. Peter Juviler, *Freedom's Ordeal: The Struggle for Human Rights and Democracy in Post-Soviet States* (Philadelphia, Pa.: University of Pennsylvania, 1998): 154.

9. Jeffrey Waggoner, "Discretion and Valor at the Russian Constitutional Court: Adjudicating the Russian Constitutions in the Civil-Law Tradition," *Indiana International and Comparative Law Review,* vol. 8, no. 1 (1997): 227, 229; Juviler, 156; and William E. Pomeranz, "Judicial Review and the Russian Constitutional Court: The Chechen Case," *Review of Central and East European Law,* vol. 23, no. 1 (1997): 9–48.

10. Maksim Zhukov, "Law on Undercover Investigation Gets Off Lightly," *Kommersant-DAILY* (July 15, 1998): 2; translated in the *Current Digest of the Post-Soviet Press* (hereafter, *CDPSP*), vol. 50, no. 28 (1998): 11.

11. See Antti Korkeakivi, *Justice Delayed: The Russian Constitutional Court and Human Rights* (New York: The Lawyers Committee on Human Rights, 1995); Konstantin Katanian, "The Propiska and the Constitutional Court," *East European Constitutional Review* (Spring 1998): 52–57; Rachel Denber, "Moscow: Open Season, Closed City," *Human Rights Watch Report,* vol. 9:10(D) (September 1997); Chris Panico, "Ethnic Discrimination in Southern Russia," *Human Rights Watch Report,* vol. 10:8(D) (July 1998).

12. Livshits, 635.

13. Peter Krug, "Departure from the Centralized Model: The Russian Supreme Court and Constitutional Control of Legislation," *Virginia Journal of International Law* 37 (1997): 725–787.

14. Peter H. Solomon, Jr., noted this in a phone conversation on February 2, 1999.

15. Krug, 772–776.

16. Konstantin Katanian, "Sam sebe sudia: Konstitutsionnyi sud RF utochnil sobstvennye polnomochiia," *Nezavisimaia gazeta* (June 17, 1998): 3; Dmitri Zharkov, "Proizvol chinovnikov uzakonen Konstitutsionnym sudom Rossii," *Kommersant-DAILY* (June 17, 1998): 2.

17. Gordon B. Smith, *Reforming the Russian Legal System* (Armonk, N.Y.: M. E. Sharpe, 1996): 144.

18. See Todd Foglesong, "The Reform of Criminal Justice and the Evolution of Judicial Dependence in Late Soviet Russia," in Solomon, 282–324.

19. John Reitz, "Progress in Building Institutions for the Rule of Law in Russia and Poland," in Robert D. Grey, ed., *Democratic Theory and Post-Communist Change* (Upper Saddle River, N.J.: Prentice Hall, 1997): 148, 178, n7.

20. William Patrick Murphy, Jr., "The Russian Courts of General Jurisdiction: In Crisis, Undergoing Reform, or Both?" *Parker School Journal of East European Law* 4 (1998): 214–215.

21. For a copy of the opinion in Russian, see <www.supcourt.ru:8000/cyrillic/dl/other/gkpi98-440_15-09-98.htm.>

22. A. M. Zhuikov, *O novellakh v grazhdanskom protsessual'nom prave* (Moscow, 1996): 25–31.

23. People's assessors, the two lay judges who sit alongside a judge in deliberating on some first-instance cases, are still functioning. However, they now seldom hear civil cases and do not hear cases involving minor criminal offenses.

24. The only criminal defendants in these regions who are eligible to opt for jury trials are those charged with terrorist acts, sabotage, banditry, contraband, a number of felonies against the state including state secrets, certain kinds of murders, rape, kidnapping, bribery, and grand theft.

25. Stephen C. Thaman, "The Trial by Jury and the Constitutional Rights of the Accused," *East European Constitutional Review* (Winter 1995): 78.

26. "Zasedanie prodolzhaetsia, gospoda priiazhnye zasedateli?" *Novye izvestiia* (March 11, 1998): 5.

27. "Rabota sudov Ross. Fed. v 1997 g." *Rossiiskaia iustitsiia* 6 (1998): 55–58.

28. Huskey, "Russian Judicial Reform After Communism," 336–337.

29. In early 1998, the federal government attempted to reduce spending on courts by 26 percent. In July 1998, the Constitutional Court found the budget cuts unconstitutional, on the grounds that the federal budget must provide for the "complete and independent" functioning of the judiciary. See the U.S. Department of State's *Russia Report on Human Rights Practice for 1998* on-line at <www.state.gov/www.global/human_rights/1998_hrp_report/russia.html.>

30. Peter H. Solomon, Jr., noted that, in Russia, "deputy law" has replaced telephone law. See James O. Finckenauer, *Russian Youth: Law, Deviance, and the Pursuit of Freedom* (New Brunswick, N.J.: Transaction Publications, 1995): 57.

31. Konstantin Katanian, "Pravosudie ne mozhet byt' deshevym," *Nezavisimaia gazeta* (June 17, 1997): 2.

32. Huskey, "Russian Judicial Reform After Communism," 336.

33. The U.S. Department of State's *Russia Report on Human Rights Practice for 1998.*

34. Peter H. Solomon, Jr., "The Persistence of Judicial Reform in Contemporary Russia," *East European Constitutional Review* (Fall 1997): 51; "Rabota sudov RF v 1997 godu," *Rossiiskaia iustitsiia* 7 (1998): 55–58.

35. Juviler, 151.

36. Igor Petrukhin, "Prokurorskii nadzor i sudebnyi kontrol' za sledstviem," *Rossiiskaia iustitsiia* 9 (1998): 12.

37. Juviler, 149, n13, which lists this source: Valery Abramkin, Rachel Denber, Richard Schimpf, and Clare Hughes, eds., *In Search of a Solution: Crime, Criminal Policy and Prison Facilities in the Former Soviet Union* (Moscow: Center for Prison Reform, 1996): 80.

38. The U.S. Department of State's *Russia Report on Human Rights Practice for 1998.*

39. Anna Feofilaktova and Aleksei Grishin, "But If You Really Want to, You Can Still Put People in Jail for 30 Days," *Segodnia* (June 18, 1997): 1; translation in *CDPSP* (July 16, 1997): 20.

40. The 1998 *Human Rights Watch Russia Report* (covering developments in 1997) can be retrieved at <www.hrw.org/hrw/worldreport/>.

41. The U.S. Department of State's *Russia Report on Human Rights Practice for 1998.*

42. The U.S. Department of State's *Russia Report on Human Rights Practice for 1998.*

43. The survey was written by Peter H. Solomon, Jr., and Todd S. Foglesong and administered between spring and fall of 1997 under the joint auspices of the Institute of Constitutional and Legislative Policy (Budapest) and the Center of Constitutional Research of the Moscow Public Science Foundation. Three-hundred and twenty-one judges throughout Russia completed the survey.

44. William Reisinger, Arthur H. Miller, and Vicki L. Hesli, "Russians and the Legal System: Mass Views and Behaviour in the 1990s," *Journal of Communist Studies and Transition Politics*, vol. 13, no. 3 (September 1997): 24.

45. Juviler, 176; report outlined in *Pravo cheloveka v Rossii: informatsionnyi set'* 11 (1995):14–23.

46. Jenik Radon, "Permitted Unless Prohibited: The Changed Soviet Mentality," *Fordham International Law Journal* 20 (1997): 369.

47. See Radon, 370.

48. I make this assessment based on my own interviews with Russian participants in Western-funded legal reform programs, such as CEELI and the Vermont-Karelia Rule-of-Law Project, as well as on information I have accessed about Russians' reception of other Western-funded legal training programs, such as the U.K.'s Know-How Program.

10

Stability from Without? International Donors and "Good Governance" Strategies in Russia*

CORBIN B. LYDAY

Background: A Failure of Political Institutions

In the seven-plus years that have elapsed since the unexpected collapse of the USSR and the reappearance of the Russian nation-state, international donors and policymakers alike have been compelled to grasp some very difficult lessons about the speed and ease with which postcommunist states could successfully integrate with the larger global political and economic system around them. An early euphoria that swept both Moscow and Washington has been replaced by a sober acknowledgment that the process of integration for all transition states, but Russia in particular, is not only traumatic and fraught with sudden, unexpected reverses, but fiercely resistant to short-term, piecemeal interventions. Unfortunately, the collapse of the ruble in August 1998 only confirmed suspicions by many observers that Russia was becoming, not a successful, mature market democracy, but in fact one of the weakest links in a larger, interdependent global system, one that could easily come undone by externally driven crises.

*The author would like to express gratitude to Keith Henderson of American University, Robert Herman of the State Department's Policy and Planning Bureau, and Daniel Kaufmann of the World Bank Institute for comments and inspiration. The views expressed herein do not necessarily represent official opinions of either the Agency for International Development or the State Department. Errors or omissions are the author's sole responsibility.

Russia's economic crisis, like that which swept across Thailand, South Korea, and other Asian states in 1998, has its roots in the failure of political institutions, even before economic or financial ones. This is an important lesson for many policymakers who, since 1992, have arguably been operating under the assumption that the Soviet totalitarian legacy left Russia with a "weak society" but "strong state." But the partial default of the Russian state in 1998 points to another reality: growing state weakness, even paralysis of certain functions. Measured by nearly any yardstick, whether the ability to provide for the general welfare of its citizens, the common defense of its territory, or the ability to levy taxes, regulate commerce and banking, or provide an orderly framework for federalism to take root, the Russian state is unable to do the things that all states, whether Western or Eastern, democratic or authoritarian, must do. Concurrent with this new state weakness is a society that has lost much of the optimism it suddenly found for itself at the end of the 1980s and the beginning of the 1990s. In effect, Russia is becoming *both* a "weak state and weak society" with little sign of immediate changes ahead. Given the legacy of near absolute totalitarianism under Josef Stalin, this new, postcommunist state weakness and social disorganization is a remarkable phenomenon indeed.[1]

Despite widely divergent histories, peoples, and traditions of statecraft, the current crisis in governance in Russia shares many of the same attributes as that in East Asia. In each place, "crony capitalism"—the political and economic system resulting from a clear failure to create and sustain transparent boundaries between the public and private sectors—is the primary culprit. In Russia, this failure is responsible for the absence of a coherent economic restructuring program (which would necessitate enforced bankruptcies of large Cold War–era industrial concerns that currently produce very little, other than weaponry, that has much relevance to current global and domestic markets). It has undermined judicial independence and respect for the rule of law that must accompany contested elections and freedom of the press and assembly. It has surrendered responsibility for contract dispute resolution to private mafias, and played an instrumental role in permitting vast amounts of unregulated capital to be exported to Switzerland, the Cayman Islands, and obscure islands in the English Channel—almost any place other than where it is most needed. It has invalidated the state's legitimate taxation authority, and failed to intervene to provide long-term incentives for reinvestment at home in anything other than extractive industry. In the private sector, it ultimately prevents, rather than encourages, broad-based, sustainable economic development. In the public sector, it engenders cynicism and civic apathy about "democracy" writ large, just when a new round of civic activism is needed to support the efforts of those courageous journalists, independent entrepreneurs, and political leaders who undergo harassment, extortion, and even death for daring to expose the collusion between the public and private sectors. While social organization remains weak and diffused, the state itself is slowly "bleeding" to death, a victim of the many wounds inflicted on it by those who know that they can take what they wish without fear of accountability. Without meaningful barriers between public and private sector activity, without traditions of effective governance or modern civil service expertise that includes codes of conduct and enforceable sanctions for their violation, and with scant attention to the role of nongovernmental organizations or civil society more broadly, the new Russia is becoming a "captured" state, far removed from public accountability.[2]

This was surely not the view that international donors and policymakers had of Russia at the onset of the postcommunist era. But the past ten years have gone a long way toward undermining some cherished early assumptions that seem inappropriate today. It is now extremely difficult to argue that cronyism is simply the "cost of doing business" in a transition economy. Merely privatizing state assets alone cannot substitute for normal capitalist development; a well-functioning market simply cannot take root without strong, coherent political institutions to help create, organize, and regulate it.[3] This new perspective is vitally important to understanding both what has gone wrong as well gone "right," and how Russian policymakers, with the assistance of international development organizations, can craft more coherent policies and programs for the future.

A Brief Summary of Major Donor Activity

Why are both Western and Russian analysts grappling with these "weak state" issues only ten years after the collapse of a totalitarian government? Is the present state of affairs a direct result of the longer-term collapse of Communist institutions, or did Russia's sudden political twists and turns bring about the very weakness the state is now forced to deal with? Historians, political economists, and policymakers will clearly grapple with these questions for many years to come.[4] While the answers lie far beyond the scope of this chapter, it is worth highlighting some of the major operating assumptions about Russia held by international donors, and how some those assumptions fared in practice.

The International Monetary Fund (IMF)

With regard to the IMF, the principal lending institution both directing and financing most of Russia's economic reforms, the policy prescrip-

tions proposed to the Russian government differed little from those offered to other countries grappling with de-statization issues. Indeed, one
of the mistakes the IMF may have made was to place Russia in the same
category as any other overly statist economy in the developing world. A
standard set of monetary and financial recipes designed to curb hyperinflation, substantially reduce deficit spending, and stabilize the nation's
currency has been advocated in places as diverse as Brazil and Indonesia.
Drastic austerity measures ("structural adjustment"), changes in a country's legal, tax, and bankruptcy codes, and a large panoply of accurate fiscal and monetary data must accompany such policy changes in return for
huge loans to support investment that could not be financed otherwise
through direct bilateral assistance.[5] These programs, devised and elabo-
rated in Washington and host-country capitals, directly affect the wages,
profits, and working lives of millions of people all over the world, and
have immense power for good or ill alike. While the IMF's charter prohibits the fund from becoming involved in a country's domestic politics,
some critics see this as something of an artificial divide, arguing that the
Fund's structural adjustment programs are political by definition and impact, and that the Fund is not sensitive to the need for domestic political
support for the painful austerity measures it recommends.[6]

The World Bank

Much more than its IMF counterpart, the World Bank is heavily involved
in the development side of the financial equation, and its loans are directed specifically toward poverty alleviation, economic development,
and the specific infrastructure needed to sustain it. Nonetheless, the
Bank's loans are often directly tied to the Fund's overall structural adjustment programs, as in the April 1999 announcement of an additional $2.3
billion loan package for Russia, when the Bank's promise of development and social safety net assistance was tied into larger IMF structural
adjustment packages.[7] Both the Bank and the Fund are Washington-
based institutions, and the Fund in particular receives much of its financial support through annual congressional appropriations.[8] Together,
they constitute the backbone of the international economic and financial
order that emerged out of the ashes of the Second World War, as the West
struggled to create new institutions to promote domestic economic
growth and international free trade at Breton-Woods in 1944.

Bilateral Assistance: Nunn-Lugar, the Gore Commission, and USAID

The political shock waves caused by the collapse of the USSR in 1991 led
to the first congressional appropriation of funds for technical assistance

to the countries of the former Soviet Union, Russia in particular, the bulk going to USAID through newly enacted legislation in 1992, the FREE-DOM Support Act. USAID was initially formed as a brainchild of the Truman Administration in 1947 when the White House issued a "democratic manifesto addressed to the peoples of the world," which first proposed the notion that the United States would share its technical expertise with developing countries. President Truman included the concept as the fourth point in a larger foreign policy statement that included support for the United Nations, the European Marshall Plan, and a European security system that would eventually become NATO (the North Atlantic Treaty Organization) two years later. In later years, other bilateral and multilateral government agencies (the Canadian Institute for International Development, the European Union's PHARE and TACIS technical assistance programs in Central Europe and the former Soviet Union, the United Nations Development Program, the Soros Foundation Open Society Institute, and others) would join an increasingly internationalized effort.

By 1993, the Act had funded $2.2 billion in assistance programs to the former USSR, a number that has grown every year subsequently.[9] While these figures appear large, they are somewhat more marginal when contrasted with the larger tranches of direct loans given to the Russian government by the Bank. Another chief distinction is that the overwhelming majority of USAID moneys do not go to the Russian government at any level, but to technical assistance programs (many but not all of them run by Western rather than Russian organizations) designed to support the creation of a market economy and a democracy in Russia.

USAID has not been the only player in this game, however. For several years, in the civil-military field, the United States and Russia have quietly cooperated extensively in nuclear disarmament and the resettling of displaced Russian officers from Eastern Europe—an effort whose funding has actually been increasing in recent years, even as funds for development assistance have been decreasing. Named "Nunn-Lugar" for the two senators who conceived of the idea, this particular aspect of the bilateral assistance program has been one of the most creative and unfortunately less publicized aspects of the new cold "peace" between the superpowers after the collapse of the USSR. Similarly, the ongoing Vice-Presidential–Prime Ministerial Commissions, organized jointly by the State Department and the Foreign Ministry, have managed to meet regularly (despite several new Russian prime ministers), bringing together Russian and U.S. government counterparts in an interagency setting to hammer out agreements on complex issues requiring cooperation, from safeguarding marine environments to Russian urban water purification, business development, and law enforcement issues. Other agencies, from the Departments of the Treasury, Energy, Commerce, and Justice to the FBI and the Drug Enforcement Agency, have also been working quietly with their Russian counterparts on various technical assistance programs in related areas.

Compared to the IMF's macroeconomic stabilization programs, the original impetus behind USAID's assistance program was largely political, and its programs were designed not simply to buttress the IMF's and Bank's overall structural and developmental goals, but also to alter Russia's political and social environment by helping to create and sustain the necessary political and social institutions that were considered to be part of a modern democracy. Whether these programs were originally motivated by well thought out strategies, either by Congress or the Bush and Clinton Administrations, is certainly debatable. The reality is that few American policymakers knew very much about the Soviet Union more broadly, even less about the kinds of specific strategies and sequences needed to transform it rapidly. Strangely enough, however, USAID was initially discouraged by the State Department from adopting a specific strategy in the early days of the program when a "Newly Independent States (NIS) Task Force" was virtually ordered to spend millions of dollars on both solicited and unsolicited proposals to the Agency for development work in Russia and elsewhere.[10] But by 1994, AID had created a Program Coordination and Strategy Office, and used its special authority granted by Congress to go outside the foreign and government service career structure to hire specialists with strong Russian and post-Soviet, or specific developmental, backgrounds. A special coordinator for NIS assistance with ambassadorial rank was appointed in the State Department to report directly to the secretary and oversee the growing alphabet soup of federal agencies increasingly involved in technical assistance programs in the region.

The most well known of USAID's programs was the technical support given to the privatization process conducted by *Goskomimushchestvo* (GKI), the Russian state privatization organization, which did privatize 80,000 small businesses and 14,000 medium and large enterprises by 1995. Over time, a capital market (stocks and securities) and the formal infrastructure necessary to regulate it were also created. In the political and social sphere, USAID embarked on a much wider array of technical assistance programs not directly linked to its economic assistance programs. Supporting political party development, building civil society (including training independent trade union leaders and journalists), the regularization of contested election procedures, the promotion of energy conservation, direct grants to nongovernmental organizations, environmental protection, and judicial strengthening, training, and development have been some of the major highlights of noneconomic programs that distinguish USAID's approach from that of some other donors.[11]

A Summary of Some Lessons Learned

Like large, cumbersome bureaucracies everywhere, donor institutions are slow to embark on complicated strategies, and arguably slower still to adapt to lessons learned through corrective strategic responses. With regard to USAID, the idea that nearly $1.6 billion (the original allocation of funds through the FREEDOM Support Act) would be spent without a carefully detailed, methodical strategy for assistance might strike many as inconceivable. In that sense, it is fair to argue that the initial U.S. response to the Soviet collapse was almost as poorly thought out as the collapse itself. (Indeed, one of the more intriguing ironies of the past decade is that both parties to the Cold War were caught completely off guard by its end, never having seriously contemplated the day when another set of global circumstances might prevail.) And the IMF's experience in other countries, many of the same critics have pointed out, hardly prepared it for the unique combination of economic misdevelopment and centralized political administration that was the hallmark of the Soviet era. What is less often stated, however, is that the Soviet Union's own penchant for extreme secrecy for more than half a century was very effective in preventing outsiders as well as its own citizens from knowing much about it.

Capitalism Without a Human Face

Nevertheless, what most donors probably believed at the beginning of the 1990s was that once the basic institutions of a market had been created, the regulatory mechanisms needed to sustain it would gradually take root on their own. But this assumption arguably skipped over much of the laborious, dirty history of Western countries themselves as they gradually replaced an unfettered, savage capitalism with mechanisms for ensuring *both* economic growth as well as strong social safety nets. There were also few opportunities to transfer all this accumulated experience in just ten years in Russia, no matter how strategically well designed or expertly proffered the technical advice was. Furthermore, the uniquely "Soviet" type of development that transpired in this part of the world strongly predisposed the eventual emergence of a private market toward high levels of corruption and mismanagement. Both of these are important facts that some critics of Western technical assistance have failed to take into account.

Furthermore, this inhospitable environment for genuine reform met up with technical assistance programs that were also fashioned with the need to ensure U.S. domestic political support at a time of extreme budget-cutting in foreign affairs more generally. Goals of simpler, more manageable "quick fix" programs were frequently (and perhaps unavoidably) at odds with the longer, institutionally driven needs of the new Russia.

Finally, the array of programs was accepted, when applicable, by a small group of Russian political elites who took little interest in social safety net issues, the degree of parliamentary budget expertise, or the need to maintain tight boundaries between the public and private sectors. Indeed, many in that elite had personal reasons to oppose stronger legislation separating the two sectors. The same elite has also thought comparatively little about the development of mature political institutions, both horizontal (executive, judicial, and legislative branches of power) and vertical (federal, regional, and municipal authority), and even less about the urgency of forgoing some current short-term profits for creating a new postcommunist social safety net. Indeed, the absence of a human face to support the new capitalism means that Russia has very nearly succeeded in creating a caricature of capitalism in its own country that would simply pass unrecognized in any other contemporary Western European or North American state.

An extreme view of the above would fault Russia alone for what has happened, and some, such as Harvard Institute for International Development's Jeffrey Sachs, once one of the Russian government's most well known advisers, has made this argument, claiming that the programs recommended to Russia were basically sound, but that the Russians "got it wrong," ignoring critically necessary components that eventually caused them to fail.[12] Whether this viewpoint is ultimately too harsh, releasing the West from too many of its own obligations, will be disputed for years to come. But the failure of Russian political elites to pursue genuine structural reforms (such as enacting and enforcing private property, banking, regulations, bankruptcy, and coherent tax legislation) has certainly affected every loan, grant, and technical assistance program, whether from USAID, the World Bank, or other donors.

An Absence of Political Consensus

A critically important reason why Russia's power elite has not held longer-term visions for the new state and society is a stark absence of political consensus about historical events since 1991. On one extreme, former Finance Minister Anatoly Chubais, former Prime Minister Yegor Gaidar, and others in a tiny clique of Westernized advisers who carried out drastic economic shifts in policy did so without the kind of political consensus that their counterparts in Poland, Hungary, and the Czech Republic both pursued, and received, from their own populations. Thus, Russian popular support for these kinds of "shock therapies" has always hovered around 10–15 percent, rarely greater, often considerably less, and weakening over time. On the other extreme can be found the rising chorus of "national-patriotic" political forces angry about Soviet collapse and Russia's increasing weakness in the international arena, searching for nearly any external justification for their own isolation from larger geopolitical currents. In the middle stands most of the population (as well as many local and regional political leaders), genuinely confused about what mature capitalism would look like, yet profoundly distrustful of halfhearted or clearly self-serving reform attempts. Sick of communism and Yeltsin alike, these new post-Soviet cynics seem justified in their beliefs, however unfortunate for a new democratic culture, spurred by high levels of mismanagement in both private and public sectors by elites who understand little of the tasks of modern governance.[13] Thus, whereas Americans in 1933 were treated to weekly "fireside chats" on the radio by their chief executive, who assured them that they had nothing to fear but fear itself, most Russians from 1992 onward have been largely on their own, with little coming from the Kremlin save Byzantine intrigues and frequently incoherent, reversible policies amid a general sense of overall corruption and ineptitude.

A Broad Blueprint for "Lessons Learned" and New Donor Activity

The intersection between both of these failures has underscored a conclusion heard increasingly from both the international financial community and Russian political analysts themselves. For a genuine market economy to take root and flourish, strong state institutions must be established and maintained. Before direct investment can take place in the country, whether foreign or domestic, the state must be able to guarantee a basic minimum in political stability, clear economic rules of the game, and predictable, transparent procedures for resolving legal and political disputes. Only then will Russia be able to compete with the rest of the world for capital investment flows, and only then will the management of the private sector acquire the incentives it needs to improve corporate governance and make Russia an attractive country for development, trade, and investment.

This is not an "American" or even Western perspective, but one common to all states and societies in an increasingly interdependent economic system that rewards winners and punishes losers, and favors sound economic, fiscal, and monetary policies irrespective of geography, climate, or historical uniqueness. Donors can help Russian elites to refocus their efforts toward "supply-side" state strengthening and good governance efforts. They can also redouble their efforts to support those in civil society willing to undertake the "demand side" of the development equation. Indeed, more of this is taking place all the time. Within USAID and the World Bank, strong debates over past and future policies are summoning a rethinking of strategies for assistance in the face of mutually scaled-back expectations of quick success and easy integration. Both strategies are beginning to accept as something of a new given that the state, particularly in Russia, needs not only strengthening but a fundamental transformation in its behavior toward society and the new private sector. Far from the notion that privatization and business development will solve the state's basic problems, this new perspective accentuates "bad governance" as one of the most important culprits in economic and political misdevelopment. Good governance, by contrast, must include strong barriers between private and public sector activity to prevent mafia-driven kleptocracy, yet also necessitates strong, articulate, influential civil society organizations—whether political associations, independent labor unions, or consumers' and tenants' rights groups—to form partnerships with subnational political elites in particular to create an overall enabling environment where it is more difficult for corruption to flourish openly, and where regions and cities that succeed in crafting new, more transparent approaches to attract investment are rewarded by international and domestic business alike. Three overall lessons seem to offer a framework for future donor activity in Russia.

First, *political and economic reforms in Russia cannot succeed in the absence of transparent mechanisms to separate public and private sector activity.* Technical assistance programs that build on the accumulated experience—not just of Western countries, but of other transition states in Central Europe—to help uncover the structural remedies for this problem are much more likely to succeed in ways that are of the greatest benefit to people and institutions alike.

Second, *Russians themselves, rather than Western organizations, must take the lead in articulating new incentive structures that focus on long-term investment in Russia's collapsed infrastructure.* While donor organizations neither should, nor could, do this particular task, they can help provide a "carrot" for this new incentive structure by linking positive change with Russian entry into the larger array of international financial and political organizations that Russia itself wants to be a part of—everything from the World Trade Organization (WTO) to the Organization for Economic Cooperation and Development (OECD)'s Anti-Bribery Convention. To do this, Russians must first be willing to admit that the costs to the continued short-term exploitation of resources and unchecked capital flight will ultimately undermine the country's chances for genuine recovery. Only then will a focus on institutional development have a real chance for success. Greatly assisting this process would be a unified commitment by donors to open up discussion of loan programs, conditionality, and technical assistance to a wider array of actors. Until now, IMF conditionality requirements, for example, have been negotiated virtually in secret with Russia's Council of Ministers and are far from well known even in academic and policy circles in the United States, let alone Russia. Under such conditions, Russian elite and mass cynicism can only continue unabated and "crony capitalism" will continue to thrive unchecked.

Third, Russian civil society must take upon itself the difficult task *of creating new relationships with municipal and regional authorities to create an atmosphere of good governance*, with NGOs acting both as partners and "watchdogs," rewarding political elites with new bases of electoral support. In this way, NGOs will begin to acquire real influence over policy, while politicians will be given incentives to start defining themselves more as reflections of interest groups, rather than solely by ideology or personality. More than anything, Russia is in desperate need of nonideological solutions to complex statecraft problems, which the current amorphous, fluid quality of political party formation and development cannot respond to.

Part of the "supply-side" good governance environment includes enactment of codes of administrative conduct (together with enforced sanctions for their violation) for all public sector and judicial personnel, civil service training, simplification of business licensing procedures, adoption of internationally accepted accounting standards by regulatory bodies, more coherent tax legislation, better legislative oversight of the executive branch, and specialized training for judges and officers attached to both the commercial courts and courts of general jurisdiction. These constitute only a small portion of a larger whole, but together contribute toward a stronger, more coherent Russian state and society. If reform is ever to be institutionalized, it must take place precisely where the supply- and demand-side governance environment intersects. Using the nongovernmental community to help discover the locus of that intersection is one of the more important lessons donors are belatedly beginning to appreciate. Already, USAID, the Soros Foundation, MacArthur, Ford, Transparency International, and several other donor organizations focused on issues of governance and transparency are engaged in a more systematic dialogue with the nongovernmental community as it searches for answers to the above issues. Belatedly, all donors have come to understand that governments cannot be assumed to find these answers in isolation from their people (or from the world at large), but must reach out to their constituencies in order to create political support for long-term reform.

Recent Transparency and Good Governance Initiatives: Prospects for Success

Some recent initiatives, in particular, undertaken by USAID, the OECD, and the World Bank, represent precisely such attempts, and deserve special mention. Focusing on the judiciary, on government transparency more broadly, and on the role of public-private partnerships to combat corruption, these programs represent an institutional approach to reform, one that seeks to learn lessons from the failure of first-generation privatization programs to generate broad-based economic development, and focuses on the regulatory and political environments that must be created in order to support it.

Judicial Assistance Programs

USAID was one of the first donors to recognize the importance of judicial independence as a political goal for the new Russian state, and targeted its early democracy programs on strengthening those parts of the system of justice that held the greatest promise for this. The Rule of Law Consortium, a group of several legal contractors and subcontractors, focused their efforts first around the newly created commercial court system (*Arbitrazhniy Sud*). This was not primarily a strategic decision influenced by a U.S. commercial agenda, but one based on the simple fact that commercial courts lay outside the jurisdiction of the Ministry of Justice, which was less open to institutional reforms at the time, and by the fact that the commercial courts openly welcomed U.S. technical assistance. Hundreds of judges received training in commercial law, and the assistance helped establish judicial training institutes, which have continued this work on their own. The focus on judges, as opposed to prosecutors or some other aspect of the legal system, was an appropriate decision, given the judiciary's overall low status vis-à-vis the Procuracy and the latter's belated support for legal reforms. USAID's programs have also created important institutional partnerships with the Judicial Department, promoting exchanges between the Department's training bodies and the U.S. National Judicial College (NJC)—the training arm for all U.S. federal court judges. Other donors, such as the European Union's TACIS Program (Technical Assistance to the Commonwealth of Independent States) and the World Bank's legal and Institutional Reform Project, have similarly worked to promote judicial integrity and independence in Russia.

This partnership work creates important bridges linking Russian and American legal professionals together. For instance, a joint workshop between the Judicial College and Russian commercial courts, held in December 1998 and January 1999 at the University of Georgia, brought together both Russian and American judges and experts to discuss tax law, pretrial procedure, and settlement conferencing. Afterward, the Russian Supreme Commercial Court disseminated guidelines for lower and regional courts, and produced a videotape from that workshop as part of its future judicial training curriculum.

These kinds of programs are focused on institutions, rather than personalities, and, though modest in scope, represent the kind of direct U.S./Russian cooperative efforts that are most beneficial to both sides. However, they are not a magic wand, and they will not remove major political or structural impediments to the rule of law. Many serious difficulties are only now even becoming fully apparent.[14] To begin with, a full-fledged cooperative effort by executive, legislative, and judicial personnel to attack judicial incompetence and create (and regularize) larger enforcement mechanisms for going after corrupt, inept, or poorly trained judges, and fully fund a desperately poor court system, has yet to transpire. A new Criminal Code has been adopted, but the dissemination of laws and new administrative procedures (even their comprehensive publication) downward through region and city occurs irregularly. Most egregiously, although the Judicial Department itself is independent, guaranteed a separate line item in the budget of the Federal Assembly, judicial allocations within the Department and arbitrary sequestration of funds have effectively turned the judiciary into beggars, dependent on municipal executive branch bodies for day-to-day financing. Most Russian courts cannot currently afford to pay for heating during the winter, hire court clerks to docket and calendar cases, or even cover the costs for registered mail or remuneration of servers to issue court summons for potential witnesses. The ignorance of new legislation is compounded by the simple organizational inability to enforce it, even were the judicial sector entirely free from corruption. The absence of court clerks means that judges themselves schedule (and select) their own cases; the taking of "payments" to schedule these cases in a timely fashion is a completely predictable by-product of such an unprofessional environment. Not least important, most Russian judges are both former prosecutors and women—a reflection not of equal rights for women, but of the low salary and status of most Russian judicial and prosecutorial personnel.

In addition, the changes discussed thus far all relate to civil law, not criminal, where the need for change is the most acute. The Russian criminal justice system—dominated by the militia, prosecutors, and bureaucratic concerns of the Ministry of the Interior—has not only failed to make much institutional progress, but has actually moved backward since the early 1990s. The crowding and conditions in pretrial prison detention centers have reached "explosive" levels, according to the prosecutor general himself, and have managed to become arguably Russia's preeminent human rights issue today.[15]

But it is the enforcement of judgments issue that lies at the apex of a weak rule-of-law pyramid. Only recently have Russian practitioners and donors begun to focus on its implications. The problem is part structural (a legacy of weak courts combined with poorly adapted European civil law traditions) and part political (the inability or unwillingness of top executive officials to grant the courts the necessary financing, independence, and protection to do their jobs effectively). Under Anglo-Saxon common law, by contrast, judges and courts are largely freed from the responsibility of having to go after defendants in civil cases, a task generally left up to the plaintiffs' attorneys. Well-defined property rights permit liens to be slapped on defendants' holdings, personal bank accounts, and other collateral, with the mechanisms of state and local courts used to enforce the rulings of the magistrate (the "King's Writ," in common law parlance). But under civil law, the "State," rather than a private attorney, is largely responsible for contract enforcement, using a body of court functionaries sometimes translated as "judicial executors" to compel compliance. In Western Europe, these executors are highly trained professionals operating under specific, culturally ingrained ethical standards, attached to the Ministry of Justice. Under Soviet law (where enforcement by firing squad and slave labor frequently contributed to "socialist legality"), this function was largely ceremonial and served little purpose outside of family law. By the Brezhnev era, court executors (*sudebnye ispol'niteli*) were mostly middle-aged women, limited to the occasional knocking on doors of deadbeat fathers trying to escape alimony responsibilities. But in the new Russia with its mafia oligarchies and "wild, wild West" business mentality, this system is largely a quaint reminder of a time when the Rule of Law meant little. In 1998, the Judicial Department created a new system of court enforcers (*sudebnye pristavy*), whose new tasks include the physical protection of judges themselves and the enforcement of plaintiff judgments. This new "bailiff" system is receiving technical assistance from the U.S. Marshall's Service and others, financed by USAID in recognition that some kind of Western model, whether from civil or common law, is crucial to the success of the new enforcement system.

There are structural flaws within the newly created bailiff system that may eventually undermine its intent, however. To begin with, the bailiffs receive a percentage of the judgment itself, raising strong ethical issues as to who (if anyone) is watching the watchers. This, together with admittedly poor safeguards against criminal penetration of the bailiff service itself, may create an entirely new round of incentives for judicial corruption. The term *zakuplennye sud'ia* (bought judges), having entered the post-Soviet lexicon in the early 1990s, may persist long into the future. Yet the creation of the bailiff service underscores two facts worth emphasizing: For the first time, judges and courts are important players in the civil and criminal justice systems; and unless the judiciary takes strong measures now against its *own* corruption and incompetence, it risks losing all of the gains it has achieved.

Other USAID-funded programs focus on strengthening private bar associations, revamping the academic curriculum at Russia's best law schools, and supporting public interest law "clinics" that provide legal help to entire classes of people who could not otherwise afford it. The vast majority of these projects take place in areas far from Moscow and generally operate without the intense Byzantine microscope of Muscovite politics.[16] But in Moscow itself, new outreaches to some national-level institutions not dominated by strong personalities (whether "reformist" or "antireformist") have also been taking place. A program linking the Duma's Chamber of Accounts—the auditing and investigative arm within the legislature, little known by anyone other than specialists—with their institutional counterparts in the United States, such as the General Accounting Office, the congressional equivalent to the Chamber, and various Offices of Inspectorate General (the investigative offices attached to U.S. executive branch agencies and departments that uncover fraud, waste, and abuse within the executive branch) has also begun. The premise for the latter is the same as for any Western government; namely, that the "power of the purse" and the skills necessary to retain that oversight power must reside within a well-informed parliamentary structure, not simply an executive one.

The OECD Anti-Bribery Convention

As part of the OECD's larger efforts to expand the scope of a recently passed anti-bribery convention from mostly developed Western states to include countries in transition, USAID's Bureau for Europe and New Independent States and OECD's Directorate for Fiscal, Financial, and Enterprise Affairs entered into a technical partnership to explore ways to develop support for more transparent and accountable government in the region. An OECD Anti-Corruption Network for Transition Economies—an informal structure linking donors, host-country governments, and NGOs—was created in October 1998 in Istanbul. A donor-financed Web site (www.nobribes.org) was created to collect lessons learned, and to serve as an organizer of best practices and discussion rooms for NGOs and others looking for ways to combat corruption by capitalizing on more successful experience in other countries. In the Russian city of Novgorod, the U.S. Department of Commerce and the OECD cooperated on a USAID cofinanced program in July 1999 with the Oblast Administration of Governor Mikhail Prusak to adopt a code of conduct for the private sector—an example of "good governance" pilot programs mentioned earlier. The long-term goal of the Anti-Corruption Network is to bring together members of key government institutions (procurement, business licensing, regulatory, financial audit, and judicial personnel), members of key nongovernmental organizations (policy "think tanks," consumers' rights organizations, housing tenant and labor unions, investigative journalists, and human rights workers), and members of the key multilateral and bilateral institutions (the World Bank, the European Bank for Reconstruction and Development, the OECD, the Council of Europe, the European Union, USAID, the Soros Open Society Institute, the Canadian International Development Agency, Transparency International, and others) to begin to formulate more coherent practices and recommendations for anticorruption implementations in transition economies. The mechanics of creating and sustaining public-private partnerships to monitor corruption, how to create and enforce new codes of conduct for public sector employees, and how banking reform in the former USSR might benefit from efforts made earlier in Poland and Hungary are only some of the topics of discussion before the Network. While there are no guarantees of "success" for any of these projects, it is far more likely that answers to seemingly intractable issues of governance, accountability, and corruption will be uncovered in an environment where there is open discussion of these issues by those most interested in finding answers than in one where elites and representatives of international organizations discuss multimillion-dollar programs behind locked doors without the benefit of public scrutiny.

A New Focus at the World Bank

It would be impossible to speak about the growing significance of "good governance" issues among donors without noting the sea change in attitude and behavior now taking place at the World Bank under the leadership of President James Wolfensohn. The drama of such a change came to a head during a tense meeting between Wolfensohn and a large group of Indonesian NGOs during that country's social and political upheavals accompanying the forced resignation of President Suharto in 1998. Acknowledging that the Bank's lending policies had actually a pernicious rather than constructive role, by corrupting a tiny core of Indonesian elites and thus preventing, rather than supporting, accountability for vast amounts of capital inflows over many years, Wolfensohn brought home to the international financial community a fact that has been known by NGOs for years: *that if political elites are left to their own unregulated devices, and particularly as recipients of large donor funds, their corruption is almost a given, and that this deeply undermines chances for the long-term political stability and social legitimacy of any government.* Democratization is now "officially" not only relevant, but absolutely essential to long-term, sustainable economic development.

The first steps toward achieving a "no-tolerance" perspective toward corruption in the developing world has been the holding of "integrity conferences" sponsored by the World Bank (and jointly supported by US-AID in the postcommunist region), where diagnostic research on government, business, and household perceptions toward official corruption is compiled, publicized, and disseminated before as wide a domestic audience as possible, and where nongovernmental representatives, the media, and government officials all publicly propose, and commit to, medium- and longer-term action plans for intervention. Such is also the thinking that has come from the conference "A Global Forum on Combating Corruption," hosted by Vice-President Gore in February 1999, and scheduled with a follow-up conference to be hosted by the Dutch government.

In Russia, all this has a particular importance and urgency difficult to overlook. While the immediate political landscape may not seem particularly rosy, there are some reasons to think that Russia is in a better position to pursue these kinds of changes now than it has been for several years. Between September 1998 and May 1999, when he was ousted in favor of former Minister of the Interior Sergei Stepashin, Russia's Prime Minister Primakov managed to steer clear of the Scylla of hyperinflation and the Charybdis of economic calamity, even as the August 1998 collapse of the ruble helped to undermine some of the influence of the country's leading banks and the oligarchic influence behind them. Although the financial collapse undermined much short-term investment in the country, and depleted the bank accounts of many middle-class Muscovites, there is more appreciation now than at any time in the previous five years for potential new rules of the game.[17]

Dangers to Anticorruption and
Good Governance Technical Assistance Programs

One of the drawbacks to working with largely English-speaking elites in the transition states has been their ability to quickly master the language of political reform that the international donor community has come to expect without the accompanying content. The underside of the new focus on anticorruption and good governance, particularly as long as civil society remains unengaged, is that it becomes all too easy for political elites to mouth slogans of transparency much as slogans proclaiming the unity of the Party and People in the Soviet era were, at one time, paraded at every opportunity. Donor organizations have been slow to realize how deeply political language and discourse have themselves been corrupted in post-Soviet countries, with a new cynicism toward political authority of all types the unfortunate result.[18] The public cynicism engendered by such unserious attempts to tackle corruption does great harm to elites and society at large by undermining, rather than enlisting, popular support for difficult policies. Donors must not only seek to do "good" by aiding top-down law enforcement or other initiatives; in many cases it is equally critical to "do no harm" by *not* officially sanctioning efforts designed more to protect elites from genuine transparency than to protect the public trust from abuse. The right balance between the two is rarely easy to establish, but donors must make greater efforts to find it than they have in the past.

The appeal of some of these programs, both for donors and recipients, is clear enough: the strengthening of the state, particularly in its financial and legal regulatory aspects, and the "carrot" of Russia's larger integration with Western political and economic institutions, including a corresponding increase in direct investment, both foreign and domestic. There are few guarantees that such programs will work, but it is far more likely that long-term solutions to governance and state-building issues will be found under this kind of transparent atmosphere than any other. Civic activism will hardly start without transparency, and without it, elites will fail to grasp that the price of *not* reaching out to the electorate to create a social base of support among key nongovernmental institutions—independent labor unions, civic institutions, business and trade associations, think tanks, policy institutes, and consumers' organizations—is the loss of their influence and positions. When this happens, there will finally be something of a convergence between "top-down" and "bottom-up" strategies for genuine reform.

Nonetheless, no one should be lulled into thinking that any of these programs—even if all of them were generously financed, expertly delivered by the donor community, and guided by well-organized NGOs with a strong sense of civic responsibility—could make much headway in the short term. Before this can happen, a broad societal consensus with respect to the incentive structures under which elites operate must begin to change. How to do this—how to change Russia's own incentive structure to emphasize anything other than short-term private gain at the expense of longer-term development—should be the most important question that both Westerners and Russians can now ask.

Conclusion

The premise of this chapter has been that donors must be more willing to grasp critical lessons from the first stage of Russia's economic and political transformation, and move to embrace more coherent, state-strengthening policies that offer practical ways to "stop the bleeding" of the public sector. But an equally important lesson is that longer-term solutions to Russia's institutional weaknesses will have to be proposed and put into effect by Russians themselves, not by others. The underlying concept behind both premises is that Russia's larger experiment with economic globalization seems destined to continue, however many modifications Russians themselves need to make along the way. International political and donor communities should remember that a peaceful, stable, strong, and prosperous Russian Federation added to the larger European and Eurasian landscape is not a luxury, but an urgent necessity, for Russians, their immediate neighbors, and the larger international community. Serious, far-reaching obstacles remain to this vision, but at this critical juncture in Russia's evolution, disengagement and indifference are the very last policies to be recommended.

Notes

1. See, for example, Elizabeth Teague, "Vacuum of State Power: Russian's Main Weakness," reprinted with permission in *Jamestown Foundation Prism* (October 2, 1998), and David Hoffman, "Yeltsin's Absentee Rule Raises Specter of a 'Failed State,'" *The Washington Post* (February 26, 1999).

2. Some scholars are using the term "arbitrary" rather than "captured" instead. See Celeste Wallander, "A PONARS Policy Discussion," Carnegie Endowment for International Peace (February 1999).

3. See Michael Johnston, "Corruption and Distorted Development: Competition, Institutionalization and Strategies for Reform," paper presented at a USAID Conference on Economic and Political Reform: The Costs of Corruption, May 1998.

4. Some have become articulate spokespersons for a perspective that argues that much of foreign technical assistance has been misplaced, a view that has many insights, but is both too sweeping and subjective to be of much practical assistance to program implementers. See Janine Wedel, "Clique-Run Organizations and U.S. Economic Aid," *Demokratizatsiya*, vol. 14, no. 4 (Fall 1996): 571–602.

5. The IMF and Russia agreed in 1998 to a loan package worth $22.6 billion, payable in a series of tranches directly tied to specific financial conditionality requirements. That package was interrupted after the collapse and forced devaluation of the ruble in August, when some of the debt servicing was interrupted by the Russian government.

6. For a discussion, see Carol Welch's op-ed piece, "Look Closely at the IMF's Record," *Washington Post* (December 8 and 30, 1998), and the reply by IMF Fiscal

Affairs Officer Vic Tanzi, AP (Internet), "Russia Promised $2.3 Billion in Loans" (April 15, 1999).

7. Tanzi (April 15, 1999).

8. Although it is true that the Fund is dependent on Washington political interests, it does not necessarily follow that congressional political interests determine its policies. Indeed, Congress has recently been one of the IMF's most vociferous critics.

9. By 1998, USAID had spent $9.4 billion in the former Iron Curtain states, with $5.7 billion going to the Newly Independent States (the former USSR minus the Baltic republics) and $3.7 billion to the countries of Central Europe. Over time, USAID's portion of the annual appropriation under FREEDOM Support has declined to about 61 percent of government expenditures in 1999, the rest being distributed to the U.S. Information Agency, the Department of Treasury, the Department of Commerce, the State Department, and the Department of Justice, among others.

10. "The initial grants were described as having been written 'on the back of an envelope' at a time when the Agency was specifically enjoined from conducting assessments or developing a strategy. According to an AID official, it was AID that initiated the Former Soviet Union strategy development process." *Supporting Democracy*, Management Systems International Assessment (April 20, 1994): 16, cited in Curt Tarnoff, "The Former Soviet Union and U.S. Foreign Aid: Implementing the Assistance Program," *Congressional Research Service*, U.S. Library of Congress (January 18, 1995): 38.

11. It bears mentioning that in dollar terms, funding for such programs has always lagged far behind spending for larger-scale economic programs, like privatization. For a description of the models of democratic development the U.S. government arguably operates under, see Thomas Carothers, "Democracy Assistance: The Question of Strategy," *Democratization*, vol. 4, no. 3 (Autumn 1997): 109–132.

12. See Sachs, "The Dismal Decade: Failures East and West," *Los Angeles Times* (November 22, 1998).

13. For a brief survey of Russia's little-publicized corporate governance weaknesses, see David Hoffman, "Out of Step with Russia: Outsider's Battle Over Stake in Oil Giant Offers a Glimpse of Nation's Uncertain Capitalist Ways," *The Washington Post*, Business Section (April 18, 1999).

14. For example, the principal drafter of Russia's new Tax Code (Deputy Andrei Makarov), member of the Committee on the Budget, Tax and Finance, presented a short history of the enactment of the code at the Georgia conference. In all, thirteen competing draft bills presented to the Committee reflected the overall confusion of the legislative process itself. Several provisions in the Code itself were taken verbatim from U.S. state law (Utah and New York), German law, and Canadian law, depending on the nationality of the adviser who had worked with various members and Committee staff. The Tax Code, accompanying legislation on the budget, and seven other laws that the IMF had requested passage on in 1998 were enacted and sent to the Federation Council within a single day, raising considerable criticism of the IMF regarding its pressure, through the Russian

government, to compel the legislature to ratify new codes with little overall coherence.

15. For a discussion of pretrial issues, see Andrew Meier, "One Day in the Life of . . . ," *Time* (May 25, 1998).

16. See, for example, "Developing Legal Partnerships in Northwest Russia: The Vermont/Karelia Rule of Law Project," University of Vermont, October 1998.

17. "Oligarchic businesses are no longer in a position to reconstruct the old systems and implement their old agreements. The business community objectively needs updating and needs new leaders, both corporate and individual." Mikhail Matytsin, "Russia on the Eve of the 21st Century: The New Situation in the Russian Business Community," *Jamestown Foundation Prism*, no. 7, part 3 (April 9, 1999), Internet version; and Robert Kaiser, "Rubles from the Rubble," *The Washington Post* (July 18, 1999).

18. In Ukraine, for example, where presidential contenders currently vie to outdo one another in terms of their outrage against personal corruption, law enforcement agencies' own reports to the Ukrainian Parliament's Committee for Legal Provisions for Law Enforcement and for Fighting Organized Crime and Corruption show that within the first nine months of 1998, Ukrainian courts received 2,754 reports of public sector corruption. While guilty verdicts were actually returned in 1,188 (43 percent) cases, the vast majority of cases were low-level civil servants compelled to face "administrative liabilities" (i.e., fines), most of which were below US$100. The bulk of Ukrainian corruption, at least in 1998, therefore, was confined to clerks! Cited in Corruption Watch, vol. 2, no. 8 (April 1999), Ukrainian Center for Independent Political Research, Internet version.

Index